Public Opinion in European Socialist Systems

Walter D. Connor
Zvi Y. Gitelman

with

Adaline Huszczo
Robert Blumstock

The Praeger Special Studies program, through a selective worldwide distribution network, makes available to the academic, government, and business communities significant and timely research in U.S. and international economic, social, and political issues.

Public Opinion in European Socialist Systems

PRAEGER SPECIAL STUDIES IN INTERNATIONAL POLITICS AND GOVERNMENT

Praeger Publishers   New York   London

203565/000

Library of Congress Cataloging in Publication Data

Connor, Walter D
    Public opinion in European socialist systems.

    (Praeger special studies in international politics
and government)
    Includes index.
    1. Public opinion polls. 2. Public opinion—
Europe, Eastern—Case studies. I. Gitelman, Zvi Y.,
joint author. II. Title.
HM261.C663   1977   301.15'4'0947   77-83471
ISBN 0-03-040931-4

PRAEGER SPECIAL STUDIES
200 Park Avenue, New York, N.Y., 10017, U.S.A.

Published in the United States of America in 1977
by Praeger Publishers,
A Division of Holt, Rinehart and Winston, CBS, Inc.

789   038   987654321

Printed in the United States of America

In recent years the study of Communist systems has moved beyond an emphasis on the political regime and its impact on society, and toward broader perspectives encompassing society's impacts and constraints on the polity. Initially treated as an independent variable, the regime now assumes, for some purposes, the position of a dependent variable.

This book treats it as both. It focuses on public opinion, which the state seeks to control but which, at the same time, limits to some degree what the state can do in certain areas of policy and action. Our concern is with public opinion in better-developed socialist states, and in those which are part of the "Soviet bloc." Thus, we have excluded from separate and lengthy consideration the relatively underdeveloped states of Romania and Bulgaria, as well as the "maverick" Yugoslavia, concentrating on four nations—the USSR, Poland, Czechoslovakia and Hungary—which fit our needs.

The chapters which follow describe the emergence of opinion polling in the socialist states. This involved varying mixes of action *on* the polity, from academics and journalists supporting new departures, and actions *by* it, as political leaders realized that more rational and efficient administration and control required systematic information on public moods and preoccupations, in addition to more traditional types of intelligence.

The problems of politics go far beyond rational administration, however—and a major problem for the leaders of the socialist regimes is guaranteeing the basic political status quo. Opinion research is a sensitive matter. Ups and downs of the opinion-polling enterprise are analyzed here in an attempt to gain some insight into the tensions between regime efforts to find alternatives to increasingly dysfunctional coercion, and their fears of an "overspill" of information. Those fears were grounded in the belief that too much openness imperiled the stability of polities still lacking many elements of legitimacy.

Of course polls, however badly or amateurishly conducted (as many have been) produce data—much of these data of great interest to those concerned with the state of mind of socialist citizens. The data occupy a large place in the pages to come, conveying the complexity of success and failures in centrally directed political socialization efforts, and the persistence of certain mass concerns, as well as an apolitical *lack* of concern, from pre-socialist periods. The rationales of regimes in permitting and supporting polling have been complex and at times contradictory, but our understanding of the linkage between polity and individual can only be enhanced by attention to the data thus made available.

We have attempted to give two concerns their due: first, the regime as subject, acting to maintain itself and its options by manipulating and shaping public opinion, seeking to ascertain it but limit its expression; and second, those judgments, anticipations, and evaluative orientations of the public, which place the regime in the position of object. We offer the results in the hope that the description and analysis herein will inform, and also stimulate speculation and further attention to the many questions of polity-society interaction in the socialist world which are not answered in this book.

Acknowledgments are the standard, and always inadequate, tribute paid to those without whose help and cooperation no book would ever see print. Our greatest are to our co-contributors, Adaline Huszczo and Robert Blumstock, whose patience and cooperation, over time and often at long distance, made it easier for us to cope with the responsibilities of seeing the work through early revisions and editorial negotiations.

The University of Michigan's Center for Russian and East European Studies has provided, over the years, intellectual stimulation and organizational support to us both, and did so with this work as well. Our gratitude goes to the Center and its staff; to its director, William Zimmerman, for his support and cooperation; and to Marita Kaw, who compiled the index with efficiency and dispatch.

Walter D. Connor
Zvi Y. Gitelman

CONTENTS

LIST OF TABLES

1

PUBLIC OPINION
IN COMMUNIST
POLITICAL SYSTEMS
Zvi Y. Gitelman

The emergence of a visible public opinion—expressed, measured, and reported—and of public opinion research in some Communist countries has surprised some Western observers, been dismissed by others, and been analyzed by few.[1] The relative inattention to public opinion in Eastern Europe and the USSR may be due to beliefs that opinion research in socialist systems is biased and unreliable, that opinion is largely manipulated and not "spontaneously" formed, and that public opinion has little, if any, influence on decision and policy making in Communist countries.

These beliefs were shaped largely by the realities of the Stalinist system and the claims of traditional Leninist theory. Few Westerners, and even fewer Communists, claimed that public opinion played no role at all even in the Stalinist period. But while the Soviet claim was that there was a near perfect identification of opinion between Soviet leaders and Communist masses, most Westerners argued that this was true only insofar as the leadership molded, led, and carefully controlled public opinion. In his pioneering study, *Public Opinion in Soviet Russia*, Alex Inkeles pointed out that while Bolshevik theory did not disregard public opinion,

> Its emphasis . . . more or less completely rejects following public opinion and stresses the prime need to shape and mold it. This implies that one studies public opinion primarily to determine the pace and speed of his own actions. The goal is not to cater to public opinion but to move it along with you as rapidly as possible without undermining your popular support. But one cannot determine his own pace, according to this formula, unless he knows the state of mass thinking.[2]

Lenin's revolutionary strategy was based on the premise that a vanguard of the proletariat and intelligentsia, crystallized in the Party, possessed a historical consciousness superior to that of the proletariat. The working class could by itself attain only a "trade union consciousness," but it possessed the element of spontaneity needed to make a revolution. While the proletariat was needed to make the revolution, it could not lead it. "Tailism" was the label Lenin contemptuously affixed to the notion that political action should be determined above all by the masses whose wishes the vanguard would be obliged to carry out.

Lenin moved beyond Marx in imputing a greater historical role to consciousness and pointing to the limits of spontaneity. Stalin further revised Lenin's doctrines, narrowing the scope of consciousness to one man's judgment and asserting the power of superstructure to transform, by sheer acts of will, objective elements of the "base." If the masses would not keep up with the advancing vanguard, then that vanguard should drag the masses along, no matter the cost. As Stalin put it, "The Party is no true Party if it limits its activities to a mere registration of the suffering and thoughts of the proletarian masses . . . if it cannot rise superior to the transient interests of the proletariat."[3]

This meant not that the Party completely ignored the opinions and sentiments of the masses, but rather that it took account of them in order better to manipulate them. A situation was created wherein the Party tried to suppress the expression of nonofficial opinion while simultaneously trying to ascertain it. As Andrei Amalrik has observed, "It is . . . paradoxical that the regime should devote enormous effort to keep everyone from talking and then waste further effort to learn what people are talking about and what they want."[4] The paradox is more apparent than real if one takes into account the purposes for which public opinion was to be ascertained. Totalitarian regimes are interested in tapping public sentiment, and "Popular opinion, in the sense of private views held by individual citizens, does of course exist under the totalitarian regime, and it is taken into account to some extent by the government."[5] Both the Nazi and the Stalinist regimes paid some heed to it.[6] As Rousseau and Hume observed, all political systems, even the most dictatorial, must take some account of popular sentiment if they are to survive. The distinctive characteristics of public opinion in the Stalinist system were, aside from its careful control and manipulation, its almost exclusively supportive function and its instrumental use as simultaneously a safety valve and a device for uncovering malfunctions within the system.

The instruments by which public opinion was discovered included the secret police, the party apparatus (which reported on all questions asked at meetings), letters to the mass media, and "self-criticism."[7] Letters to the media continue to be widely encouraged in the Soviet Union and other socialist countries. They can point to miscreants and malfeasance that the regime is anxious to uncover; they also have the advantage that they can be screened and edited.

Moreover, letters are individual expressions and do not entail the risk of mo-
bilizing and coalescing individuals into self-conscious opinion groups. Soviet
and East European sources point with pride to the number of letters received by
the media as testimony to the activism of the citizenry, the responsiveness of
the system, and the availability of channels for the expression of opinion. Four
central Soviet newspapers receive about 1 million letters from readers every
year; in April and May 1967, ten Bulgarian newspapers and the radio and television received 34,800 letters; in 1957 the Polish radio received 100,000 letters.[8]

A fundamental Communist assumption about the nature of public opinion
in Communist systems, challenged by some "revisionists" and, lately, by some
scholars in the Soviet Union and Eastern Europe, is that there is a near perfect
congruence between leadership policy and mass opinion. "On the basis of many
decades of struggle and victory the people have become convinced that the voice
of the Party, the opinion of the Party—this is its voice and its Party, only deeper
and clearer, more foresighted and mature."[9] A Romanian scholar typically
claims that a

> new feature of public opinion under socialism is its concordance
> with state power, [to] such a degree that between them collisions
> have completely disappeared. . . . What ensures a concordance,
> nearly an identity between socialist public opinion and the activity
> of party and state, is their common ideological orientation, the
> conscious adhesion of the whole people to the cause of Communist
> construction.[10]

In this "identification theory," the linkage between opinion and policy is
achieved through the sharing of fundamental beliefs. There should be no real
need to probe the opinions of the citizenry since they are much the same as
those of the political decision makers.

PUBLIC OPINION AND SOCIALIST
POLITICAL DEVELOPMENT

The interaction of changed political, social, and economic conditions with
changing perceptions of those conditions in the Communist states of Europe
brought about both implicit and explicit questioning of the identification theory
or premise and gave rise to a new interest in and approach to public opinion and
its apperception. While socialist scholars, like their counterparts in the West,
have devoted a great deal of attention to the definitions of "public" and "opinion"—these definitions have important implications, as shall be seen—public
opinion may be seen, paraphrasing V. O. Key, Jr., as those opinions held by
private persons that governments find it prudent to take into account.[11] By

and large we mean by "public opinion" mass opinion. Obviously, public opinion can exist independent of public opinion research, but such research is an indication not only of the existence and the nature of public opinion, but, in East European and Soviet conditions, also of the willingness of governments to acknowledge its existence and, in some way, take account of it. This is not to say that the field of public opinion research was initiated in socialist countries from above; in fact, in almost every instance, research was begun on the initiative of journalists and social scientists. But the institutional forms given to opinion research, the political uses made of it, and the issues investigated are often determined largely by the individual regimes.

The emergence of public opinion and its study must be understood in the context of political development in postrevolutionary Communist societies and of situational-cultural factors such as the political style of the leadership, the political culture, and the social science tradition of the respective countries.

Karl Deutsch, among others, has identified three kinds of information essential to the functioning of a political system: Information is needed by the governors in order to compel the governed; it is needed by the governed in order to comply with the commands of the governors; and it is needed to perform the "internal intelligence function."

> Everywhere political decisions depend for their effectiveness on the correctness with which the relevant reactions to them have been predicted. Lacking such information, they are apt to produce results quite different from those intended, and all attempts át enforcement are apt to make the danger of an eventual breakdown worse.[12]

Most basically, every political system requires a flow of information from society in order to maximize the efficiency of its policy choices. The more complex the society, the more such information must be acquired and processed.

David Apter observes that "different polities employ different mixtures of coercion and information in trying to maintain authority, achieve stability, and increase efficiency" and posits "an inverse relationship between information and coercion in a system; that is, high-coercion systems are low-information systems."[13]

While the absolute amount of information generated within the Stalinist system was probably quite high, its quality was often poor, due to the high incentives for falsification, distortion, and covering up. Certain kinds of information, such as that about consumer demands, were deliberately ignored or suppressed. "Having imposed on the masses the official conception of reality," Zbigniew Brzezinski remarked, "totalitarian leadership begins to see nothing but the reflection of that 'official' reality. . . . This position of isolation induces a simple but extremely serious defect: lack of adequate information."[14] A leading Polish student of public opinion, Andrzej Sicinski, commenting on "the problem of unrecognized social needs or even the denial of the very significance of public opinion research under Socialism," attributes the problem to the identification premise as well as to the

> emphasis on a one-way flow of information: from the center of power to the society at large. . . . The importance of the unbiased information that could be obtained was underrated. . . . [There was a] disregard of information on the direction that social processes were taking, as well as the absence of consideration of public views on certain decisions.[15]

Information obtained by the leadership was often distorted, since one of its main channels was the secret police, who had a vested interest in presenting information in a way that would maximize their own importance and virtue. The same held for information transmitted by the state and Party structures, though the amount of distortion may have been less in the case of the Party. Whatever the quality and quantity of information in the Stalinist system, since the mid-1950s coercive means have ceased to be the main information-gathering instruments. At the same time, post-Stalinist regimes have found it necessary to increase their information flows—about resource allocation, for example—from society. This means that Communist systems have had to devise and discover new, and perhaps more efficient, ways of gathering this needed information. Public opinion research is one of those ways.

Along with the decline in coercion, Communist political development has involved increased functional differentiation and social complexity.[16] Two consequences of this are the transformation of masses into publics and the changed role of the Leninist party from mobilizer to integrator of society. The modernization of East European society has resulted in the partial emergence of publics—collectivities that confront issues, discuss them, and divide over them—in place of masses—heterogeneous collectivities composed of anonymous individuals who engage in little interaction or exchange of experience.[17] The peasants of Eastern Europe—traditionally the objects, not the subjects, of politics—were brought into the political arena as masses, but, as a consequence of their increasing sophistication, awareness, and self-consciousness, they are slowly approaching the status of publics. "The presence of an issue, of discussion, and of a collective opinion is the mark of the public,"[18] the obvious prerequisite for the existence of public opinion. Indeed, in almost all socialist societies a third and "higher" type of collectivity has become visible and politically relevant; interest groups are stable publics that have a permanent nexus of concerns as their integrating force. The issues and opinions associated with publics shift constantly; interest groups concern themselves consistently with a defined issue or set of issues, and their general attitudes tend to be stable and, hence, more predictable. A third developmental consideration is the economic reform and decentralization that has been carried out, to varying degrees, in all socialist states, excluding Albania. The new system, or in some cases direct consumer pressure expressed in a variety of forms, including violent ones, forces producers to take consumer demand into account and to engage in some forms of market research. The consumer public acquires new influence over production and distribution planning.

As the socialization of the citizenry in a Communist system proceeds, the leadership may gain greater confidence in the diffuse support it enjoys and be more willing to allow a controlled expression of opinion by the publics. The Soviet leadership, for example, has expressed this confidence by postulating that coercive means of social regulation and control can give way to persuasive means as a result of the deepening consciousness of the citizenry, the vast majority of which supports the fundamental goals and institutions of the system.[19] "The role of public opinion increases also because the consciousness of the workers increases linearly."[20] It should be recognized, however, that the habits of manipulation and distrust of the masses, reinforced by the sanctity of Leninist proscriptions against tailism, are not easily unlearned. With the possible exception of Yugoslavia and the short-lived regime of Alexander Dubcek in Czechoslovakia, Communist governments maintain a stance of distrust or at least caution toward their populations.

European Communist systems were established mostly in societies where the prevailing beliefs were that it was not the business of the public to criticize the government or even formally participate in political life. One of the powerful appeals of Communist parties was their proclamation of a system belonging "to the people" and a stress on participation in state affairs. Communist regimes consciously constructed institutions and developed behavioral patterns that led to the formal involvement, if not the genuine participation, of most of the population in civic affairs. "Preemptive" organizations and structures serve for a time to give citizens the feeling of genuine participation, but experience and sophistication often lead to the realization that this "participation" is without efficacy, voluntarism, and responsiveness.[21] This realization conduces to apathy and withdrawal from even formal participation (as in the declining membership of officially sponsored youth organizations in Czechoslovakia and Poland), or to alternative explanations of the system (Milovan Djilas). At other times, attempts are made to infuse existing institutions with meaning and to turn formal involvement into efficacious participation (as in the Czechoslovak trade unions in 1968-69). What V. O. Key said about a democracy seems to apply in some degree to a Communist system as well:

> If a democracy is to exist, the belief must be widespread that public opinion, at least in the long run, affects the course of action. In a technical sense that belief may be a myth or an article of faith, yet its maintenance requires that it possess a degree of validity.[22]

While a growing disbelief in the myth may not be as dangerous to a Communist system as it is to a democratic one, at the very least it results in widespread apathy, and under certain conditions it may feed active rebellion. The participatory myth of Communist systems, even though hedged by Leninist elitism, thus generates pressures for the formation and expression of public opinion, pressures that may be unintended, but nonetheless real, consequences of ideology and policy.

In democratic societies, Key has suggested, public opinion may be supportive on some issues, permissive on others, and decisive on still others. Mass public opinion in Communist systems performs different functions at different stages of Communist development. In the totalitarian, or mobilization, stage, mass opinion is allowed to be only supportive and only on issues selected by the regime. The relaxation of totalitarian controls and the emergence of publics at a second stage enables mass opinion to play both supportive and permissive roles, in the sense that it must now be taken into account to a greater degree when making policy decisions. In reform systems, such as the Yugoslav and Czechoslovak (1968), mass opinion can even play a decisive role, in addition to the other ones, at least on selected issues. Thus, the development of some Communist systems away from the Stalinist model expands the functions of public opinion, possibly to a point not very dissimilar from the function of mass opinion in democratic systems. Naturally, Communist systems can move back to the Stalinist model or evolve other highly authoritarian forms.

The differential recognition accorded to public opinion and its study is due also to such considerations as leadership style, political culture, general level of societal development, and the social science traditions of each country. A political leadership that favors a "populist," pseudoconsultative, or genuinely consultative political style will be more likely to play up the role of public opinion and attempt to bring it into the system in some way, while a more elitist leadership will not find it necessary to "go to the people" as often. The difference between the political styles of a Joseph Stalin and a Nikita Khrushchev, an Antonin Novotny and an Alexander Dubcek, or a Wladyslaw Gomulka and an Edward Gierek, are cases in point.

With the exception of Czechoslovakia, the pre-Communist political cultures of Eastern Europe did not highly value participation and consultation with mass public opinion. The relative impact of Communist participatory myths and the differential success of socialization, interacting with traditional political culture, help determine the amount of pressure that will be produced "from below" to allow the expression of spontaneous opinion. Perhaps even more important is the developmental level of a society—how far the process of transforming masses into publics has gone, the general level of literacy and exposure to mass media, the extent to which political authorities and issues have penetrated the lives of individuals, and the attainment of an economic level above that wherein the individual must devote most of his time to keeping himself and his family alive and cannot afford such luxuries as opinions on political and social issues. Finally, countries with established social science traditions are more easily able to rationalize the reestablishment of public opinion research and can draw on survivors of pre-Communist social science to aid in the rebirth of the disciplines. Bulgaria and Romania, with weakly developed traditions in empirical social science, wait until other socialist countries show the way before initiating their own efforts. A brief overview of the rise of opinion research in socialist countries illustrates this point.

Poland is the country with the richest sociological tradition in Eastern Europe. Decimated by the Nazi slaughter of Polish intellectuals and suppressed during the Stalinist period, Polish sociology nevertheless managed to begin a new productive era after 1956. The international reputations of such men as Jan Szczepanski, Stanislaw Ehrlich, and Stanislaw Ossowski are testimony to the prestige enjoyed by Polish sociology. Public opinion research was begun on a rather nonscientific basis by several newspapers in 1955, but social scientists quickly entered the field and produced a great number of interesting and illuminating studies, especially between 1958 and 1964.[23]

In the Soviet Union, public opinion research was also initiated by a newspaper, *Komsomol'skaia pravda*, in 1960, and, in the words of B. A. Grushin, the moving spirit behind the newspaper's public opinion institute, it was regarded as "an illegitimate child" by academic institutions.[24] The newspaper has conducted over a score of mass surveys, many of them of dubious scientific validity. A short-lived Center for the Study of Public Opinion was established in the USSR, and various institutions and individuals have conducted sample opinion surveys of different scopes and compass. The center was established in 1969 within the Academy of Sciences' Institute for Concrete Social Research and was headed by Grushin. In 1970-71, it researched such topics as alcoholism and means to combat it, sports, audience preferences in phonograph records, and the like. "Aside from this, in this period there were a series of local studies commissioned by Party organs."[25] According to an emigre Soviet sociologist, Ilya Zemtsov, as early as 1962 the KGB (Soviet security police) had a functioning "public opinion research institute." He asserts that the *Komsomol'skaia pravda* institute had to present its findings very selectively and that Grushin reported to the Propaganda Department of the Party Central Committee, "I have not one, but two books [resulting from studies of Soviet youth], one completely anti-Soviet and fit for a bourgeois publishing house, and the other . . . matches the profile of the ideal personality."[26] Zemtsov claims that Grushin was pressured by the KGB to identify at least the localities where the least acceptable replies to his questionnaire had been obtained and that sometimes questionnaires were secretly coded so that respondents could be identified. Much of the work of Grushin's center was classified "secret," and by 1971 it had ceased functioning altogether, its materials were seized by the KGB, and its work was characterized as "having lost its political vigilance." The center's fate demonstrates the narrowness of the boundaries within which Soviet social science, even that designed to serve regime purposes, must operate.

What Merton and Riecken say of Soviet empirical research in general seems to apply, by and large, to opinion surveys as well:

> The Soviet orientation toward empirical social research might be described as "practical empiricism:" As an effort to obtain just enough systematic information on which to base recommendations for policy and action, with little interest in pursuing, through empirical research, the more theoretical implications of what has been observed. In spirit and outcome, it is most like market research in the United States: on a low level of abstraction and largely confined to ferreting out facts that can be taken into account in making practical decisions.[27]

As I hope to demonstrate, this is too severely limited a view of the functions of Soviet sociology, but it makes an important point.

While empirical sociology had developed in Czechoslovakia before World War II, it was only after the war that an Institute for Public Opinion Research came into being. The institute was actually a government agency, and its directors saw it as a "tool for democracy."[28] In 1947-48, the findings of the institute showed declining Communist electoral strength and undoubtedly hastened the coup in Prague in February 1948. With the onset of the Stalinist era, the institute was dissolved, to be revived only in 1967. The former head of the institute, Cenek Adamec, "rehabilitated" it in two 1966 articles about the history of opinion research in Czechoslovakia.[29] The new institute spent its first year in recruiting interviewers, training, and planning. It began full-scale operations in late 1967, but until mid-January 1968, its research was done "in keeping with the still valid rule that all research and its results must be approved by the high Party organs."[30] Shortly after Dubcek became Party first secretary, the institute was freed from this restriction and, as we shall see, played an important role in further political developments. Political surveys continued into the early spring of 1969, when the attention of the institute shifted to research on health and consumer matters. As in Poland, Czechoslovak opinion research has diminished greatly in quantity, scope, and political relevance.

In Hungary, opinion research was again begun in an informal way by newspapers and magazines, but a growing network of academic institutions has also conducted sample surveys, particularly of young people's attitudes. An early start was made by the Audience Research Department of the Hungarian Radio and TV, organized in 1963. "Public opinion polls and surveys of numbers of listeners . . . are primarily for concrete, practical aims: to aid in making timely decisions."[31]

In such less economically developed countries as Bulgaria and Romania (not to speak of Albania, which has probably not reached the stage where there are large publics), opinion research has lagged, not for economic reasons alone. In both countries empirical sociology is a recent phenomenon, though Romanian rural sociologists used some empirical techniques before the war. Most Romanian studies focus on industrial and agricultural questions and are clearly intended to aid in the improvement of production. A Romanian journalist has suggested that the channels of dialogue between the leadership and the mass public ought to be improved, and, in this connection, "it would be very useful to the development of socialist democracy to create instruments for rapid soundings of public opinion, using contemporary sociological techniques adapted to the conditions of our country."[32] Given the relatively mass nature of Romanian society and the ability of the present leadership to achieve rapport with the population while still maintaining a traditional Leninist leadership style, it is doubtful whether such "instruments" will be created in the immediate future.

Youth journals and newspapers were again the initiators of opinion research in Bulgaria, and once more sociologists were slow in adopting empirical research methods in the study of public opinion. Only after a 1961 conference of socialist sociologists, sponsored by the journal *Problems of Peace and Socialism (World Marxist Review)*, did the Bulgarians begin to do empirical research, and even then there was some opposition to this method.[33] A sociological institute was established in 1967, and a major study has been done of religiosity in Bulgaria, with studies of workers, peasants, and youth carried out in the late 1960s and early 1970s. The first Bulgarian monograph on public opinion, originally a dissertation done in the USSR, was published in 1969.[34] Bulgarian opinion research is closely linked with the more conservative of the Soviet schools in this area, as we shall see.

Yugoslavia, as always, is something of a special case. Sociology in Yugoslavia did not suffer a long Stalinist repression, and empirical methods were used rather early, especially in the Serbian, Croatian, and Slovenian republics. There are centers for public opinion research in Beograd, Zagreb, and Ljubljana, and they have published extensive public opinion studies done in their respective republics and in the country as a whole.[35] Even in Yugoslavia, however, opinion research is a delicate political issue and is directly affected by shifting political winds in the various republics. There are special problems, too, attendant upon opinion research in a federal republic.[36] Because of Yugoslavia's distinctive political system, federal structure, and opinion research experience, it cannot be treated as an integral part of this chapter.

The diffusion of public opinion research in Eastern Europe is surely partially explained by a process of mutual learning and the spread of innovation. No doubt, the Poles and Yugoslavs were the initial inspiration for some of the other countries. In the case of the Bulgarians, it is clear that not until the 1961 conference had given approval to empirical research were they willing publicly to adopt the Polish and Yugoslav "innovations."[37] A casual perusal of East Euro-

pean sociological journals will demonstrate the importance of scholarly inter-
change in the development of social science in socialist countries.

This brief overview of the evolution of opinion research in Eastern Europe
illustrates the stages of its development. By no means universally accepted in
Communist countries, opinion research usually begins as a rather amateurish
effort of the mass media and sometimes is adopted and adapted by social scientists. The Poles, Yugoslavs, Czechoslovaks, and Hungarians all report an initial
suspicion not only by some social scientists, and presumably politicians as well,
but also by the general public. "Even the avoidance of 'delicate' questions,"
Sicinski observes, "extensive press and radio propaganda explaining the survey
technique was insufficient to eliminate resistance in the early stages."[38] In
Yugoslavia, special problems were encountered in "backward areas," where
husbands would not permit wives to be interviewed or where some regarded "the
interviews as on opportunity to complain about personal problems, alleged
injustices suffered by them, and the like. More educated people often gave
stereotyped answers, particularly in earlier years, considering it a 'matter of
honor' to reply to each question."[39]

Nevertheless, the universal experience has been that following a period of
"acculturation" to opinion research, East European publics respond very eagerly.
Many volunteers come forth in response to calls for interviewers, and the response rate in surveys is by and large very high. The suspicion of respondents,
clearly a protective reflex acquired in earlier times, is probably compensated for
by the growing distance from the years of terror as well as the feeling of participation and importance that the respondent undoubtedly feels. This, of course,
compounds problems of respondent bias, since some may be impelled to say
"profound" things or to demonstrate their loyalty by giving "correct" answers.
Much depends on the political context in which the survey is being conducted,
the type of subject the survey investigates, and the type of respondent being
queried. These considerations must be borne in mind when examining the results of any survey conducted in Eastern Europe (and elsewhere).

In Poland and the Soviet Union, and to a lesser extent in the other countries, the initial stage of at least partial legitimation was followed by a stage that
might be called "faddism." Opinion surveys became fashionable, and, in Adam
Schaff's phrase, a "polling mania" seemed to grip not only academics but
journalists, students, managers, politicians, and just about anyone who wanted
to show his sophistication and modernity. Problems that could legitimately and
more effectively have been handled in traditional ways were suddenly exposed
to the new panacea, an opinion poll. This did not necessarily affect the scholarly
work that continued to be done, but it had the dual effect of cheapening the
value of polls and of dulling the original glitter of the technique. Indeed, it may
be that in addition to more important political reasons, most easily understood
in connection with Poland and Czechoslovakia, the surfeit of polls and pseudo-
polls has helped opinion research in one or two countries into a third stage of

fading interest and political reversals, wherein institutes are dissolved or areas of interest sharply circumscribed.

PUBLIC OPINION, IDEOLOGY, AND METHODOLOGY: TWO SOCIALIST APPROACHES

In the West there have been many discussions in the learned journals about the definitions of "public" and "opinion," and no end of articles and books on the methodology of public opinion research. Scholars in socialist countries have also taken up these questions, frequently differing quite sharply with each other.[40] Practically all American scholars maintain that public opinion is pluralistic, rarely decisive in political decisions, frequently amorphous, often poorly informed, susceptible to manipulation, and shifting, in the sense that

> there are many publics, and each consists of those individuals who have an interest in the matter (idea, institution, behavior) that provides their focus and definition as a public. The publics of public opinion are defined by the issues, with each issue having its own public.[41]

A minority has taken the view that "the public opinion survey performs the tremendously important function of an auxiliary ballot box. . . . Sooner or later the opinion poll is going to be used by government as a day-to-day public opinion audit," and this will check "pressure groups . . . forcing them to put their alleged popular support in evidence."[42] Less naive is Albert Cantril's statement that

> the challenge is to work toward their [polls'] responsible integration into the policy process. . . . The point is not that public opinion is to be followed at every turn in decision-making. Rather, the point is that decisions will be more informed—and in the long run wiser—if public opinion is at least taken into account early in the formulation of a substantive policy.[43]

Leaving these normative statements aside, most Western students of public opinion seem to agree with V. O. Key that policy is formulated in the context of opinion and is broadly constrained by it, but, except at election times, mass opinion rarely has a directive impact on political decisions.

Soviet, Bulgarian, and Romanian scholars have criticized American and West European opinion research on the grounds that it is mired in a swamp of empiricism in which it will be bogged down until rescued by a theory that would make sense of all the data accumulated over the years. Needless to say, Marxist scholars have such a theory at their service. The East Europeans also object to conceiving of public opinion as a simple arithmetic sum of individual opinions. Rather, they argue, public opinion is a social force with dynamics and properties that allow it to be an actor in the social and political arenas. Furthermore, it is argued, the idea popularized by Walter Lippmann that mass opinion is frequently irrational and amorphous is an improper denigration of man, typical of bourgeois social science, which seeks to serve its capitalist masters by proving the masses unworthy of serious consideration. Concomitantly, the public becomes a mere plaything to be manipulated by the state. Only in voting is there

> the sad remnant of the former democratic principles of the liberal democracy . . . the mass gradually turns into a passive observer, into an object of manipulation, into a depoliticized crowd which is a mechanical aggregate of individuals, a simple sum of semi-dead figures deprived of their will and of the awakening of their own selves.[44]

These criticisms are not without merit, and the last argument is ironically reminiscent of many Westerners' views of the masses of Communist societies, but it is not our aim critically to examine these assertions.

Rather, we shall describe two schools of thought that emerge from the recent Marxist literature on public opinion and examine the operational consequences deriving from the theoretical assumptions of each school.

The fundamental cleavage dividing the two schools is the answer to the question, What is socialist public opinion?—assuming that public opinion in capitalist countries is the opinion of the ruling class forced upon everyone else. The two most divisive issues are whether socialist public opinion is homogeneous or pluralist, and what is the best way to study it. One group maintains that socialist public opinion is homogeneous and nonantagonistic and ought to be studied mainly by the traditional method of examining letters to the editor, the resolutions of political and social organizations and institutions, the press, parliamentary decisions, and the like, with sample surveys serving only as an ancillary tool. The other group contends that socialist public opinion is pluralistic on all but the most fundamental issues, that it is not necessarily class determined, that it can reveal important cleavages in society, that the best tool for studying and understanding public opinion is the sample survey, though the traditional methods should also be employed. One way of viewing this cleavage is in terms of the distance traveled from the identification premise: The monist-traditionalist school asserts the basic validity of this premise but qualifies it by saying that it holds the "basic interests" and values in socialist society, whereas there can be differences among people, and even between the people and the political leadership, on secondary issues. The pluralist-modernist school departs further from the identification premise, implicitly or explicitly rejecting it and arguing that disagreement on almost any issue in socialist society is conceivable, though it may not be desirable.

A basic presumption of much of Marxist social science is that it must have immediate and direct utility. One of the leaders of the sociological revival in the Soviet Union states:

> Empirical social analysis makes it possible, firstly, to reveal defects in the functioning of social systems and relations, secondly, to establish a connection between the functioning of a social system and the social organism as a whole, thirdly, to eliminate the defects in the functioning of the social mechanism, and, fourthly, to contribute to the successful functioning of a social system or (if it has outlived itself) to help to eliminate it.

Further,

> Sociological studies are intended to reveal the factors determining deviations of the wills and strivings of individuals from their results in a specific social system. This, in turn, combined with a knowledge of the laws of social development, enables us to find the best way to coordinate individual aspirations and the progressive development of the social system as a whole.[45]

It is in this spirit that some Soviet and East European, particularly Bulgarian and Romanian, observers treat public opinion research.

> The task of such research is not to gather testimony about the existence of different opinions, but to explain their origin, penetrate into the essence of the formation of opinion and to give appropriate recommendations for practical use. It arises from the most urgent problems of social life and serves as an objective orientation for practical purposes, especially in the solution of problems of Communist socialization (*vospitanie*).[46]

As we shall see, the proper functions of public opinion research are a matter of controversy among Marxist scholars.

The emphasis on the collective—traditional in Marxist thought—is extended to the study of public opinion by some scholars' assertion that individual opinions have no intrinsic worth, and public opinion, by definition, exists above and beyond individual opinion. Public opinion can be borne only by the people as a whole. Grushin, on the other hand, maintains that public opinion exists also within smaller collectives, and Czechoslovak, Polish, and Yugoslav scholars clearly assume the importance of individual opinion.[47]

A. K. Uledov, one of the first Soviet scholars to write about public opinion, maintains that while there may be differences of opinion in a socialist society, they exist on secondary issues, and besides, they represent nothing more than the differences between "the old and the new," between "progressive and backward forces." Therefore, "public opinion is the opinion of the majority. Public opinion does not include the opinion of the minority."[48] Other Soviet, Bulgarian, and even Yugoslav scholars uphold the same view.[49] In contrast, Soviet political scientist R. A. Safarov states that there are no "antagonistic contradictions" between the people and the governmental organs but at the same time urges that opinion surveys be conducted in order to "discover in time contradictions (within each social group and among them, between the public will and the law . . .) and take measures for their resolution by democratic methods inherent in socialist government." In a later work, Safarov explicitly states that even under socialism there can be contradictions between the positions of government administration, on one hand, and public opinion, on the other. Such contradictions are a result of lack of information, unrealistic goals, or lack of governmental resources for meeting the demands of the public.[50]

Grushin criticizes Uledov explicitly for asserting the monism of socialist public opinion as an absolute, falling into the same kind of error as bourgeois scholars who take the pluralism of public opinion as an absolute. There is, says Grushin, a monistic opinion on some issues, and he cites the dubious example of Soviet elections, but in all surveys conducted by *Komsomol'skaia pravda* a pluralism of opinions was observed. While Uledov maintains that pluralism exists in the process of opinion formation but resolves itself into a unity, Grushin denies that there are "objective boundaries" between "process" and "result."

> The process of opinion formation goes on without interruption, at all times. It may have different directions: going from pluralism to monism, or the opposite—from unity to differentiation. . . . The differentiation of opinion under socialism is a fact. . . . The principal difference in the functioning of public opinion under socialism does not consist in the fact that monism reigns and the pluralism of opinion is impossible, but in that the existence and possibility of such pluralism are *limited in principle*, limited, in particular, by the *absence of opposition*.[51]

Yugoslav, Polish, and Czechoslovak commentators go further in their assertions of the pluralistic nature of socialist public opinion. One Yugoslav even writes that nonconforming opinion in socialist societies is an essential condition of social progress. Opinion conforming to the messages carried by the mass media cannot contribute to the development of the system for it offers no new ideas: "This role, however, can be played by unconformable opinions, which are those of the minority. . . . The feedback of these opinions is not a confirmation of the system but a [foreshadowing] of new possibilities for development."[52] A Hungarian journalist argues that "As long as public opinion as a whole was not united in support of the basics of socialism, it was feared—and rightly so—that any discussion might simply release a dormant urge to restore capitalism . . . and therefore there was no possibility of true discussion." But since agreement on fundamentals has been reached, differences of opinion on other issues can be acknowledged and sanctioned, for "If public interest exists as a matter of course, then why bother to engage in discussion at all? As long as a debate is going on, there are individual and group interests; it is only the final decision which has to serve public interest."[53]

The monist-traditionalist school sees public opinion as class-determined, content-determined, and properly guided by conscious efforts of the leading forces of a society. In a class society, public opinion is the opinion of the progressive class; therefore, the opinion of the capitalist class (and the assumption is that there exists such an undifferentiated opinion) cannot be considered genuinely public. "It follows that the bearers of public opinion are those social classes whose interests are congruent with the public interest, those classes interested in social progress."[54] Grushin rejects this thesis and points out one of the many logical contradictions in Uledov's theory (the latter prefers to call them "dialectical"): If the opinion of reactionary classes is not truly public opinion, how can Uledov simultaneously maintain that capitalist opinion is pluralistic? Grushin argues that whether opinion is objectively true or false is irrelevant; it is still public opinion irrespective of its content and regardless of whether or not it is "in conformity with the interests of the people" (Uledov's phrase).[55]

The Romanian Mihail Ralea contends that the chief tendency of socialist public opinion

> is to conform itself as exactly as possible to the objective laws of society. . . . The leading role belongs to the Marxist-Leninist parties which endeavor to raise the opinion of the masses to the standard of the scientifically founded opinion. . . . Public opinion does not represent a mere group of persons . . . but a special collectivity which acts conformably to the interests of communist construction. Whatever contradicts such interests . . . should not be considered an action of the real public opinion, but as a pseudo-action of it.[56]

A Soviet scholar states simply that socialist public opinion has two features: it expresses the actual interests of the people, and "these interests coincide with the objective path of historical development."[57] To make sure of this coincidence, it is necessary to guide the formation of public opinion. As Uledov puts it,

> Spontaneously formed public opinion exists on the level of the everyday and . . . is not always free of faults and misconceptions. This is precisely the point where conscious, guided aspects of opinion formation must play an effective role. The Party educates the

masses in the spirit of Marxist-Leninist ideology and raises the level of mass opinion to that of a theoretically grounded public opinion.[58]

France Vreg, Jerzy Wiatr, and, to a lesser extent, B. A. Grushin, reject these assumptions and prefer to assume, as Grushin puts it, that public opinion is simply the crossroads of all forms of social consciousness. This passive definition of mass opinion is unacceptable to those who impute to public opinion anthropomorphic properties. A reviewer of both Uledov's and Grushin's books criticizes Grushin's definition and argues that public opinion is a "specific phenomenon," an active force. "It is the concrete historical mechanism connecting evaluation with human activity, the mechanism of converting opinion into practice."[59]

These differences in conceptualizing public opinion are closely associated with different methodological preferences. Uledov's pioneering article criticized Western opinion studies for their biases arising from several sources—among them that samples were chosen on a random basis, the topics surveyed were "extremely narrow," and questionnaires could be manipulated to produce the desired result. "Bourgeois researchers" were afraid to use the Soviet method of "popular consultation and discussion" since these might allow antibourgeois attitudes to surface. Since it is "erroneous to base public opinion research solely on social psychology, which is nothing but the everyday consciousness of the masses," opinion surveys are of limited utility.[60] The basic method of opinion research in socialist societies is examination of national discussions (*obsuzhdenie*). Pavlova, too, denigrates opinion surveys and claims that a more efficient way to study opinion is through public documents. "In documents there is fixed the kind of opinion which, thanks to prior discussion and deliberations, has been cleansed of the subjective elements of its expressors and has retained primarily that which is really public (*obshchi*)."[61]

Safarov, on the other hand, considers such materials "far from always sufficient" and calls for more widespread use of survey techniques, especially in political-juridical areas, including citizen attitudes toward domestic and foreign policy, administrative problems, and legal questions. He even suggests that citizens themselves take the initiative in conducting such surveys and, more significantly, urges the establishment of a national institute of public opinion (presumably with more official standing and more rigorous methods than those of *Komsomol'skaia pravda's* institute). Citing the example of the Czechoslovak Institute for Research on Public Opinion as a model for the USSR (for obvious reasons, his 1975 book does not cite this precedent), Safarov suggests that the Soviet institute be attached to the Academy of Sciences wherein it could conduct surveys "on the most diverse problems" both of its own choosing as well as at the behest of Party and state organs. This is a prerequisite to the formation of a Marxist-Leninist conception of public opinion, Safarov says, implicitly expressing his dissatisfaction with the concepts of Uledov and others. Safarov acknowledges the utility of the traditional "juridicial" means of opinion research, but focuses his attention mainly on the newer "sociological" methods.[62] Grushin devotes approximately 50 pages to the defense of the survey method; Adamec carefully dissects and criticizes the methods favored by the monist-traditionalist school, pointing out, for example, (1) that letters to the media may be atypical or the work of habitual letter writers and (2) that reports of meetings do not reflect the opinions of those who do not speak up and the reports say nothing about distribution of opinions and so on.[63] It might be noted in passing that Adam Schaff's well-known polemic against opinion polls was not an attack on polls per se but rather on their misuse in studying complex problems and the tendency of overenthusiastic pollsters and students of public opinion to lapse into "mathematical cretinism."[64]

THE FUNCTIONS AND USES OF SOCIALIST PUBLIC OPINION

Different concepts of socialist public opinion lead to different conclusions about the proper use and function of public opinion in socialist societies. The general view of social research is to see it as a tool for the enhancement of societal (that is, regime) goals, a view more characteristic of the monist than of the pluralist school, but at least formally subscribed to by members of both. Grushin sees the uses of public opinion as providing practical information, particularly about "negative phenomena," for decision makers; providing information about the level and structure of "mass consciousness"; regulating the behavior of individuals and groups; improving socialist government, especially by providing opportunities for direct democracy and by checking on the mistakes of officials and the "backwardness" of mass publics; and, finally, helping participants in opinion surveys strengthen their civic sense and interest in social affairs. The functions of public opinion are evaluative, constructive, and regulatory ("Narrowly construed, this [last] is the socialization [*vospitanie*] function").[65] While Sicinski lists the function of opinion research as an instrument for measuring the achievement of societal goals and "the agreement of such objects and goals with social needs," his colleague, Anna Pawelczynska, defines the function of public opinion as a source of information but also as "a mouthpiece for democratic standards in public life, that is, a research tool which conveys public views and opinions . . . to those institutes responsible for social, political, and economic activities." Sicinski comments that "this definition of the function of social research in Socialist countries would be acceptable to most Polish sociologists."[66] The American Paul Hollander adds to the information-gathering function the purposes of combating apathy and educating people by holding up for emulation "correct" attitudes, while Allen Kassof also mentions the possibility of using polls not so much to measure opinion as to create it.[67]

In general, the Soviet and East European literature discusses the following uses of public opinion and opinion research, obviously not always in these terms: (1) democratic inputs into the political system; (2) enhancing the manipulative capacity of the political elite; (3) improving economic, political, and social efficiency; (4) serving as a source of information about society; (5) serving as a means of social control and socialization; (6) providing psychological support for the political leadership; (7) developing a sense of political efficacy among the citizenry and promoting national and political integration; and (8) promoting genuine political efficacy. Obviously, the pluralist and monist schools stress different uses of public opinion and opinion research.

Opinion research as a means of enabling the mass public to influence the formation of public policy is stressed by the pluralist school and almost entirely ignored by the monists. As noted earlier, Safarov explicitly states that public opinion should be taken into account by government organs when deciding "basic questions" and suggests that public opinion be surveyed before any administrative rearrangement is undertaken. It should be surveyed at all stages of policy making, both before and after decisions are taken. Safarov makes so bold as to suggest:

> It is advisable to give a constitutional character to the institution of political mandates and obligatory referenda . . . an institution which would be used on the initiative of citizens themselves. . . . It is advisable to supplement the Soviet constitutional mechanism of discovering public opinion with the establishment of a public opinion institute [since present channels of information are limited]. By no means do [these channels] give a full picture of the actual state of public opinion. Forms of public opinion expression have constitutional significance. Therefore, they should be fixed in the constitutional order. This pertains, in part, also to such sociological forms as questionnaire surveys and the conduct of legal experiments.[68]

Dzinic, like his compatriot Vreg, considers "systematic research into public opinion" as "essential for modern political decision making,"[69] while Stefan Nowak argues that the Gomulka regime got into trouble and ultimately fell because it had no way of gauging public opinion and lost touch with it. Adamec asks, "What could help the process of democratization more than systematic public opinion research and publication of its results?" And Dr. Zapletalova expresses the same sentiments, adding that "democratic socialism . . . cannot be imagined without public opinion research."[70] In this vein, Czech journalist Helena Klimova remarks:

> For twenty years the citizens' consciousness suffered from a sort of schizophrenia, conducting two monologues: a monologue of genuine, but not public opinion. . . . The spring and summer of 1968

cured this schizophrenia to such an extent that in the tragic August week ninety-five percent of the citizenry evaluated highly the activity of journalists and identified themselves with their opinions. ... The entire development from January to August, as seen in the [public opinion] research can be understood as the rapprochement of the name "socialism" with its content, the will of the people expressed in life. If this is so, *who dares then to speak of counter-revolution?*[71]

It is significant that Andrei Sakharov, the Soviet scientist who has called for fundamental reforms of the Soviet political system, included the establishment of a public opinion research institute in his proposed program.[72]

Adherents of the monist school prefer to emphasize the ways in which the functioning of the present political arrangements and approved behavioral patterns could be enhanced through the use of public opinion. "Empirical research directed toward working out the problems of the scientific management and control of social processes" is one of the main "tasks" of public opinion mentioned by Pavlova. Examples of research in this vein would include a Romanian study of three Bucharest enterprises, reported by Bellu, where the main question was "What are in your opinion the main directions along which socialist emulation influences the workers in your workshop?", or studies in Leningrad that attempted to determine how many people studied current political literature before and after a campaign, to increase the number of people doing so. Jerry Hough observes that some local Party organs use sociological investigations in an effort to improve their effectiveness. "Survey investigation has become almost the symbol of the scientific approach to problem-solving which the Party officials have incessantly been instructed to follow in the post-Khrushchev period."[73] A Soviet source reports that the central committees of four republic and three *oblast'* Party organizations adopted measures to improve ideological work "on the basis of research findings of projects done by sociological groups."[74] Opinion surveys have been used to study the behavior and effectiveness of deputies to governmental organs on several levels, as well as to improve planning and production of books and of radio and television receivers.[75] The Western analogy to this type of research is market surveying and perhaps polls taken by candidates for election who want to know which issues to emphasize and which to play down. This kind of research enables one to know in order better to manipulate.

A more obvious function of opinion research is to uncover information not easily obtained by other means, particularly politically relevant information. "The results of enquiries ... often serve as a warning that some attitudes, which political actors consider to be generally accepted, and on which they thus act, have not yet been adopted by public opinion," writes Bogdan Osolnik. "Such misunderstandings can be extremely harmful—and dangerous. [And, in particular,] leadership of organizations, if they rely only on indirect sources of information, can become prisoners of their own visions and concepts."[76] A study done in the Siberian city Irkutsk showed that "only a part of the voters could recall the name of the deputy they voted for. . . . All these facts testify to the necessity of further strengthening the ties between deputies and voters. Also, they permit the observation of several shortcomings in the electoral system."[77] The Bulgarian survey of religious adherence throughout the nation enabled those interested in atheist propaganda to judge some of the effects of their work and to make more precise plans for the future.

The deliberate use of public opinion for the purpose of social control occupies a prominent place in the writings of contemporary socialist scholars, especially adherents of the traditionalist persuasion. According to Pavlova, all opinion research must be relevant to "the use of public opinion as a regulator of relations among people."[78] Uledov and Igitkhanian assert that this function of opinion will expand as Soviet society approaches communism, since governmental coercion will wither away and the establishment of "Communist norms" will depend upon "the activization of public opinion."[79] Rachkov devotes two of the four chapters in his book to public opinion as an influence in the formation of morals and ethical relations, and Ralea discusses the usefulness of public opinion in bringing pressure to bear on "lazy fellows" who are not overly enamored of work.

Some Soviet scholars go further and seem to view public opinion as a possible functional equivalent of terror, insofar as it can be employed in a police function. But while one observer argues that public opinion should influence judicial proceedings ("We stand for the broadest influence of 'public passions'"), another cautions that this can lead to serious abuses, as in the case wherein judges, pressured by public opinion to impose a death sentence, did so despite the fact that the criminal code did not prescribe death in such a case. "Public opinion may be right and it may be wrong. . . . It may also happen that the petitions of individual persons who have a personal interest in the outcome of the case are offered as 'public opinion.'"[80]

A long-range form of social control is socialization. Igitkhanian, writing in the Party's ideological journal, states that "In our country public opinion is one of the most effective means of Communist socialization [*vospitanie*]."[81] If public opinion is conceived of as an active force, with a legitimate ideological component introduced by the Party, it would seem to be a natural instrument to be used in the socialization process.

Though it is rarely made explicit in Communist literature, opinion research plays a "self-affirmation" role in the sense that some studies seem to be carried out merely to confirm what the leadership wants to hear. Some scholars point to the results of studies of dubious validity as proof of a priori assumptions. Ralea draws such conclusions from Romanian studies, and Igitkhanian does the same on the basis of the early *Komsomol'skaia pravda* youth surveys, which even Grushin, their chief designer, admits were methodologically poor. People like

Safarov, on the other hand, admit that such studies can serve as little more than invalid, but comforting, messages of support to the directing forces of the system.

Public opinion might also be useful as a weapon in factional struggles within the political elite. While it is more important for a political aspirant to rally elite and interest-group support, he may also find it beneficial to have the backing of larger, more diffuse publics. Khrushchev seemed particularly sensitive to this use of public opinion, and, in other socialist systems, public opinion has been used as an input, though not a decisive one, in political combat within the elite. Public opinion played a significant role in the intra-Party struggle in Czechoslovakia in 1968.

Without imputing cynical motives to any of the Marxist opinion researchers, one can say that a consequence of opinion research, perhaps unintended, is to give some respondents a sense of their own political efficacy and increase their identification with the system. Grushin claims that the percentage of "no opinion" or "don't know" type answers has been lower in Soviet than in most Western surveys. (In the second *Komsomol'skaia pravda* survey only 30 of 1,500 refused to participate.)[82] This phenomenon may be partially explained by Osolnik's perceptive observation that in the formation of public opinion every individual is at the same time a subject and an object. "The ability to choose freely among several possible solutions not only instills in people a feeling of responsibility for the adopted attitudes but also increases their general social commitment."[83] Safarov, too, notes that "an informed and consulted people has more trust in the political course of its government, its institutions and functions."[84] James Oliver has suggested that in the Soviet Union "active participation such as stating demands will vary according to the citizen's perception of the efficacy of his actions."[85] Mere statement of opinions to someone seen as semiofficial, such as the survey interviewer, may increase one's sense of political efficacy.

In 1968-69 one of the ways Czechoslovak citizens felt they could influence the turn of events was by participating in opinion polls. Since these polls were widely publicized in the press and on the radio, it was possible for Czechoslovak citizens, like the Poles before them, to develop what Edward Keenan has called a "sense of statistical community."[86] The knowledge that large numbers of people share one's opinions undoubtedly helps one believe that his opinion may count, or, at least, that his opinion is "legitimate." Firdus Dzinic sees this as a force for integration in a multinational state, as well as a way of making people realize just how widely accepted their opinions are.

There is no linear progression in the development of genuine or perceived political efficacy in Communist systems. In some East European countries, the prewar period was one in which there was no political involvement and no political participation for the majority of the population. After the Communist ascension to power, many became involved in political life for the first time, and their sense of efficacy developed rapidly. This sense has probably waned over the years in such countries as Romania and Bulgaria, as people begin to realize that their involvement is falling short of the promises of the participatory myth. In Yugoslavia, with the expansion of genuine participation in workers' councils and an ever more meaningful electoral system, involvement may have turned into genuine participation. The pattern in Poland, Hungary, and Czechoslovakia is different. In 1956 in the first two, and in 1968 in the third, involvement was rapidly replaced by participation; in the case of Czechoslovakia participation began to assume stable institutional forms. Yet, in all three instances, the trend toward participation was reversed to the point that there was even less participation or involvement than in the pre-1956 or pre-1968 eras.

In Hungary, this trend was so pronounced that Kadar reconciled the regime to it in his famous formula, "He who is not against us is with us." The maximum that could be expected of a great number of citizens was neither participation nor involvement, but simply abstention from activity against the system. As regards public opinion, when the possibilities of influencing politics and social life appear to be expanding, there is a growing interest in public opinion surveys among the population as a whole. When the activist period is ended, polls cease to be taken at all or are concentrated on more specialized and less controversial issues, and interest in public opinion wanes, as does belief in its importance and efficacy. In a Czechoslovak poll reported in August 1969, just one year after the Soviet invasion,

> 43.1 percent of the younger generation declared that they were not interested in politics at the moment but that they were interested in the period between January and August 1968; 33.8 percent are interested in politics in a passive way. . . . Altogether 68.6 percent of Party members in this cross-section do not believe that the post-January policy could be realized under the present circumstances (among the university students the figure is actually 83 percent); 57.1 percent of these young people (66.6 percent of the university students) have no confidence in the present Party leadership. The question of whether political engagement is of any use was answered by 60.2 percent positively, but 69.7 percent of the young people included in the poll take a pessimistic view of the future development of our society.[87]

In Poland, too, by the mid-1960s, when it had become clear that the promise of the Polish October would not be fulfilled, there was a decline both in the sense of efficacy and in interest in opinion polls as a means of influencing policy. The decline may have been halted, but not reversed, by the Gierek regime. As Key says, "Attentiveness with its correlative behaviors will wane unless it is associated with a belief that watchfulness and articulateness ultimately have some bearings on what government does or does not do."[88]

Growing disbelief in the ability to exercise meaningful influence is certainly not the only cause of political apathy in Communist systems. It may well be that in some political cultures, such as the Soviet, there is no great value attached to participation as a means of influence. Quite often one hears from Soviet citizens that "political affairs are for the Central Committee to decide, and I am perfectly content to let them do so." It is impossible to know how widespread this feeling is, but in view of the traditional cultural values prevalent in much of the USSR and Eastern Europe, and taking account of many years of conditioning away from the expectation of high political efficacy, it would not be surprising if many East Europeans would not actively engage in meaningful politics, even when given the chance. In any case, under present conditions in most socialist countries, the populations are aware that they face the "dilemma of the one alternative," that there is no realistic alternative to the present system that they could bring about. This realization is conducive to apathy.

A third consideration that ought to be borne in mind is that "for a sense of political involvement to be widespread within the population, the conditions of life must be such that the struggle for subsistence does not monopolize the efforts of most men."[89] As noted earlier, one must be able to afford political interests, or, on the other hand, be so discontent as to be unable to avoid such interests. Where people feel they must spend most of their time making ends meet—that is, when living conditions are tolerable but not satisfactory—political interest is likely to decline, as *altagsleben* becomes the major focus of most people's interests. Political disinterest may also occur in a situation where, for the first time, large numbers of people perceive the possibility of radically altering their life-styles and raising their socioeconomic status. The promise of a luxurious life, just as much as the pursuit of what is perceived as the minimal existence, is enough to distract people from political affaris. In the United States it seems that those who are far from having attained what American commercialism has set out as the "good life" and those who are well beyond it form the initial core of political dissenters, while those who see themselves as being in the process of attaining this level, or have recently attained it, are not politically active until they feel themselves threatened by groups that, directly or indirectly, might take away their gains. This simplistic generalization, even if it contains some elements of truth, should by no means be taken as an "iron law." The workers of Czechoslovakia, who could not be fired and were secure in a very egalitarian wage structure, were initially suspicious of the economic and political reforms of 1968, but they were won over by the reformers, aided by a powerful dose of "fraternal aid" given by the Warsaw Pact forces.

Opinion surveys, especially if they are hampered by political considerations, are likely to fade from prominence as interest in political affairs declines. In a stable system, such as the USSR, interest in opinion polling probably declines as more becomes known about the structure and content of mass opinion. If it becomes obvious that opinion polls have no influence on policy but remain simply collections of possibly interesting information, interest in polls and surveys will wane. In any case, the Polish and Czechoslovak instances would alert us to the fact that the widespread surveying of opinion is not an irreversible trend, nor is it necessarily the herald of a new, more democratized political system.

Having examined some of the functions and uses of public opinion research in socialist societies, we may now point out the utility to Western observers of examining the results of such research, aside from the intrinsic interest they have. If we are to make anything of this research, we must be keenly aware of the methodological and other shortcomings of opinion research in socialist contexts. The major difficulties in opinion sampling are (1) dishonest responses; (2) problems of recall; (3) "response set"; (4) response norm; and (5) salience.

With reference to Communist countries, the problem of dishonest responses is probably greater than in democratic countries, since respondents may feel more impelled to tell an interviewer what they think he wants to hear, fearing sanctions for "inadmissible" answers. One emigre Soviet social scientist claims that Soviet surveys are largely invalid because "The majority of the people questioned do not express their sincere opinions. . . . In the majority of cases sociological surveys are viewed by Soviet citizens as yet another extension of official form filling which accompanies them from the cradle to the grave."[90]

Problems of recall may be illustrated by the finding that more Americans recalled voting for Dwight D. Eisenhower than actually did; there seems to be no a priori reason to say that this problem would be of a different magnitude or significance in a socialist country.

"Response set" is the tendency of people to respond affirmatively to questions, to agree with the interviewer, all other factors being equal. It might be hypothesized that in less developed countries, and in countries with strong authoritarian traditions where the interviewer, like the census taker, may be seen as an important official, response set would be a major difficulty. Some of the early Soviet polls used members of the Komsomol as interviewers, and this undoubtedly made people very cautious about their responses. However, the Czechoslovaks, to cite one example, made a conscious and successful effort to recruit ordinary people as interviewers, attempting to reduce this difficulty. However, when Polish interviewers were drawn from communities being studied, they selected the sample on their own, and this procedure raised obvious problems.[91]

"Response norm" means that a person says what he thinks is expected of him, even if no conscious dishonesty is involved. This is probably a significant problem in Eastern Europe and the USSR where expectations are relatively well known, owing to the pervasive flow of cues from official sources.

Finally, "saliency" connotes whether or not the respondent really cares about the issue he is being presented with or whether the question itself, and only the question, elicits interest and response. Especially under conditions of low political interest, this may be an important consideration. It might also play a significant role in cultures where tradition and events combine to produce a conscious withdrawal from political concern.

Grushin discusses some of the methodological shortcomings of the Soviet polls, shortcomings that have been pointed out in the West as well, and admits, for example, that the fact that questionnaires are published in a newspaper reduces the reliability of response.

> The ambitious striving to "be published," especially in a central newspaper, compels some people to write not what they really think but what, in their opinion, will please the editors more and will get published. So in their responses they show off their courage and their original thinking, flaunting their erudition . . . passing from contemptible prose to poetry. . . .[92]

More sophisticated and reliable surveys, such as those conducted in Poland, Czechoslovakia, and Yugoslavia, also have their problems. Dzinic found that quota samples—a method used also by the Prague Institute for Research on Public Opinion, but not much favored among American survey specialists—could not be checked for accuracy, and the Yugoslavs have gone through several revisions of their sampling methods. The real meaning of national figures in a multinational, federated republic is also hard to fix with precision. If 60 percent of the Yugoslav population responds "x" on question "y," it may be that in three of the six republics, less than half the respondents responded with an "x." "The fact remains that it has not yet been theoretically established what constitutes objectively, rather than statistically, the public opinion of a federal state," since it is clear that though peasants constitute 48 percent of the Yugoslav population and Yugoslav survey respondents, they do not wield proportionate influence in the society as a whole.[93]

The impact of the immediate political situation on survey research is demonstrated in Slovak surveys reported in August 1969, when the percentage of "don't know" answers became quite large in relation to the frequency of this type of answer in 1968. To the question "Are you in favor of the efforts to intensify the leading role of the CPCS in public life" (that is, are you in favor of moving away from some of the changes brought about in the reform period), 50.1 percent answered affirmatively, 14 percent answered negatively, 19.6 percent said they did not know, and 16.2 percent gave no answer. Thus, a total of 35.8 percent did not commit themselves. It is interesting, by the way, to note that the "Cabinet" of Public Opinion and Cultural Research in Bratislava was now formulating questions in a leading way that was not at all typical of the survey questions posed before the invasion and even after it by the Prague Institute. For example:

> At the CPCS CC session Gustav Husak emphasized the desire of the majority of our people to be able to live in a calm atmosphere, and

> their demand that the activities of those people who spread chaos
> and intensify social disintegration should come to a halt. Is this also
> your view?

Despite the loaded nature of the question, only 58.9 percent of the replies were affirmative. Embarrassing results were dismissed: When over three-quarters of the respondents stated that those who stayed abroad after the invasion should be granted amnesty, in line with the position taken by President Svoboda, a Slovak journalist commented that "the question itself was not a suitable one" since the right of granting amnesty is the president's alone, and "public opinion, whatever it may be, cannot influence the president's decision."[94]

To be aware of the shortcomings of opinion surveys and polls in Communist countries is not to dismiss their usefulness. On the contrary, it enables us to use them more judiciously and productively. The most basic and obvious utility of survey data from socialist countries is to provide us with information about these societies that is among the most unyielding of objective data. A second benefit to be derived from opinion data is an ability to measure, if only indirectly and by means of secondary analysis, the effectiveness and impact of Communist socialization efforts. Studies of behavior and attitudes, such as the surveys of religiosity in Bulgaria, Poland, and Czechoslovakia, may provide insights into such areas as continuity and change in societies where Communist systems have been constructed. Thirdly, studies of political attitudes and opinions may serve as indicators of the level of political integration in any given society, as well as of feelings of solidarity with other socialist, or nonsocialist, states. One might add that the incidence and nature of opinion surveys could be an indicator of the political style of the regime, the confidence it displays in the population, and its general responsiveness to and evaluation of masses and publics.

The kind of information that is provided by opinion surveys, information that must be supplemented by other kinds of sources if significant conclusions are to be drawn, may be illustrated through an examination of data from Czechoslovakia. The crisis of confidence that existed before January 1968, a phenomenon discussed at length by Westerners only in retrospect, is reflected in surveys of young people taken in 1966. One study showed that only 11.3 percent of students who were members of the Party "joined out of conviction." Over a quarter joined for reasons closely connected with material advantage and social pressure. In answer to the question "Has our society gotten the full advantages out of socialism?" only 2 percent thought it had completely, and 18 percent partially. Only 7 percent of the student respondents said that the Party influenced the majority of students either consistently or from time to time.[95]

Public opinion data also dramatically illustrate the revival of political interest and the overwhelming and growing support for the changes initiated in January 1968. The data are rich and fascinating and are treated more extensively in another chapter.

There is no need to dwell on the usefulness of attitude surveys as indirect indicators, when compared to official policies and values, of the effectiveness of socialization efforts. The near sensational poll of Warsaw students in 1958, surveys of the attitudes of Hungarian and Bulgarian youth, and studies of religiosity in Poland, Czechoslovakia, and Bulgaria, as well as data from the USSR on the same subject, provide the raw material for those interested in Communist socialization. Similarly, Yugoslav studies of interethnic relations and Czechoslovak research on Czech and Slovak views of history offer interesting material for the study of attitudinal continuity and change in their respective societies.[96] These same data, added to other kinds of information and survey data, can be of use to those interested in studying political and national integration in these societies.

OPINION-POLICY LINKAGES IN SOCIALIST SYSTEMS

American students of public opinion generally agree that, except in elections, mass opinion rarely influences policy decisions directly. Harwood Childs, Gabriel Almond, V. O. Key, James Rosenau, and Pendleton Herring all maintain that public opinion acts as a context conditioning, but not determining, policy choices. The opinions of mass and attentive publics set broad limits within which political elites are free to make a wide variety of choices. Neubauer and Kastner point out that opinion may also serve political leaders as a "gauge of compliance."[97] Almond's formulation is representative:

> The function of the public in a democratic policy-making process is to set certain policy criteria in the form of widely held values and expectations. It evaluates the results of policies from the point of view of their conformity to those basic values and expectations. The policies themselves, however, are the product of leadership groups ("elites") who carry on the specific work of policy formulation and policy advocacy. The public share in policy decisions may be compared, with important qualifications, to a market. It buys or refuses to buy the "policy products" offered by competing elites.[98]

While most American formulations of the opinion-policy linkage are so vague as to apply just as easily to Communist systems, Almond's statement at least suggests some differences in the linkages within democratic and Communist systems. First, values and expectations, set in both types of systems by elites as well as mass publics, are shaped more consciously and intensively by Communist than by democratic elites, especially in the immediate postrevolutionary period. Second, Communist elites have more powerful instruments for use in overcoming resistance from mass publics and changing values and expectations. Third, the availability of goods on the policy market, to continue Almond's metaphor, is more limited in Communist systems due to the lack of competing parties and the less frequent public discussion of alternatives. The illegitimacy of dissent makes it difficult explicitly to "refuse to buy 'policy products,'" though indirect refusal is possible, as the great piles of unsold political literature in Soviet bookstores will testify. In both kinds of systems, the elites tend to claim legitimate right sometimes to violate the values and expectations of publics ("Only the President has all the information and he knows best"; compare: "The Party leads the masses on the basis of its superior consciousness"). As then President Richard Nixon told C. L. Sulzberger, "I am certain a Gallup Poll would show . . . that a great majority of the people would want to pull out of Vietnam. But a Gallup Poll would also show that a great majority of the people would want to pull three or more divisions out of Europe. . . . Polls are not the answer. You must look at the facts."[99]

The statements of Soviet and East European scholars on the linkage between opinion and policy are as vague as those of their American counterparts. For those who cling to the identification premise, even in slightly revised form, the entire question does not arise. Grushin, on the other hand, sees the issue as more complicated and writes of the expressive, consultative, and directive functions of public opinion. On the most general level, public opinion takes sides on every issue and thereby generates the power to constrain the decision makers' actions. Opinion is consultative when it can be interpreted to offer advice for the solution of problems. It is directive in elections and referendums. Here, according to Grushin, opinion acts as a "dictator."[100]

While these may be neat, formal, perhaps even normative distinctions, one must be skeptical as to their operational relevance to the Soviet system. Uncontested elections are directive only in the most formal (and meaningless) sense. Safarov, in his essentially normative argument, stated explicitly that the opinion-policy linkage is at present weakly developed and that it must be strengthened by institutionalization. He adopts much the same classificatory scheme as Grushin ("informational, consultative, recommendatory, imperative") but goes far beyond Grushin in demanding a closer tie between unmanipulated mass opinion and public policy.[101] By 1975 he was even advocating polls to evaluate the performance of "leading, responsible people," so that the public "can express its views not only on the activity of a government institution generally, but also on the work of responsible leaders of these institutions." He also suggested that each ministry have a department for opinion research.[102]

Leaving aside what Marxist scholars think ought to be the opinion-policy relationship and examining what they think it presently is, we find that, aside from the adherents of the identification premise, most feel that there is little correlation between them. Sicinski's judgment is typical of most Polish (and post-1969 Czechoslovak) views. He points to the "lack of properly organized and institutionalized channels for conveying the data and conclusions from the research centers to the executive authorities. As yet, no satisfactory mechanism has been developed for introducing research data into the policy-making process."[103] This despite the fact that the Center for Public Opinion Research of the Polish Radio and TV made it a practice to send copies of every study to the relevant government and Party organs.

Grushin, on the other hand, reports that the results of the survey on the change in standards of living of Soviet citizens were taken to "a group of government leaders," and they took these findings "seriously." It is true that several high officials publicly commented on the survey, but a brief glance at their reactions is instructive. Reacting to findings that showed dissatisfaction with the availability of refrigerators, furniture, and the like, one minister stated that a shortage undoubtedly existed, but "this shortage (a temporary one, of course) at the same time serves as a striking illustration of how the well-being of Soviet people has grown and how their requirements have risen." He assured the public that it was their right to raise the question of the improvement of the supply system but consoled the dissatisfied with the comforting reminder that the Central Committee had adopted a decree "on measures for the further improving [of] trade. This decree contains a full-scale program for lifting trade to a new and higher level."[104] Stefan Nowak described a "period of general good will toward public opinion studies . . . typical of the late 1950s and early 1960s. Afterward, the atmosphere clearly began to change." He concludes that

> The basic role in the change of atmosphere . . . was played by the lack of understanding of the function of sociology interpreted narrowly as a propaganda function of social research, rather than its usefulness as a source of information. This was particularly true of public opinion studies where certain "controversial" results, meaning those which did not tally with ideological stereotypes, either awakened ideological mistrust in a given piece of research (and researcher)—or—much worse—mistrust of scientific methods of studying public opinion in general.[105]

Obviously, hard evidence of the nature of the opinion-policy relationship is difficult to obtain, although some Yugoslav researchers note that "opinion-makers" had no accurate picture of and sensitivity to mass opinion,[106] and there are a few instances when public opinion caused the government to reverse its policies.[107] Some attempt can be made at least to identify the realities that ought to be considered. First, mass opinion probably differs both in substantive nature and in effect on policy when it deals with foreign policy, where it will probably be "approving and amorphous," and when it deals with domestic issues, where it is more likely to be "critical and precise."[108]

Second, opinion relates to policy in different ways, depending on which policy areas are involved. There are issues on which public opinion seems to be congruent with official policy—condemnation of fascism, imperialism, crime, war—and on such issues opinion is given relatively wide leeway for expression. There are also issues on which mild and restricted expressions of displeasure are tolerated, as long as neither the system nor the regime are blamed for failures or shortcomings. Thus, complaints about consumer shortages, bureaucracy, nepotism, corruption, and the like are allowed limited expression as long as individual functionaries or impersonal forces, such as the weather, are blamed. In some issue areas, the individual is allowed to express dissatisfaction, but his views are condemned only indirectly, as a general criticism of certain classes of people. For example, few people are persecuted for criticizing regime policy toward the church though believers in general are labeled as backward and obscurantist. Finally, there are issues on which masses are made to express opinions that are probably contrary to those they truly hold—for example, their attitude toward the USSR, their love for the Party—or where the very raising of the issues is impermissible—for example, whether it is advantageous to have a multiparty system.

Third, public opinion can play a significant role in supporting a leader and a program, particularly in a period of leadership instability or changeover. The support Dubcek enjoyed helped him against his domestic enemies and made it more costly for his foreign detractors to remove him. Gomulka's lack of support among the mass public facilitated his removal. Finally, the constraints on policy choice that are imposed by mass opinion are weaker in Communist polities than in democratic ones and can be ignored or weakened more easily. Communist regimes are able to do this because their putative superior consciousness provides them with an ideological rationale for ignoring mass opinion. They can mobilize more powerful coercive instruments; they may be able to withhold and manipulate information more easily; they do not operate within a tradition of constitutional restraints on power; and they are less accountable to mass opinion in that they do not have to stand for reelection and are not as exposed to the countervailing power of organized interest groups. In most East European countries, political cultural factors also work to permit governments greater leeway in deciding and implementing policy.

Rosenau identifies three types of publics operating in the political arena: mass, attentive, and opinion-making. Their power to influence policy is unevenly distributed, with mass opinion having least power and opinion-making groups obviously having most power. In socialist societies, the raw material of opinion-making, and to some extent, attentive, publics, exists, but it is prevented from becoming a legitimate political force. Interest groups and their opinion-making leaders may exist, but they are often denied the standing of organized political actors. They are frequently denied access to information and to the political leadership, and they are subverted by the overlapping Party membership of their leaders, creating interlocking directorates where every interest group leadership is constrained by its dual identity and potentially conflicting loyalties. It may be that in Eastern Europe many individuals and collectivities, which in a democratic that in Eastern Europe many individuals and collectivities, which in a democratic system would be part of the opinion-making public, are forced into the roles of attentive or mass publics—amorphous, relatively passive, groups with limited influence.

Mass publics in East Europe and the USSR cannot effectively wield what Key calls the "ultimate weapon of public opinion," the majority party and the decisive election. Communist systems in Europe appear now to allow more articulation of individual interests than in earlier times, but, except for the Czechoslovaks (1968) and the Yugoslavs, they do not appear to permit the formation of interest-articulating groups. As Francis Castles notes, Communist systems "are not so much antipathetic to the articulation of interests as to the formation of groups . . . a group's current interests may not be objectionable, but its possession of an independent organizational structure and leadership implies a potential for opposition . . ."[109] Oliver points to the significance of interest groups as the crucial component of a public opinion that will have political influence:

> The lack of any autonomous groups . . . capable of aggregating and processing the specific raw citizen demands into a program that can serve as an alternative . . . weakens the impact of citizen demands on official deliberations and policy making . . . Raw citizen demands are processed entirely within the political system. This imposes a burden on officials, but it also assures the leadership a greater amount of decision-making autonomy by sharply reducing the pressures of public opinion.[110]

The critical role of interest groups was well understood by the Czechoslovak reformers, and for this reason people such as Vaclav Havel and Michal Lakatos urged the legitimation of interest groups in the policitcal system. Havel explicitly pointed to the ineffectiveness of public opinion in the absence of groups that could aggregate and articulate it.[111] The formation of new groups, such as KAN and Club 231, and the transformation of the hollow shells of the youth, labor, and minor party organizations into powerful, vibrant, and articulate interest groups is what frightened Communist traditionalists more than any other development in reformist Czechoslovakia, with the possible exception of the related abandonment of censorship. This is the real meaning of the complaints about the weakening role of the Czechoslovak Communist Party.

Surveys of public opinion may be regarded as standing midway between traditional Communist channels of opinion expression, the individualized forms such as letter writing, and the still inadmissible system of interest groups. Surveys, though they may engender a sense of statistical community, elicit responses not from groups but from aggregates. The element of self-conscious group membership and the organizational component are absent. Polls are, however, more sensitive gauges of public opinion than have heretofore been used in Communist systems, though, as we have seen, they can easily be used for manipulative purposes. In and of themselves, opinion polls and surveys are ambiguous entities, as easily used for manipulative as for democratic ends. A comparison of opinion surveys in the USSR with those in Czechoslovakia ought to make this clear. But perhaps just the fact that there is more experimentation with, and arguing over, opinion surveys is a significant component of political development in Marxist-Leninist systems. The phenomenon of opinion surveying in Eastern Europe and the USSR should sensitize us to some of the changes that have taken place in the relationship between the state and society. Those changes are evolutionary, rather than revolutionary, and they are usually masked as aspects of continuity. But there is a process of incremental change in these countries, which is sometimes obscured by more dramatic and visible changes, such as the Polish October, the Prague Spring, or the Polish events of December 1970. Because of the controversial and highly visible nature of such change, it may be more likely to be reversed by internal or external force: The Czechoslovak experiment was halted by outside intervention, while the Hungarian experiments of recent years have not been interfered with, partially because of their lower visibility and more gradual introduction. One way of discovering incremental change is to examine the small stones, such as public opinion, in the emerging mosaic of political development in Eastern Europe and the USSR.

NOTES

1. Paul Shoup's stimulating essay on "Comparing Communist Nations: Prospects for an Empirical Approach"—*American Political Science Review* 62, no. 1 (1968): 185-204—called attention to the unexplored possibilities of using the empirical data produced by researchers in socialist countries to expand and enhance our knowledge of socialist systems. Among the few Western studies of public opinion research in Eastern Europe are: Allen Kassof, "Moscow Discovers Public Opinion Polls," *Problems of Communism* 10, no. 3 (1961); the brief report on "Public Opinion in Communist Countries," in *Public Opinion Quarterly* 27, no. 4 (Winter 1963); Emilia Wilder, "Opinion Polls," *Survey* no. 48 (July 1963); Ithiel de Sola Pool, "Public Opinion in Czechoslovakia," *Public Opinion Quarterly* 34, no. 1 (Spring 1970); Jaroslaw Piekalkiewicz, *Public Opinion Polling in Czechoslovakia, 1968-69* (New York: Praeger, 1972); and Rene Ahlberg "Theorie der Offentlichen Meinung und Empirische Meinungsforschung in der UdSSR," *Osteuropa* 19, no. 3 (March 1969). The studies done in the 1950s by the Russian Research Center at Harvard (Bauer, Inkeles, Kluckhohn, et al.) dealt with the opinions of refugees from the USSR. Studies of emigres from Poland, Czechoslovakia, and Hungary (1951-52) were reported in Siegfried Kracauer and Paul L. Berkman, *Satellite Mentality* (New York: Praeger, 1956). The Hungarian Refugee Project (1956 ff.) at Columbia University and the Special Operations Research Office surveyed attitudes of Hungarians who left after the revolt of 1956. (See the articles by Henry Gleitman and Joseph J. Greenbaum, "Hungarian Socio-Political Attitudes and Revolutionary Action," *Public Opinion Quarterly* 24 (Spring 1960); and "Attitudes and Personality Patterns of Hungarian Refugees," *Public Opinion Quarterly* 25 (Fall 1961). The major Western study of public opinion in an East European country, not a typical one, is by Allen

Barton, Bogdan Denitch, and Charles Kadushin, eds., *Opinion-Making Elites in Yugoslavia* (New York: Praeger, 1973). Finally, Radio Free Europe has conducted many studies of the attitudes of East Europeans visiting West European countries on tourism or business.

2. Alex Inkeles, *Public Opinion in Soviet Russia* (Cambridge: Harvard University Press, 1950), p. 24.

3. "Foundations of Leninism," quoted in Alex Inkeles, "The Totalitarian Mystique: Some Impressions of the Dynamics of Totalitarian Society," in Carl J. Friedrich, ed., *Totalitarianism* (New York: Grosset and Dunlap, 1964), pp. 96-97. On Lenin's attitude toward the masses, see his *What Is to Be Done*. See also Alfred G. Meyer, *Leninism* (New York: Praeger; 1962), chap. 2. On Stalin's belief in the possibility of "subjectively" transforming "objective" reality, see Robert C. Tucker, *The Soviet Political Mind* (New York: Praeger, 1963), chap. 5.

4. Andrei Amalrik, *Will the Soviet Union Survive Until 1984?* (New York: Harper and Row, 1970), p. 32.

5. Paul Kecskemeti, "Totalitarian Communications as a Means of Control," *Public Opinion Quarterly*, Summer 1950, p. 225.

6. See Aryeh L. Unger, "The Public Opinion Reports of the Nazi Party," *Public Opinion Quarterly* 29, no. 4 (Winter 1965-66).

7. Anon, "Public Opinion Inside the U.S.S.R.," *Public Opinion Quarterly* 11 (Spring 1947): 23.

8. For Soviet data, see Mark W. Hopkins, *Mass Media in the Soviet Union* (New York: Pegasus, 1970), pp. 303-4; the Bulgarian figures are given in Rachko Rachkov, *Obshchesvenoto Mnenie* (Sofia, 1969), p. 74; the Polish figures are in Andrzej Sicinski, "Public Opinion Surveys in Poland," *International Social Science Journal* 15, no. 1 (1963): 93.

9. "Obshchestvennoe mnenie kak factor kommunisticheskogo vospitanii," in *Sotsializm i kommunism: stroitel'stva kommunizma i dukhovnoi mir cheloveka* (Moscow, 1966), p. 393.

10. Mihail Ralea, "Success in Socialist Society," *Romanian Journal of Sociology* 1 (1962?): 42-43.

11. Key's definition is "Those opinions held by private persons which governments find it prudent to heed." V. O. Key, Jr., *Public Opinion and American Democracy* (New York: Alfred A. Knopf, 1961), p. 14.

12. Karl W. Deutsch, *The Nerves of Government* (New York: Free Press, 1963), p. 154.

13. David Apter, *The Politics of Modernization* (Chicago: University of Chicago Press, 1965), p. 40.

14. Zbigniew K. Brzezinski, *The Permanent Purge* (Cambridge: Harvard University Press, 1956), pp. 14-15.

15. Andrzej Sicinski, "Developments in Eastern European Public-Opinion Research," *Polls* 3, no. 1 (1967): 3-4.

16. See Chalmers Johnson, ed., *Change in Communist Systems* (Stanford, Calif.: Stanford University Press, 1970).

17. For the distinction between publics and masses, see Herbert Blumer, "The Mass, the Public, and Public Opinion," in Bernard Berelson and Morris Janowitz, eds., *Reader in Public Opinion and Communication* (Glencoe, Ill.: Free Press, 1953), p. 43 ff.

18. Ibid.

19. This is the tenor of the 1961 Program of the CPSU. For an explanation of this thesis, see T. N. Torbiak, "Sootnoshenie metodov prinuzhediia i ubezhdeniia v deiatel'nosti sovetskogo sotsialisticheskogo gosudarstva," in G. M. Gak, et al., *Voprosy teorii sotsialisticheskogo obshchestva* (Moscow: AON pri Tsk KPSS, 1960). Paul Hollander, commenting on the appearance of public opinion polls in the USSR, suggests that they "may also conceivably reflect an increased confidence on the part of the leadership in the masses under

the conditions of de-Stalinization" ("The Dilemmas of Soviet Sociology," *Problems of Communism* 14, no. 6 [November-December 1965] : 44). On similar changes in Poland, see Jerzy J. Wiatr, "Niektore zagadnienia opinii publicznej w swietle wyborow 1957 i 1958," *Studia socjologiczno-polityczne*, no. 4 (1959).

20. G. A. Aleshinoi, et al., *Obshchestvennoe i lichnoe* (Voronezh: Izdatel'stvo voronezhskogo universiteta, 1961), p. 212.

21. These are the defining characteristics of the Western notion of participation, as identified by Robert Sharlet, "Concept Formation in Political Science and Communist Studies: Conceptualizing Political Participation," *Canadian Slavic Studies* 1, no. 4 (Winter 1967). For different views of participation in Communist systems, see Jerry Hough, "Political Participation in the Soviet Union," *Soviet Studies* 28, no. 1 (January 1976); and D. Richard Little, "Mass Political Participation in the U.S. and the U.S.S.R.," *Comparative Political Studies* 8, no. 4 (January 1976).

22. Key, op. cit., p. 547.

23. For a list of approximately 100 opinion studies done between 1958 and 1964 by one institute alone (OBOP, the Center for Public Opinion Research of the Polish radio and TV), see Andrej Sicinski, *Spoleczenstwo Polskie w Badaniach Ankietowych* (Warsaw: PWN, 1966). Sicinski categorizes the OBOP studies as follows: problems of labor and industry— 12 percent; rural and agricultural problems—14 percent; views on urban and small town living—16 percent; consumption, services (one-third of these studies were devoted to "alcohol addiction")—17 percent; "Weltanschauung and general social attitudes"—17 percent; "problems of mass culture"—24 percent. "Developments," op. cit., p. 4.

24. B. A. Grushin, *Mneniia o mire i mir mnenii* (Moscow: Izdatel'stvo politicheskoi literatury, 1967), p. 12.

25. Andras Sekfiu, ed., *Obshchestvennoe mnenie i massovaia kommunikatsiia: Rabochee soveshchanie v Budapesht, 1972* (Budapest, 1972), p. 206.

26. Ilya Zemtsov, *IKSI: The Moscow Institute of Applied Social Research* (in Russian) (Jerusalem: Soviet and East European Research Centre, Hebrew University, Soviet Institutions Series no. 6, April 1976), p. 24.

27. Robert K. Merton and Henry W. Riecken, "Notes on Sociology in the USSR," *Current Problems in Social-Behavioral Research*, Symposium Studies no. 10, Washington, D.C., 1962, p. 4.

28. Cenek Adamec and Ivan Viden, "Polls Come to Czechoslovakia," *Public Opinion Quarterly* 11 (Winter 1947-48): 550.

29. Cenek Adamec, "Pocatky vyzkumu verejneho mineni u nas, *Sociologicky casopis* 2, nos. 1 and 3, (1966).

30. "Verejne mineni v objektach vyzkumu," *Reporter* 3, no. 14 (April 3-10, 1968):8.

31. "Kozvelemeny kutatas: Public Opinion Research" (Budapest, mimeo., 1968), p. 1.

32. N. Ignat, "Reflections on Socialist Democracy," *Lupta de Clasa* no. 5 (1970), Radio Free Europe (RFE) Romanian Press Survey, no. 844 (June 19, 1970), p. 6.

33. See "Marksistskaia sotsiologiia i konkretnye sotsiologicheskie issledovaniia v Bolgarii," *Vestnik moskovskogo universiteta* series 8, vol. 33, no. 4 (July-August 1968); Zhivko Oshavkov, "Opyt sotsiologicheskogo issledovaniia religioznosti naseleniia v Bolgarii," in G. E. Glezerman and B. G. Afanasev, *Opyt i metodika konkretnych sotsiologicheskikh issledovanii* (Moscow: Mysl', 1965); and K. Goranov and O. I. Zotova, "Marksistskaia sotsiologiia i opyt konkretno-sotsiologicheskikh issledovanii v Bolgarii," *Sotsiologiia i ideologiia* (Moscow: Nauka, 1969).

34. Rachkov, op. cit. I am indebted to Professor Stoian Mikhailov, the assistant director of the Sociological Institute, for sharing with me his extensive knowledge of Bulgarian sociology. Of course, he is not responsible for any of the views expressed here.

35. The publications are so numerous that only a few examples can be cited: Mladen Zvonarevic, *Javno mnijenje gradana SRH o samoupravljanu* (Zagreb, 1967); Zvonarevic, *Politicka i socijalna orijentacja seoske omladine u SR Hrvatskoj* (Zagreb, 1967); Institut Drustvenih Nauka, *Javno mnenje o prednacrtu novog ustava* (Belgrade, 1964); and the series of the (Belgrade) Institute of Social Science, *Jugoslovenski Javno Mnenje o . . .* , as well as the series of its public opinion department, "Izvestaji i studije."

36. See Firdus Dzinic, "Opinion Surveys in a Federal Republic: A Review of Yugoslav Experience," *Polls* 3, no. 3 (1968).

37. See Zygmunt Bauman, "The Influence of East European Social Science on Soviet Social Science," in Roman Szporluk, ed., *The Influence of East Europe and the Soviet West on the USSR* (New York: Praeger, 1976). See also Zvi Gitelman, "The Diffusion of Political Innovation from East Europe to the USSR" in the same volume.

38. Sicinski, "Developments," op. cit., p. 99.

39. Dzinic, op. cit., pp. 6-7.

40. The uses and abuses of the concept of "public opinion" are discussed in Floyd H. Allport, "Toward a Science of Public Opinion," *Public Opinion Quarterly* (1937), reprinted in Daniel Katz, Dorwin Cartwright, Samuel Eldersveld, and Alfred McClung Lee, eds., *Public Opinion and Propaganda* (New York: Dryden Press, 1954).

41. Bernard C. Hennesy, "Public Opinion and Opinion Change," in James A. Robinson, ed., *Political Science Annual* 1 (Indianapolis and New York: Bobbs-Merrill, 1966), p. 249.

42. Julian Woodward in ibid., p. 82.

43. Letter to the New York *Times*, July 1, 1970.

44. France Vreg, "Structural and Functional Changes in the Public and the World Community," in *Mass Media and International Understanding* (Ljubljana: School of Sociology, Political Science, and Journalism, 1969), pp. 39, 42.

45. G. Osipov, *Sociology* (Moscow: Progress, 1969), pp. 31, 34.

46. I. T. Pavlova, "O nauchnoi metodologii issledovaniia obshchestvennogo mneniia," *Vestnik moskovskogo universiteta* series 8, vol. 23, no. 4 (July-August 1968): 7. For examples of how opinion research is made policy-relevant in the USSR, see Ellen Mickiewicz, "Policy Applications of Public Opinion Research in the USSR," *Public Opinion Quarterly* 36, no. 4 (Winter 1972).

47. Grushin, op. cit., pp. 96-198.

48. A. K. Uledov, *Obshchestvennoe mnenie sovetskogo obshchestva* (Moscow, 1963), pp. 156-80.

49. See Rachkov, op. cit., p. 177; B. A. Erunov, "Kharakternye cherty obshchestvennogo mneniia v usloviakh perekhoda k kommunizmu," *Uchenye zapiski kafedr obshchestvennykh nauk vuzov g Leningrada: Problemy nauchnogo kommunizma* (Leningrad: Leningrad University, 1964), pp. 150-51; and Bodgan Osolnik, "Socialist Public Opinion," *Socialist Thought and Practice*, no. 20 (October-December 1955), p. 120.

50. The first quotation is from R. A. Safarov, "Vyiavlenie obshchestvennogo mneniia v gosudarstvenno-pravovoi praktike," *Sovetskoe gosudarstvo i pravo*, no. 10 (1967), pp. 48 and 47. Safarov's later work is *Obshchestvennoe mnenie i gosudarstvennoe upravlenie* (Moscow: Iuridicheskaia literatura, 1975) and the quotation is from pp. 65-66.

51. Grushin, op. cit., pp. 168-86.

52. Ana Barbic, "(Ne) Konformizam i javno mnenje," *Sociolgija* 11, no. 1 (1969): 93 (English summary).

53. A. Bor, "Conditions for a Discussion," *Magyar Nemzet*, November 2, 1972, translation in RFE, Hungarian Press Survey, no. 2243.

54. Uledov, op. cit., p. 77.

55. Grushin, op. cit., pp. 192-96. See also pp. 59-62.

56. Ralea, op. cit., pp. 42-43. The frequency with which Ralea approvingly refers to and quotes Uledov should be noted. It is significant that not one poll is cited in a Romanian monograph on public opinion in a "generally developed socialist society." See A. Bondrea, *Opinia Publica in Procesul Fauririi Societatii Socialiste Multilateral Dezvoltate* (Cluj: Dacia, 1973).

57. Erunov, op. cit., p. 155.

58. A. K. Uledov, "Obshchestvennoe mnenie kak predmet sotsiologicheskogo issledovaniia," *Voprosy filosofii*, no. 3 (1959), p. 52.

59. M. Ia. Koval'zon, "Issledovanie obshchestvennogo mneniia," *Voprosy filosofii*, no. 9 (1968), p. 155.

60. Uledov, "Obshchestvennoe mnenie," op. cit., p. 44, n. 1 and p. 46.

61. Pavlova, op. cit., pp. 9-10. Similar views are expressed by Osolnik, and by M. Kh. Igitkhanyan, "The Spiritual Image of Soviet Youth," *Voprosy filosofii*, no. 6 (June 1963), translated in *Current Digest of the Soviet Press* (CDSP) 4, no. 39 (October 23, 1963): 18. A milder expression of similar views is found in G. Osipov and M. Yovchuk, "Some Principles of Theory, Problems, and Methods of Research in Sociology in the USSR," *American Sociological Review* 28, no. 4 (August 1963): 622.

62. Safarov, "Vyiavlenie," op. cit., pp. 49-53.

63. "Rozhovor o verejnem mineni," *Nova mysl* 12, no. 12 (December 1968): 1519. (Interview by Jan Hysek of three members of the Institute of Public Opinion: Jaroslava Zapletalova, Milan Benes, and Cenek Adamec).

64. For Schaff's criticisms and some replies to it, see "Professor Schaff and the Sociologists," *East Europe* 11, no. 7 (July 1962): 24-29.

65. Grushin, op. cit., chap. 6, and pp. 90-93.

66. Sicinski, "Developments," op. cit., pp. 3 and 6. Indeed, in calling for a revival of opinion research in Poland, Stefan Nowak stressed precisely this point. "The Social Usefulness of Studies of Public Opinion and Attitudes," *Nowe Drogi*, September, 1971, translation in RFE Polish Press Survey, no. 2333.

67. Hollander, op. cit., p. 45; Kassof, op. cit., p. 55.

68. Safarov, "Vyiavlenie," op. cit., pp. 51-54. In his book, Safarov suggests that surveys be conducted that would evaluate the work of "leading, responsible people" (p. 86). He further suggests that citizens should not only help decide on alternatives presented to them, but should themselves be able to present alternatives; not only to decide questions, but to determine the methods by which decisions will be implemented (pp. 89-90).

69. Dzinic, op. cit., p. 8.

70. Adamec in "Verejne mineni," op. cit., p. 8 and Zapletalova in "Rozhovor," op. cit., p. 1511.

71. "Co si myslime u nas doma?," *Listy*, no. 6 (1969), p. 3.

72. See the letter of Sakharov, Turchin, and Medvedev, published in *Saturday Review*, June 6, 1970, pp. 26-27.

73. Jerry F. Hough, *The Soviet Prefects* (Cambridge: Harvard University Press, 1969), p. 181.

74. G. V. Osipov, "Tseli i opyt sotsiologicheskikh issledovanii v SSSR," in *Sotsiologiia i ideologiia* (Moscow: Nauka, 1969), p. 306.

75. On the work of deputies, see "Effektivnost' deputatskoi deiatel'nosti (Opyt konkretnogo sotsiologicheskogo issledovaniia na materialakh Armianskoi SSR)," *Sovetskoe gosudarstvo i pravo*, no. 1 (1969), and I. Kalits, A. A. Laumets, and Kh. Kh. Shneider, "Izuchenie deiatel'nosti deputatov s pomoshchiu konkretno-sotsiologicheskogo metoda," *Sovetskoe gosudarstvo i pravo*, no. 9 (1965); on market research for book and radio-TV production, see R. Orlova and L. Kopelev, "Kniga i obshchestvennoe mnenie," *Literaturnaia gazeta*, January 23, 1962, and Grushin, op. cit., p. 84, respectively. A Hungarian example of this type of opinion research is reported in E. Szluka, "Performance, Wages,

Conduct, Party Work—The Success of Sociology in the Lenin Metallurgical Works," *Nepsza-badszag*, August 16, 1969, RFE Hungarian Press Survey, no. 2049. Safarov, in his book, reports a study in Kalinin *oblast'* involving 1,500 citizens and 1,000 local administrators whose aim was to discover whether the administrators were taking account of public opinion. Mladen Zvonarevic found a high degree of accuracy in the perception of public opinion by Yugoslav "opinion-makers." See his "The Relationship Between Public Opinion-Makers and Public Opinion," in Barton, Denitch, and Kadushin, eds., op. cit.

76. Osolnik, op. cit., pp. 125-26.

77. V. A. Pertsik, "Puti sovershenstvovaniia deiatel'nosti deputatov mestnykh sovetov," *Sovetskoe gosudarstvo i pravo*, no. 7 (1967), p. 17.

78. Pavolva, op. cit., p. 5.

79. Uledov, *Obshchestvennoe mnenie*, op. cit., pp. 338-48; Igitkhanyan, op. cit., p. 18.

80. I. Galkin, in "The Court and Public Passions" (*Izvestiia*, April 17, 1966) expresses the first view, and I. Perlov ("Justice and Public Opinion," *Izvestiia*, June 30, 1966) the second. Both articles are translated in *Soviet Review* 8, no. 1 (Spring 1967). See also A. B. Sakharov, "Rol'obshchestvennosti v ukreplenii sovetskogo pravoporiadka i zakonnosti," *Voprosy filosofii* 14, no. 3 (1960). A Bulgarian judge publicly criticized attempts by various groups, speaking in the name of "public opinion," to influence court proceedings. See RFE, Situation Report, Bulgaria, May 17, 1973.

81. M. Igitkhanian, "Sila obshchestvennogo mneniia," *Kommunist*, no. 8 (May 1962), p. 97. See also Grushin, op. cit., p. 95; Pavlova, op. cit., p. 7; and A. K. Uledov, "O vliianii sotsialisticheskogo obshchestvennogo mneniia na soznanie lichnosti," in D. M. Ugrinovich et al., *Obshchestvennaia psikhologiia: Kommunisticheskoe vispitanie* (Moscow: MGU, 1967).

82. Grushin, op. cit., pp. 85-86.

83. Ibid., p. 127.

84. Ibid., p. 47.

85. James H. Oliver, "Citizen Demands and the Soviet Political System," *American Political Science Review* 63, no. 2 (June 1969): 473.

86. In a discussion of a paper by Zev Katz, "Political and Industrial Sociology in the Soviet Union," Russian Research Center, Harvard University, December 5, 1969, p. 13.

87. F. Motycka, "Notes on a Public Opinion Poll," *Tribuna*, no. 30 (August 6, 1969), RFE Czechoslovak Press Survey, no. 2249. The results of a survey of about 1,000 Hungarian workers on their interest in politics are reported in *Delmagyarorszag*, February 6, 1972, and are discussed by F. Baktai, "On the Right Wave Length," *Nepszava*, March 5, 1972, RFE Hungarian Press Survey, no. 2191.

88. Key, op. cit., p. 546.

89. Ibid., p. 548.

90. Alexei Yakushev, "Are the Techniques of Sociological Surveys Applicable Under the Conditions of Soviet Society?" *European Journal of Sociology* 13 (1972): 143, 145.

91. See Antoni Sulek's review of Gostkowski and Lutynki, *Analizy i proby technik badawczych w socjologii*, in *Polish Sociological Bulletin 1973*, nos. 1-2 (Warsaw, 1975), p. 125.

92. Grushin, op. cit., p. 273.

93. Dzinic, op. cit., pp. 8-9.

94. M. Mitosinska, "Verejna mienka ako sociologicka snimka," *Noveslovo* no. 33 (August 14, 1969): 9. English translation is to be found in RFE Czechoslovak Press Survey, no. 2254. For another example of "loaded" questions used in an East German youth survey, see Heinz Lippmann, *Honecker and the New Politics of Europe* (New York: Macmillan, 1972), p. 213.

95. "Studenti o sobe," *Student*, March 27, 1968, p. 11; and Galia Golan, "Youth in Czechoslovakia," *Journal of Contemporary History* 5, no. 1 (1970). See also the survey on local government in Olga Vidalkova, "Dormant Activity," *Nedele* no. 8 (April 1967), RFE Czechoslovak Press Survey, no. 1916. For a Hungarian poll of secondary school students, see S. Daroczy, "The Social and Political Knowledge of High School Students," *Partelet*, November 1971. Translated in RFE Hungarian Press Survey, no. 2166. See also Koroly Varga, "The View of Life of Hungarian Students," *New Hungarian Quarterly*, no. 35 (Autum 1969).

96. For the relevant Polish studies, see Sicinski, ed., *Spoleczenstwo*, op. cit., and the journals *Kultura i spoleczenstwo* (for example, X, nos. 1 and 4), *Studia socjologiczno-polityczne*, nos. 19 and 24. See also Stefan Nowak, "Equalitarian Attitudes of Warsaw Students," *American Sociological Review* 25, no. 2 (April 1960). On Hungarian youth, see the study by Varga, cited in the previous note, and the studies cited in Bennett Kovrig, *The Hungarian People's Republic* (Baltimore: Johns Hopkins Press, 1970), p. 143. The major Czechoslovak study of religiosity (in North Moravia) is Erika Kadlecova, *Sociologicky vyzkum religiozity severomoravskeho kraje* (Prague: Academia, 1967). See also P. Prusak, "Some Results of a Survey on Religiousness in Slovakia," *Sociologia*, no. 1 (1970), RFE Czech Press Survey, no. 2308). On Czech and Slovak views of their history, see Ustav pro vyzkum verejneho mineni, *Vztah cechu a slovaku k dejinam* (Prague, 1968) (data from this study were published in *Prace*, November 27, 1968 and by de Sola Pool). A Yugoslav study of religiosity is dragomir Pantic, *Neki aspekti religijskog fenomena u nasoj zemlji* (Belgrade: Institut drustvenih Nauak, 1967). The same author and institute have published a study of ethnic relations, *Etnicka distanca u SFRJ* (1967).

97. Deane E. Neubauer and Lawrence D. Kastner, "The Study of Compliance Maintenance as a strategy for Comparative Research," *World Politics* 21, no. 4 (July 1969): 634-35; Harwood H. Childs, *Public Opinion: Nature, Formation, and Role (Princeton, N.J.: Van Nostrand, 1965)*, p. 318; Gabriel Almond, *The American People and Foreign Policy* (New York: Harcourt Brace, 1950), pp. 5-7; Key, op. cit., pp. 14, 29, 423-24, 552-57; James W. Rosenau, *Public Opinion and Foreign Policy* (New York: Random House, 1961), pp. 33-34, 72; and E. P. Herring, *The Politics of Democracy* (New York: Rinehart, 1940), p. 309.

98. Almond, op. cit., p. 6.

99. New York *Times*, March 22, 1971.

100. Grushin, op. cit., pp. 86-90.

101. Safarov, "Vyiavlenie," op. cit., p. 54.

102. Safarov, *Obshchestvennoe Mnenie*, op. cit., pp. 90, 94-95.

103. Sicinski, "Developments," op. cit., p. 9.

104. V. A. Kucherenko, "Joyous Results, Valuable Suggestions," *Komsomol'skaia pravda*, October 8, 1960. Translated in CDSP 12, no. 45 (December 7, 1960): 14-15.

105. Nowak, op. cit., p. 3.

106. Mladen Zvonarevic, "The Relationship Between Public Opinion-Makers and Public Opinion," in Barton, Denitch, and Kadushin, eds., op. cit., pp. 263-81. A Polish study in six cities showed "marked differences between leaders' and public's support for developmental goals." See Jerzy Wiatr, "Political Elites and Political Leadership," *Indian Journal of Politics* 7, no. 2 (December 1973): 149, n. 11.

107. See, for example, "Angry Public Makes Hungarian Government Think Twice," Radio Free Europe, *RAD Background Report* 21, (Hungary), January 21, 1976.

108. Alexander Dallin et al., *The Soviet Union, Arms Control, and Disarmament* (New York: Columbia University: School of International Affairs, 1964), p. 80.

109. Francis G. Castles, "Interest Articulation: A Totalitarian Paradox," *Survey*, no. 73 (Autumn 1969), p. 127.

110. Oliver, op. cit., p. 474.

111. Vaclav Havel, "On the Subject of Opposition," *Literarni Listy*, April 4, 1968 (RFE, Czech Press Survey, no. 2055).

2

PUBLIC OPINION
IN POLAND
Adaline Huszczo

Of all the Eastern European countries, Poland enjoyed by far the richest and most varied sociological tradition during the interwar period. Though the intellectual community in which it flourished was decimated by the Nazis and opportunities for its further development were suppressed during the postwar Stalinist period, that tradition did survive. On that score alone, it is not surprising that it should have been in Poland that the ferment of the 1950s brought with it new emphasis on the study of people and society.

Indeed, one of the first overt signs of the "thaw" that developed in the Soviet bloc after Stalin's death was the establishment by the Polish Academy of Sciences in 1954-55 of a Center for Sociological Research. As ferment in Polish intellectual circles continued through the mid-1950s, Jozef Chalasinski, a respected scholar and a disciple of the internationally known Polish sociologist Florian Znaniecki, published articles openly criticizing the "unanimity of intellectual opinion" that had stifled serious controversy among Marxist philosophers and seemed to imply that present dogma could not stand the test of empirical investigation.[1] Responding firmly to an answering polemic from the Marxist philosopher Adam Schaff, who emphasized the need to resist contamination by "bourgeois sociology and philosophy," Chalasinski continued to attack the absence of empirical investigation and strongly urged empirical study of "mass processes."[2]

However, it remained for newspapers and other periodicals to break the ice and make the first attempt at empirical investigation of mass opinions. The first attempts at polling public opinion in the Soviet bloc—and they were very amateurish ones, without a doubt—were journalistic enterprises. Perhaps the very first was one by the major Warsaw daily, *Zycie Warszawy*, in November

1955, in which the paper asked its readers to respond to the question "What is your opinion of your newspaper?" From the answers received, *Zycie Warszawy* noted the following complaints: "the lack of factual information on life in Western Europe and America"; the stereotyped propaganda on the USSR and the desire for a "report which does not consist merely of a few sentences expressing the highest admiration"; the suppression of information about the defection to the West of important persons such as Jozef Swiatlo and others.* The paper quoted one reader's response as follows: "It is a shame that Poles know so little about what is going on in the world; this is the fault of our press, which forces those who are eager to get some information to listen to the 'Free Europe' broadcasts."

In fact, this first "public opinion poll" does not differ in many respects from the type of voluntaristic "self-criticism" that has always been practiced, and indeed encouraged, in the Soviet bloc countries, but the sensitive political content is striking, and it was a significant indicator of what was to come.

In the events that led up to the establishment of the Gomulka regime in October 1956, segments of the Polish press played a crucial role in bringing problems to the fore and focusing attention on important issues. Gauging reader interests and evaluation of their own efforts became important to the media, and it is hardly accidental that the eventual institutionalization of public opinion research came in the form of an arm of Polish Radio and Television Center. Nor is it surprising that a large proportion of the polls conducted by the Public Opinion Research Center in its earliest and most active period dealt with the functions, receptivity, and general quality of the press and radio as perceived by the public.[3]

In the freer and more open atmosphere of post-October Poland, press polling efforts soon spread to a wide variety of social, economic, and political topics. The youth magazine *Dookola Swiat* published a survey on the sexual mores of teenagers. *Polityka* cooperated with the Paris paper *l'Express* in a survey comparing the attitudes of French and Polish children toward war. A number of polls were done on the literary and film tastes of various groups. The youth paper *Sztandar Mlodych* conducted an extensive survey among young married couples dealing with budgets, living conditions, children, and relations with in-laws. *Przeglad Kulturalny* polled rural readers on their mood and feelings. In addition, Polish newspapers reprinted many polls from the Western press.

---

*Swiatlo was a high-ranking secret police official whose broadcasts to Poland after his defection provided many with their first insights into the scope and nature of the Stalinist terror.

Few of these press polls would stand any test of methodological rigor. Even when the press polls were at their peak, complaints were voiced about this, and though "Gallupism" became a term of reprobation, some bore more resemblance to "man-on-the-street" or "inquiring reporter" type features than the rather rigorous techniques employed by the George Gallup organization. The organ of the Polish Journalists Association, *Prasa Polska*, noted in October 1959: "The question of method, or rather the lack of it, is the cause of many clashes between sociologists and journalists . . . who are so eager to use various polls. . . . Materials derived from them [most often] produce nothing and explain nothing."

But by this time the question of method was already being dealt with and public opinion research was being shifted away from the press and into official and academic institutes with greater capacities for methodological rigor. The Center for Public Opinion Research of Polish Radio and Television (Osrodek Badania Opinii Publicznej—hereafter OBOP) was founded in 1958. And in spite of Adam Schaff's worries about contamination by bourgeois sociology, the Polish October witnessed a rapid proliferation of sociological institutes attached to the Polish Academy of Sciences, to university chairs, and to various party and government agencies. Most of them openly engaged in research on a broad range of topics, employing empirical and statistical methods used extensively in Western sociological research but ignored in Eastern Europe since the establishment of the Communist regimes and in the USSR since the 1920s.

Having noted this shift, however, we would be remiss in not emphasizing the extent to which the early newspaper polls anticipated the subject matter of the later efforts by official and academic institutes, and also the important role played by the continuing zeal of the press for publicizing the results of such surveys.

Public interest in polls and surveys during this period was intense. When the OBOP, operating on a limited budget, asked in 1958 for volunteer interviewers to do the field work for its surveys (work that is paid in Western countries), it was overwhelmed with applicants from all over the country. As a result, according to its director, it was able to pick and choose a highly competent field staff. The volunteer interviewers took special training and did the work of interviewing and writing periodic reports on problems and additional needs with great enthusiasm.[4] When the OBOP polled its interviewers in 1959 for suggestions on topics for future surveys, it received 1,450 replies containing over 20,000 suggestions.[5] The most frequently suggested topics were negative social behavior (theft, drunkenness), by 80 percent of the poll takers; problems of the governmental system, 77 percent; standard of living, 76 percent; international affairs, 73 percent; and relations between Church and state and religious instruction in lay schools, 69 percent.

All these topics and more received attention in the heyday of Polish public opinion studies, which roughly spanned the years between 1958 and

1963. (Reference can even be found to a study "On Sexual Life."[6]) The OBOP continued to operate after that time, and empirical sociological studies have been undertaken by various academic institutes as well. But public and journalistic interest in them has faded, in no small part because of the significant changes that have occurred in their nature and function.

It is beyond the scope of this chapter to examine any or all of these studies in the depth they deserve. The aim is rather to provide a broad survey of the studies conducted, their findings, and the political context in which they occurred in order to suggest that these studies constitute a rich resource for understanding many aspects of the social and political life of Poland, and to illustrate the potential value of such studies in other socialist countries.

THE YOUTH STUDIES

One of the newspaper polls published during the early post-October period inspired a series of more rigorous studies that proved to be of the utmost importance, not only because of their findings, but because of their political repercussions—then and later. A survey of the youth organ *Sztandar Mlodych* in 1957 indicated that young people had been deeply influenced by the October events, that they overwhelmingly preferred some kind of "national communism," that they were pro-Western in their literary tastes, and that they considered better living conditions their major personal aspiration. In addition, the *Sztandar Mlodych* survey indicated that over half of the young children, with their mothers working, were being brought up by grandparents who instilled religious and other pre-Communist values. Said the paper, "The generation of today's parents tried to break away from the influence of the older generation; now their children are being subjected to the self-same influence. The circle closes."[7]

In 1958, the Warsaw University Department of Sociology carried out a carefully constructed and detailed survey of the religious and political attitudes of a representative sample of 730 undergraduates from all Warsaw University faculties, in what was described by the researchers themselves as "an attempt to confront . . . the student myth with the reality which a sociologist finds when he attempts to look at it through spectacles which are neither rose-colored nor black."[8] The "rose-colored" myth, they explained, was the one in which the hero "broke a date to be on time for a lecture on Marxism"; the "black" myth was that in which "he broke it in order not to be late for his rosary circle."

The results of this survey confirmed the striking implications of the *Sztandar Mlodych* poll. It showed that while many of them did not practice regularly, 69 percent of the students, including 70 percent of those of worker origin, were religious believers.

The students' attitudes toward "socialism" and "Marxism" were extremely interesting. A substantial majority (nearly 70 percent) indicated a preference for "some form of socialism," while an almost equally decisive majority (68 percent) declared that they were not "Marxists." Over 600 of the polled students belonged to the Socialist Youth Union, but only 8 percent claimed to have joined out of conviction.

In order to determine in more detail the extent of their socialist attitudes, the pollsters asked the students specific questions on various ideological issues identified with socialism, such as the economic model, the function of Workers' Councils (an issue being hotly debated in Poland at the time),* and economic egalitarianism.

With regard to the socialist economic model, nearly 85 percent of the students agreed that private enterprise could not be admitted to heavy industry without any limitations. But when asked to indicate whether it could be permitted "without limitations" in any of eight other listed fields, majorities of from 96 percent to 62 percent said "yes" for handicrafts, retail trade, and light industry. In the remainder of the categories, the number favoring unlimited private enterprise decreased with the importance of the activity to the economy as a whole. An unexpectedly high number (16 percent) approved unlimited private enterprise in agricultural estates, a phenomenon that the researchers attributed to "the fairly universal opinion that the socialist economic forms so far applied in agriculture are ineffective, particularly on the big estates."[9] As the researchers noted, "The picture here is not that which the supporters of outworn political conceptions would wish to see; but it has one virtue: it is true."

On the question of Workers' Councils, the majority of the students (55 percent) felt that they should be "the real master of the enterprises."

The students reacted rather negatively to all but the most obvious slogans of economic egalitarian ideology. The majority (52 percent) even disagreed that "a wide range of salaries and wages constitutes an indirect form of the exploitation of some people by others"; 49 percent considered the postulate that all citizens' incomes should be roughly equal "fundamentally wrong," while an additional 25 percent thought it right, but said that it should be postponed to the distant future; and 64 percent felt that professions requiring higher education should be "much higher" rewarded than those that do not.

(When asked to indicate what the highest and lowest monthly income of a working person should be, however, the students' attitudes did begin to look more egalitarian. More than half confined the permissible income range, measured in concrete terms, to a three-to-one ratio.)[10]

---

*Workers' Councils had been formed spontaneously in 1956, and the regime was struggling to transform them and bring them under its political control.

As a further gauge of the meaning that the students attached to the term socialism, they were asked to cite various countries where socialism could be found in its ideal form. The responses to this question were not given in any of the reports on the study reviewed by this writer, but one report indicated that individual responses "depended a good deal on the student's 'knowledge of the world.'"[11]

Another area probed in the study was the students' attitudes to civil liberties. When asked if they considered it permissible for the state to place limitations on civil liberties for the purpose of carrying out aims of great social importance, 52 percent declared it permissible only under exceptional circumstances and only for very brief periods of time, while 22 percent said it was not permissible at all. When asked to indicate if they would favor applying certain specified sanctions to people whose opinions they considered harmful to the community, however, a somewhat different perspective emerges on the students' "libertarian" attitudes. A majority opposed only the application of penal sanctions for expressing such opinions. The majority favored rendering their accession to power impossible, preventing them from influencing public opinion, barring them from important positions in society, and even barring them from any kind of public activity. In a later elaboration of these results, in which a scale of tolerance was constructed, 50 percent of the students fell in the low-tolerance range and another 32 percent in the medium range.[12]

Finally, the students were asked which of a list of possible aims in life came closest to their own profound desires. On the basis of these answers, the researchers drew the following picture of the "typical" student:

> He desires, while being assured of a reasonably decent existence, to live a quiet life in the midst of friends, enjoying their respect and acknowledgment of his modest but useful activities. . . . He feels very little necessity for bringing his ideological values to bear on life; he is not attracted by a great professional career, attended with responsibility. And in no case . . . does he aspire to either a great fortune or political power.[13]

The researchers concluded:

> The relative unimportance of social and political principles in the students' scheme of values seems to suggest that such principles, though fairly thoroughly imbibed, do not call into play the emotions of the students. They consider them to be simply a normal and accepted social background, against which their personal affairs, their conflicts and private life, take place. And it is these personal issues which are of most importance and interest to them.[14]

These findings of widespread religious belief, attachment to a less than orthodox model of socialism, and lack of ideological engagement were very distressing to the regime. While Marxist theory, as formulated by the Soviet party leadership and followed by the East European regimes, does not deny the possible existence of such attitudes and opinions, a consistent pattern would be expected only within "hostile classes." Among youth raised under socialism and educated in the Marxist tradition, they could not be expected as more than random and minimal "carryovers from the past."

The OBOP, which had been established as an autonomous survey research center attached to Polish Radio in 1958, was asked to explore the situation further. In 1959, it carried out another series of studies on a representative national sample of youth from 15 to 24 years of age, using a questionnaire entitled "My World View." These studies again sought to gauge the political, religious, and moral attitudes of youth and their aspirations for the future. Again, the results confirmed the unorthodox findings of the earlier studies. Still another survey among younger children (12 to 13 years) revealed that a large majority showed "ritualistic" attitude patterns, characterized by a tendency to condemn transgressions of Catholic precepts, as opposed to an "altruistic" pattern, characterized by condemnation of acts injurious to others.[15]

The regime took steps to counteract these disturbing trends. Religious instruction, which had been compulsory (!) in the state schools since October 1956, was banned from the school premises, and a new, "more scientific" approach to atheistic propaganda was developed. Marxist theory was reintroduced as a mandatory subject in schools, while ideologist Adam Schaff led a new, humanistically embellished Marxist indoctrination campaign. The regime expanded training of Marxist teaching cadres and passed a retirement law to remove noncommunist professors. Membership in the Socialist Youth Union had dropped from one million to 100,000 after October 1956 and remained at that level at the time of the Warsaw University study in 1958. Party organizations at institutions of higher education were ordered to draw more students into membership.

In 1961, the Warsaw University Sociology Department carried out what was said at the time to be the first in a series of periodic follow-ups on its original study. It would provide, for one thing, a short-term test of the effectiveness of the regime's measures. The follow-up survey was given to only 355 students, compared with 730 in 1958, and unlike the earlier study, which had encompassed students from all fields, it was restricted to students at the technological institute. About half of the subjects in the 1961 study had also been subjects in the earlier one. No significant differences were found between this group and the new subjects.

In some respects, the results would appear encouraging to the regime. The overall number of religious believers declined by 8.5 percent and religious practice by 14 percent. Seven percent more of the students were willing to have civil liberties restricted to attain important social goals, and 9 percent less considered such limitations not permissible at all.

The already large number who preferred some form of socialism increased by 5 percent, but more satisfying to the regime was the fact that approval of nationalization of the economy also increased markedly. While a majority in 1961 still approved unlimited private enterprise in handicrafts, this was no longer the case in any other field. The researchers attributed this change to "the real improvement in light industry production and the functioning of trade which has occurred in Poland in the last three years."[16]

Thus, the students' view of the economic model of socialism had come somewhat more into line with the orthodox model. On the other hand, while the number of self-proclaimed Marxists had doubled from 9 percent to 18 percent in the three years, this still constituted a distinct minority. Sociologist Stefan Nowak attempted to discover the meaning that the students in the sample attached to the two terms "socialism" and "Marxism" by cross-tabulating all the ideological items in the survey with the indicators of prosocialist and of pro-Marxist orientation and taking statistical measures of correlation and contingency for each item. He found that the items that his statistical analysis revealed to constitute "nuclear meaning" were the same for both terms, both in content and in rank order. So while a number of Western analysts had concluded from the survey results that "Marxism" and "socialism" had quite different meanings for the Polish students, Nowak concluded that the terms had the same denotative meaning but that the term "Marxism" represented a higher intensity of conviction.[17]

Whether or not this conclusion is correct (it is possible that the questionnaire did not include a sufficient variety of ideological items to reveal other differences between socialist and Marxist positions), the lack of political and ideological engagement of the Polish students was even more marked in 1961 than in 1958. On the question of the function of Workers' Councils, the proportion who felt they should be "the real master of the plants" declined by 16 percent; rather than switching to a more moderate or negative position, however, most of the loss showed up in the "no opinion" section, which constituted over 20 percent of the sample. This was undoubtedly due to the emasculation of the Workers' Councils, which had been transformed beyond recognition.

Though membership in the Socialist Youth Union had increased to 600,000 by this time, the frequency of political discussions reported by the surveyed students declined sharply; and 40 percent of the students, as opposed to 30 percent in 1958, felt that "those who do not care about such things" constituted the majority among their peers. This tendency was also confirmed by another survey reported in the professional journal *Zycie Szkoly Wyzszej* (Life of Higher Schools) of October 1960. Out of 500 freshmen at the Warsaw Polytechnic asked what daily and weekly newspapers they read, only four named such intellectual weeklies as *Polityka*, *Przeglad Kulturalny*, and *Nowa Kultura*. Eighty-five percent had not attended a school celebration of the 15th anniversary of the establishment of the Communist regime, and not one respondent reported taking part in any program of the student political organization.

On the other hand, the students did seem to be happier and more optimistic about their own personal prospects. Large majorities responded positively to the questions "Do you think you will obtain a job in your profession easily after completing your studies?" (73 percent) and "Are you pleased with life in general?" (83 percent). These represented a 20 percent and 10 percent increase, respectively, over 1958.

Thus, though the Polish students seemed to be conforming more to ideological orthodoxy and finding a personally satisfying adaptation to the social system under which they lived, they showed little inclination to take an active part in the "building of communism." They still did not fit into the mold of the "new Communist man."

RELIGIOSITY

Historians mark A.D. 966, the year in which the pagan Piast king Mieszko I adopted Roman Catholicism for himself and his people, as the year of the formation of the Polish state. (The "Millennium" was celebrated with much fanfare in Poland in 1966, with the Communist regime finding itself faced with the necessity of belatedly staging counter-celebrations to offset mass festivities planned and carried out by the Church.) Roman Catholicism remained throughout Poland's tangled history the religious persuasion of the vast majority of ethnic Poles, though the Protestant Reformation made small inroads and the well-known marches of mid-European history at various times resulted in the inclusion of significant minorities of Jews, Russian Orthodox, and Uniate Catholics within Poland's shifting borders. One of the effects of World War II was the virtual elimination of that historical ethnic and religious diversity. The extermination of the sizable Polish Jewish community by the Nazis and the postwar emigration of most of its remnants, the westward shift of Poland's boundaries and the concomitant massive transfer of the German population out of the Western Territories and of ethnic Poles from the ceded Eastern Territories into the new Polish state, resulted in a population that was not only almost completely ethnically homogeneous, but religiously homogeneous as well. Most sources, including the present Communist regime, consider 97 percent of the present-day Polish population to be Roman Catholic, at least by heritage.

The extent to which various studies conducted in the post-October period revealed Roman Catholicism to be a still active force in modern Polish life, in spite of its relegation to the position of a dying historical carryover by Marxist orthodoxy, was another distressing fact for the Communist regime.

The Roman Church, despite severe circumscription of its activities, has remained the sole (and painfully visible) formal organization contending openly with the Polish United Worker's Party (PUWP) for the support of the masses. The post-October studies proffered little hope to the regime that this historical carryover would soon fade away.

The 1957 *Sztandar Mlodych* poll had noted the phenomenon of a young generation being raised in religious traditions by grandparents and had remarked ominously, "The circle closes." The Warsaw University sociologists had set out to examine the "black myth" in which the hero broke a date in order not to be late for his rosary circle and found that 69 percent of the students in their sample, including 70 percent of those of worker origin, considered themselves religious believers. In an all-Poland survey conducted in 1959, 78 percent of the respondents classified themselves as Roman Catholic.[18] Nor should it be forgotten that 69 percent of the OBOP volunteer interviewers in 1959 wanted studies done on the future of relations between Church and state and of religious instruction in lay schools.

Such general findings led to further studies attempting to examine the structure of religious belief and practice in more detail.[19] It may be indicative of the growing intolerance of the regime for more bad news on the subject of widespread religiosity (as well as of the "enlightened" perspective of the researchers themselves), that these reports tend to be couched in terms emphasizing a tendency towards "moderation" of religious belief, along with identification of sociodemographic factors that correlate with greater or lesser religiosity.

With regard to the former, Tadeusz Jaroszewski notes that the tendency to moderation of religious belief in Poland was taking two forms: (1) the loosening of formal ties with the Catholic Church, and (2) the subsidence of strong religious attitudes.[20] Anna Pawelczynska, too, notes the decline in numerical affiliation with the Church and subsiding intensity of belief, and postulates that a religious structure similar to that of France is evolving in Poland.[21]

Various studies cited by these two authors indicate that Poland is similar to many other modern societies in that religious sentiment and attachment appear to decline with education. For instance, Pawelczynska contrasts an OBOP poll taken in 1960 in which 78.3 percent of all youths in Poland between 18 and 24 years of age classified themselves as religious believers,[22] with the Warsaw University studies, which found a somewhat smaller proportion (69 percent) of youths of the same age group—who were students in Warsaw institutions of higher education—considering themselves believers of varying intensities, though not necessarily churchgoers.[23] In attempting to identify education rather than such other factors as urban-rural background as the critical variable, Pawelczynska cites data from the latter studies that suggest a shift from believer to nonbeliever status among the university students.[24]

Studies cited by Jaroszewski also point to education as an important variable in religiosity (see Table 2.1).

In a 1959 poll of 1,000 teachers by M. Kozakiewicz, cited by Jaroszewski, 38.6 percent of the teachers declared themselves to be practicing Roman Catholics and 34 percent "nonbelievers."[25]

TABLE 2.1

Religious Believers, Poland, 1961
(percent)

Examined Strata of Population	Believing Deeply or Simply Believing	Not Believing (Atheists, Indifferent, etc.)
Intelligentsia with higher education	60.1	39.9
Intelligentsia in gcneral	66.1	34.0
Skilled workers	75.0	25.0
Unskilled workers	82.2	17.8

Source: Tadeusz Jaroszewski, "Dynamika i funkcje postaw wobec religii," *Studia socjologiczno-polityczne* no. 10 (1961): 138.

Irena Nowakowska examined the representatives of various teaching disciplines in more detail and found the greatest percentage of those "believing and practicing" located in the disciplines of agriculture and forestry (33.8 percent) and in technical studies (33 percent), and dropping to a low of 14 percent among biologists.[26]

Education was not the only factor in religiosity pointed up by the Polish studies, however. Czeslaw Staciwa, reporting on in-depth studies of a less educated segment of the male population—draftees in the Polish army—presents indices showing that the attitudes of male acquaintances and of parents both outranked education as molders of religious attitudes.[27]

Even with the emphasis on a tendency to moderation of religiosity, certain findings of the studies remained difficult to explain away. Jaroszewski notes the fascinating characteristic of religious life in Poland, in which many who consider themselves nonbelievers nevertheless continue to attend church services and participate in religious activities,[28] including baptism of their children and church marriage. He mentions social pressure, fear of recrimination from fanatical religious elements, psychological or esthetic gratification, and the lack of anything else to do on religious holidays as possible motivations for this behavior, but does not mention other possibly significant factors, such as the identification of Catholicism with Polish nationality, or religious practice as political protest. Nor does he mention that the "social pressure" or "fear of recrimination" may have produced the self-description of nonbeliever.

Further, Pawelczynska notes that acceptance of Catholic moral principles remains widespread in Poland, extending even to those who classify themselves as nonbelievers.[29]

STANDARD OF LIVING

It is hardly surprising that the standard of living should be a problem in a country that had not, even before the war, attained the level of economic and industrial development of most Western nations, which had suffered immense physical and human destruction during the war and which suffered additional displacements with the imposition of a new and different political and economic system after the war. That it was an issue of great political and social interest to the Polish populace in the October and post-October period has already been indicated by the fact that some 76 percent of the OBOP's volunteer interviewers wished to see the subject dealt with in future surveys. The OBOP did do a number of surveys on this topic from its inception up until about 1963, and, as might be expected, the survey results revealed a great deal of dissatisfaction.

A 1959 survey found only 16 percent of the respondents reporting that their cultural needs were satisfied, while 44 percent indicated that they were not.[30]

A 1960 survey of the urban population found that some 25 percent of the respondents considered the food situation in their families "good" or "very good," while 16.7 percent considered it "bad," and fully 71.5 percent indicated that if they should have any increase in income, it would be used for additional food.[31] A second survey that same year found that even among families with high incomes, only 48 percent were able to satisfy fully their food desires.[32]

The first of these two 1960 surveys also found that only 20.9 percent of urban residents considered their clothing needs adequately met, while 21.7 percent said their clothing budget was totally inadequate. Seventy-two percent of the respondents would set aside part of any additional income for clothing.[33]

Dissatisfaction with material aspects of life extended to retail outlets, the primary site of the consumer's frustration. In a 1961 survey of Warsaw residents, respondents indicated that the worst stores were food stores. Complaints included paucity of goods (36.1 percent), rude service (31 percent), and dishonesty (24.2 percent).[34]

General dissatisfaction with the economic situation and its effects on the personal standard of living continued to be evident later in the period as well. In 1963, survey respondents found increases in the prices of consumer goods the most unfavorable occurrence of the year. And more detailed studies about such specific areas as agriculture, employment, and satisfaction with location of residence broadened the picture of the standard of living.

AGRICULTURE

The first of the Warsaw University studies in 1958 revealed that a surprisingly large proportion of the students (16 percent) held the decidedly un-

Marxist view that unlimited private enterprise should be permitted in agricultural estates. The researchers bluntly attributed the phenomenon to "the fairly universal opinion that the socialist economic forms so far applied in agriculture are ineffective, particularly on the big estates." The inadequacy of socialist forms in agriculture is hardly limited to Poland, of course, but was much in evidence in Poland by the time of the October events. Agriculture continued to occupy a rather large proportion of the Polish population, while contributing significantly less than its share of the national income.

In fact, however, though the socialist system had circumscribed and burdened the agricultural sector in numerous ways, little headway had been made toward "socializing" it. The deep attachment of the Polish peasantry to its land had made collectivization politically unpalatable, even during the Stalinist period. About 85 percent of the productively utilized agricultural land remained in private hands, and it employed the bulk of the farm population. The tradition of subdividing land among one's descendants, according to Polish government figures, had resulted in a significant decline in the average size of individual farms even in the decade between 1950 and 1960.[35]

A 1960 poll of farmers' attitudes reported by Boguslaw Galeski revealed a rather bleak picture of the farmers' economic condition. Over one-fifth (21.7 percent) reported that their income was not sufficient to provide even the bare essentials. Another 32.5 percent said their income was barely sufficient to cover essentials, while another 35.6 percent declared simply that it must be sufficient, and only 9.2 percent considered it siffucient.[36]

An even starker picture of the Polish farmer's economic condition is suggested by portions of Galeski's data that suggest that the farmers themselves overestimated the sufficiency of their income relative to the estimations of urban dwellers. Galeski found that the farmer's definition of "sufficient" or "satisfactory" income was not related to the degree to which he could satisfy certain consumer needs (radios, motorcycles, other staples) or personal needs such as education for his children or provision for his old age, but rather to the ability to meet basic human needs for food, clothing, and shelter, to his level of indebtedness, and to the level of farm taxes.[37]

Something of the primitive technological state of Polish agriculture was revealed in a 1959 poll conducted by the OBOP, which queried farmers with regard to their greatest immediate needs. As reported by Zdzislaw Szpakowski, 63.2 percent of the farmers singled out the necessity of constructing adequate roads as the most urgent requirement of Polish agriculture. For their own individual farms, the greatest number of farmers (36.5 percent) reported a need for building materials above all else, with a cow following a close second at 34.8 percent. Only 24.3 percent mentioned any kind of farm machinery, and more farmers (20 percent) expressed the need for a horse than for a tractor (16 percent).[38]

Galeski found that fully 85 percent of Polish farmers had no professional agricultural training and, further, that many displayed a rather high degree of resistance to it. Thus, in a 1961 national survey of farmers owning a minimum of two hectares of land, 72 percent of the farmers canvassed believed that some form of agronomic instruction would be helpful, but one-fifth firmly insisted that formal training was unnecessary and not helpful in raising farm productivity. (Galeski found that attitudes toward agricultural training correlated strongly with the size of the farm and with the educational experience of the owner. Generally, the larger the farm and the more extensive the agronomic training of the farmer, the more likely he was to value vocational agricultural instruction.) And even among the 72 percent of farmers who favored "some form of agronomic instruction," Galeski found more emphasis on less formal means of dissemination of information than on formal education. Radio programs were most valued by the farmers, with 73 percent reporting that they listened to them. Seventy-one percent reported that they read newspapers as well, and many said they attended local lectures about agriculture. Their interest and motivation, according to Galeski's data, was solely the improvement of their farms, and their concern with nonagricultural topics was insignificant.[39]

The most significant findings of the many surveys of the agricultural population, however, were those that showed no abatement of the Polish peasantry's strong resistance to the notion of giving up private ownership of its land, in spite of the hardships suffered.

In a 1959 OBOP poll reported by Waclaw Makarczyk, the Polish peasantry showed itself well aware of the abovementioned criticial problem of fragmentation of farm plots. Over three-quarters (76 percent) of those polled indicated that the problem already existed or would exist within ten years on their own homesteads.[40] Their concern about this problem did not, however, extend to a willingness to give up control of the disposition of the holdings. In a 1963 OBOP survey reported by Makarczyk and Danuta Markowska, 25.6 percent of the farmers owning two or more hectares of land favored banning the partition of any farms; 46.3 percent recognized the need for some restrictive legislation but thought that larger farms should be excepted; and 18.6 percent were against any such restrictions.[41] Nearly half (42.6 percent) of the farmers wished to bequeath their entire farm to their offspring, being reciprocated with care in their declining years; 30.9 percent wished to retain a piece of land on which they could remain until the end of their lives; and only 18.6 percent were willing to hand over their land to the government in return for a guaranteed lifetime pension.[42] A majority (60.2 percent) of the farmers were of the opinion that they should be allowed total freedom in the selling of their land.[43] In Makarczyk's 1959 study, the farmers' own suggested solutions to the fragmentation problem included transfer of agricultural youth to work in urban areas, a legal ban against divisions of land below a certain number of hectares, and the construction of industrial enterprises in rural areas.[44]

The strong attachment of the Polish peasantry to the traditional form of private land holding showed up repeatedly in different ways in various surveys taken over a number of years. Makarczyk's 1959 survey found 61.4 percent supporting independently worked private holdings, with an additional 36.1 percent, however, willing to consider joining "agricultural circles."* In 1960, of those replying to a questionnaire, 49.2 percent agreed that "individual peasant farms are and always will be the best form of agricultural system" and 25.6 percent felt that "the future belongs to various forms of cooperation *between the owners of individual farms*."[45] Even in later years, when farmer attitudes on specific farm problems that were receiving much government attention were measured, the rural population showed itself highly sensitive to any action that might jeopardize their control over their holdings. In 1962, the government passed legislation allowing government seizure of neglected, dilapidated, or unproductive farms. Farmers polled on various aspects of the "neglect" problem proved decidedly lenient toward the unsuccessful farmer, blaming the phenomenon of the neglected farm on small size or poor quality of holdings, sickness and old age, and excessively large costs.[46] The farmers proposed various forms of aid to the distressed farmer and considered seizure of his land by the government justifiable only when there existed no hope of rehabilitating the farm under its current ownership, and then only with fair reimbursement.[47] The most frequently mentioned means of disposal by the government of land acquired through such seizures was sale or lease to private farmers.[48]

Another problem that elicited much concern from the government in the early 1960s was that of part-time farmers, whose number was estimated in 1964 at 824,000 and growing.[49] In a 1962 survey, however, Dyzma Galaj found the prevalent opinion among farmers to be that such part-timers were forced by the difficulty of making an adequate living on farms into dual occupational roles in order adequately to support their families.[50] Galaj found that part-time farmers were generally more enterprising, better educated, and better prepared for life, came from smaller farms, and participated more often in activities outside the family group than their full-time counterparts.[51] Moreover, their agricultural productivity was only slightly below the national average and did not appear to suffer markedly from their occupational duality.[52] And, in spite of the government's concern, the rural population found part-time farming rather attractive and encouraged its further growth.

What about the stability of the farm population, as reflected in satisfaction or dissatisfaction with farm life? In 1959, a representative sample of adult rural inhabitants were asked if they were satisfied with life on the farm. Over half (53.6 percent) answered an unqualified yes, 13.4 percent, "yes, more or less," 13.5 percent, a qualified no, and 17.6 percent, "no."[53] In 1960, a survey of farmers owning more than two hectares of land asked, "Do you like your work

---

*These were cooperative forms seen by the regime as an initial step on the long road to socialist forms of agricultural organization.

on the farm?" Twenty-two percent said they "liked it very much," 51.3 percent said they simply liked it, 17.7 percent that they really didn't care, and 7.4 percent that they did not like it.[54] Considering the preceding data on the economic hardships prevalent on Polish farms, the fact that majorities appeared satisfied with farm life and farm work may seem surprising. Makarczyk found in his studies, however, that the better-educated rural inhabitant was more likely to have migratory tendencies than the poorly educated and that intention to migrate was also more frequent among the young and among those from larger peasant families.[55]

JOB SATISFACTION

Polish sociological researchers appear to have encountered some forms of "blue-collar blues" rather early on. Analyses of a 1962 survey of steel workers in six plants by Aleksander Matejko and Franciszek Adamski reveal a sad picture of the steel workers' milieu and the apparent demise of the once proud "steel worker's tradition."[56] Heavy labor, difficult working conditions, strict discipline, and the monotony of their jobs had produced severe disillusionment among a large number of the steel workers, the surveys found,[57] but the modestly educated laborers were disinclined to take extra time and effort to pursue training necessary for upgrading their positions, and the majority saw "no possibility for advancement" within their own plants.[58] Their disillusionment did not, however, lead to overt expression of dissatisfaction, according to the studies, but rather showed up in a passive, apathetic resignation toward their mode of living, combined with a hope that their children would not follow in their footsteps, but would get an education and pursue other career opportunities.[59] Matejko found the occupational apathy of the steel workers, and of their counterparts in other industrial enterprises as well, reflected in the fact that they attached the greatest weight to "personal relationships" within their work locale.[60] He also found that foremen, caught between production demands from above and unfulfilled expectations for remuneration and satisfactory work conditions from below, had ceased to function as a mediating force and simply did their day-to-day jobs and stayed "above" worker-management conflicts.

The problem of morale within factories was also the subject of a number of surveys conducted within individual enterprises by the OBOP. Jozefowicz and Sufin reported that factory workers themselves blamed the rise of negative characteristics such as theft and absenteeism and a "general moral breakdown within factories" on poor organization of work and conditions of labor.[61] They found "implicative evidence" that factories had ceased to function as units and were operating instead as loosely linked collections of isolated brigades, each more interested in the tasks and well-being within its own ranks than that of the whole factory.[62]

Research carried out among office workers also revealed a general lack of job satisfaction. Krystyna Lutynska reports that when asked to place their occupation in a hierarchical listing that included doctor, engineer, teacher, technician, foreman, factory worker, tailor, and shop assistant, the office workers ranked themselves somewhere between foreman and factory worker.[63] Among the reasons the office workers gave for assigning such low value to their own occupation were that their work could not legitimately be classified as an "occupation," that it involved little responsibility, that it required no skill, that it was nonproductive in character, and that it did not help the community as a whole.[64] Lutynska also noted that among the small percentage of office workers who assigned a higher value to themselves and their work, the satisfaction stemmed from non-work-related factors, such as believing that they were of a higher cultural and intellectual level.[65]

One occupational group that studies revealed to have a high level of job satisfaction (in spite of a relatively low level of remuneration)—and esteem for which was shared by the population as a whole—was primary-school teachers. In a representative sample of 2,050 teachers asked to place themselves in a hierarchy of professions, the teachers ranked themselves far ahead of doctors, and second only to research personnel. Sixty percent of the teachers considered the intelligentsia, in which they included themselves, as the most important stratum in the country. As an additional indicator of satisfaction, 35 percent of the teachers surveyed wished to see their children become teachers.[66] Surveys among parents who were not teachers revealed that as many as 40 percent of them would also like to see at least one of their children enter the teaching profession.[67]

WORKING WOMEN

Women have constituted a significant portion of both the professional and manual work force in the Soviet Union since 1918 and in the Soviet bloc since 1945. While it may be interesting to note that certain basic tenets of "feminism" have long received at least lip service in Marxist-Leninist orthodoxy, the more obvious roots of the phenomenon lie in the economic and demographic situations with which these countries have been faced. The drives for economic modernization required massive doses of "manpower," which would have drawn more women into the labor force in any event. But the substitution of "womanpower" was made inevitable by the heavy losses brought on the European population by World War II, losses that were, of course, disproportionately heavy for the male population. In fact, most of these countries have not yet recovered a normal demographic balance between male and female populations, though it approaches normal in the postwar generations. On the more personal domestic level, the difficult postwar economic situation often made it necessary for all able-bodied adults in a family, male and female, to be employed just to provide the basic necessities of life.

The currency given by the women's movement in Western countries to issues concerning the employment of women may make one study done in Poland of some special interest. According to a report of a 1960 OBOP survey by Zygmunt Drodzek and Anna Preiss-Zajdowa,[68] 56.1 percent of the women queried cited the need for additional funds as the primary motivating factor in their seeking employment. A large portion of the remainder also cited reasons of a material nature. Those women who were not employed cited such reasons as child rearing (58 percent), their husband's status (27 percent), or poor health (24 percent) as the reasons why they were not currently working.[69]

When asked to indicate which occupations on a given list were most appropriate for women, the respondents chose teacher, clerk, saleswoman, or doctor. Those occupations considered least appropriate for women were steel worker, grinder, and lathe operator.[70]

Some questions that might be of great interest to Western feminists, such as the relative status and remuneration of women in the work force and the domestic adjustments their employment has entailed, appear not to have been studied in these surveys.

SOCIAL STATUS

In addition to these studies of satisfaction within different occupational strata, Polish sociologists delved deeply into the questions of social status among occupations and other sources of social divisiveness. Among the most impressive of the studies done must be included a survey conducted in December 1958 among selected Warsaw inhabitants,[71] one carried out in the summer of 1959 on a randomly chosen national sample of 1,400,[72] and one conducted in 1961 among urban males above 18 years of age.[73] While it is hardly possible to do justice here to the highly regarded and sophisticated work done by Polish sociologists in the complex area of social stratification, some of the findings of these three studies are of interest in themselves.

Subjects in the Warsaw survey were given a list of 30 occupations and asked to rank them in a hierarchy on the basis of the material rewards attached to each occupation. They were then asked to construct a second hierarchy according to the social prestige of the occupations.

The overall results, shown in Table 2.2, indicate the high regard accorded to occupations requiring a significant amount of professional training, and also the divergence that is perceived between the social prestige of some occupations and the remuneration they receive. (It should be kept in mind, of course, that the levels of remuneration shown for each occupation are what the subjects believed them to be, and not necessarily what they actually were.)

TABLE 2.2

Occupational Rankings, by Material Rewards and Social Prestige

Occupation	Rankings	
	Material Rewards	Social Prestige
Member of government	1	8
Lawyer	2	7
Shopkeeper	3	20
Doctor	4	2
Tailor (with own shop)	5	17
Locksmith (with own shop)	6	16
University professor	7	1
Aircraft pilot	8	5
Priest	9	12
Journalist	10	10
Skilled metallurgical worker	11	9
Mechanical engineer	12	3
Carpenter	13	11
Small farmer	15	18
Factory foreman	16	14
Agronomist	17	6
Section head in office	18	19
Accountant	19	15
Sales clerk	20	26
Militiaman	21	23
Teacher	22	4
Unskilled building tradesman	23	27
Office clerk	24	24
Typist	25	25
Railway conductor	26	22
Nurse	27	13
Unskilled farm laborer	28	29
Domestic servant	29	28

Source: Adam Sarapata, "Poglady mieszkancow Warszawy na strukturze spoleczna," *Studia socjologiczno-polityczne* 6 (1960): 98 and 105.

The 1959 national poll was similarly constructed, with the additional feature that the subjects were asked to construct a third hierarchy based on what the relative material remuneration for each occupation should be. While the occupational categories that the subjects were asked to rank differed slightly from those in the earlier Warsaw study, the results (see Table 2.3) are remarkably similar. And it is interesting to note that when given the opportunity to postulate a proper level of financial reward for each occupation, the subjects of the study corrected many, but not all, of the divergences they perceived between the social status of an occupation and its existing level of remuneration.

TABLE 2.3

Occupational Rankings, by Financial Rewards, Present Prestige, Postulated Remuneration

Job	Evaluation of Job According to		
	Present Financial Rewards	Present Prestige	Postulated Remuneration
Cabinet minister	1	5	2
Physician	2	2	3
Fitter (owner of shop)	3	12	12
University professor	4	1	1
Skilled steel worker	5	6	5
Priest	6	7	14
Mechanical engineer	7	4	4
Fitter (employed in factory)	8	9	9
Army officer	9	13	7
Private farmer	10	10	13
Bookkeeper (accountant)	11	11	8
Shop assistant	12	15	16
Policeman	13	14	11
Teacher	14	3	6
Unskilled building worker	15	16	17
Nurse	16	8	10
Farm laborer (on state farm)	17	18	15
Cleaner	18	17	18

Source: Adam Sarapata, "Iustum Pretium," *Polish Sociological Bulletin*, no. 1 (1963), p. 46.

The third survey mentioned above was part of an ambitious and complex series of studies[74] on questions of social stratification.

TABLE 2.4

On Postwar Lessening of Class Distinctions
(percent)

Social-Occupational Groups	Are distinctions between people of different groups in Poland generally greater or smaller today than before the war?*				
	Much Smaller	A Little Smaller	About the Same	A Little Greater	Much Greater
Unskilled workers	22.3	29.2	13.5	7.6	7.3
Skilled workers	28.2	29.6	13.9	5.7	7.3
Nonmanual workers	37.9	31.2	10.8	4.3	5.2
Creative intelligentsia and free professions	30.9	36.0	16.0	2.2	3.6

*Nowak notes that 14.1 percent of the respondents answered "hard to say" and that most of these replies came from the younger age groups.

Source: Stefan Nowak, "Changes of Social Structure in Social Consciousness," *Polish Sociological Bulletin*, no. 2 (1964), p. 48.

As indicated in Table 2.4, all strata within Polish society perceived a lessening of social divisions since the war, and that perception was most common among the higher-status groups.

Table 2.5, however, indicates that all classes of Polish society claim to desire an even further lessening of social differences in the future, though that desire is less strong, predictably, among the higher-status groups.

The overriding importance of income or wealth as a perceived source of both objective societal division and of "divisiveness" (dislike), was apparent in all Polish studies dealing with income and wealth. It is particularly clear in the survey results presented in Table 2.6, though the significant proportions attributing divisiveness to differences in religious outlook and political views as opposed to objective social division are also notable.

THE WESTERN TERRITORIES

At the end of World War II the borders of the Polish state were substantially redrawn. A large portion of prewar eastern Poland was ceded to the Soviet Union and incorporated into the Soviet Republics of Lithuania, Byelorussia, and the Ukraine. In compensation, the Polish western border was moved westward to the Oder-Neisse Rivers, incorporating territory that had been German East

TABLE 2.5

On Further Lessening of Distinctions
(percent)

Occupational Categories	Would you like to see the social differences in Poland in the future			
	Entirely Disappear?	Decrease?	Remain Unchanged?	Increase?
Unskilled workers	44.0	38.2	4.0	3.7
Skilled workers	52.7	36.9	2.8	2.8
Nonmanual workers	48.0	41.2	3.2	2.2
Free professions	38.1	43.2	3.6	7.2
Total sample	45.5	38.0	3.2	2.8

Source: Stefan Nowak, "Changes of Social Structure in Social Consciousness," *Polish Sociological Bulletin*, no. 2 (1964), p. 52.

TABLE 2.6

Perceived Causes of Division
(percent)

Basis of Differentiation	Do these differences divide people in our society?		Which of the listed differences in your opinion are the cause of dislike in our society?
	Very Strongly	Rather Strongly	
Earnings or wealth	45.7	36.9	71.5
Education	26.1	45.0	45.5
Managerial or nonmanagerial	25.0	33.1	41.8
Manual or nonmanual	15.9	41.1	35.4
Manner of behaving in company	16.7	39.8	28.0
Religious outlook	21.3	26.9	41.3
Political views	13.8	27.4	43.6
City and country	10.9	33.3	30.2
Social origin	6.4	16.2	16.7

Source: Stefan Nowak, "Changes of Social Structure in Social Consciousness," *Polish Sociological Bulletin*, no. 2 (1964), p. 49.

Prussia. The German population of the so-called Western Territories was forced to emigrate, and the ethnically Polish population of the ceded Eastern Territories was given the option of resettling within the new Polish borders. The vast majority of them were resettled in the newly acquired Western Territories.

The sociological impact of such a large-scale demographic phenomenon would seem of obvious interest to the researcher, and, indeed, a number of studies of the psychological development of the inhabitants and the character and mechanics of social ties taking shape within the new environment were undertaken.[75] Other motivations for the research were also apparent. The regime (indeed, the populace as well), ever sensitive to any evidence of German revanchism, has an obvious stake in proving that the Western Territories have been successfully integrated into the postwar Polish state. In addition, a marked tendency to migration out of the Western Territories and into the major cities, which had already resulted in the closing of the cities of Warsaw, Poznan, and the tri-city ports of Gdansk, Gdynia, and Sopot to in-migration, indicated the need for insights into the sources of satisfaction and dissatisfaction with life in the Western Territories.

Research reports on these studies have generally stressed high levels of optimism and feelings of stability. While findings support this overall contention to some degree, a comparative study done in the town of Pulawy in eastern Poland suggests that such feelings may not be as strong in the Western Territories as they are in areas that have had greater historical continuity of identification with the Polish people. The Pulawy study, for example, showed that 96.1 percent of the residents were satisfied with their habitat, and 71.5 percent to the extent that they wanted their children to remain there.[76] In comparison, the highest degree of satisfaction in the Western Territories was found in Slupsk (an industrial town in northwest Poland, west of Gdansk), where 90.7 percent of the inhabitants expressed satisfaction.[77] In Szczecinek, 86 percent expressed contentment with their decision to settle there.[78] In Swinoujscie (a port city on the German border), 89 percent of those surveyed in 1959 were glad they had settled there, though only 51.7 percent were eager for their children to remain there upon reaching adulthood.[79] (The number glad they had settled in Swinoujscie declined slightly to 86 percent when a second survey was taken in 1961.[80]) In Zlocieniec, 75.2 percent were happy with their residence, though 47.7 percent of the sample indicated that they would migrate to another town if given the opportunity![81]

In the Swinoujscie study, 51.7 percent of the respondents indicated they had "a strong feeling of stability,"[82] while only 6.6 percent felt no stability and 11.6 percent very weak stability.[83] The greatest source of satisfaction with life in Swinoujscie, cited by 46.8 percent of the survey respondents, was the town's "natural-esthetic" quality—its climate, the nearby sea, the surrounding countryside.[84] The greatest source of dissatisfaction was the paucity of amusements, followed by low wages (27.3 percent), and the small size of homes (25.1 percent).[85] Ninety percent of the respondents in the 1959 survey were optimistic that further development of the town would lead to improved living conditions for all the inhabitants.[86]

In Zlocieniec, where dissatisfaction was rather more pronounced, the desire to migrate (47.7 percent indicated such a desire) was found to be strongly correlated with material conditions and to be initially aroused by lack of schools and forms of amusement.[87]

WORLD OUTLOOK

It may be recalled that in the first "public opinion poll" mentioned in this chapter—that conducted by the newspaper *Zycie Warszawy* in 1955 on the question "What is your opinion of your newspaper?"—the major complaints included "the lack of factual information on life in Western Europe and America"; "stereotyped propaganda on the USSR"; and "It's a shame that Poles know so little about what is going on in the world." It may also be recalled that 73 percent of the OBOP interviewers in 1959 wanted to see studies on questions of international affairs undertaken.

The number of studies conducted by Polish researchers on "problems of world outlook" was, in fact, relatively limited,[88] but, interestingly enough, continued for some time after political conditions had brought a near halt to public opinion studies in other areas.

The impact of twentieth-century history was clear in a 1961 OBOP survey that posed the question "Which countries are you interested in most?" Over 50 percent of the respondents named the Soviet Union and the United States, while 46 percent also mentioned Germany. Great Britain and France were mentioned significantly less.[89]

A poll of Warsaw residents in 1961 revealed some aspects of Polish interest in those countries. Respondents were given a list of 12 positive traits and asked to indicate "Which country do you think of first when the preceding are mentioned?" Germany was assigned only two positive traits by a significant number of the respondents: order and thriftiness, by 45.7 percent, and welfare (West Germany only), by 15.9 percent. The United States and USSR each were attributed six positive traits by a significant number of respondents: the Soviet Union—military power, 71.9 percent; wise foreign policy, 35.4 percent; equality, 29 percent; opportunities for making a career, 26.4 percent; an equitable social system, 21.3 percent; and particularly friendly toward Poles, 15.1 percent; the United States—military power, 68.2 percent; opportunities for a career, 27.2 percent; colorful and interesting life, 22.3 percent; high cultural level, 9.9 percent; wise foreign policy, 8.5 percent; equitable social system, 7.6 percent.[90] (The omissions here are perhaps as interesting as the given data. For instance, on the important question of "friendliness to the Poles," the largest number of respondents—59.2 percent—mentioned Hungary.[91]) A breakdown of the data by the researchers revealed that positive attitudes toward the United States were more frequently held by less educated and non-Party respondents, while more educated and Party people were more likely to view the Soviet Union positively.

By 1963, when national and international conditions both were already significantly different than they had been in the early post-October era, leaders of the three nations in whom the Poles showed most interest were compared as follows: Of 67 percent of the respondents who replied to the question, 66 percent felt that West German Chancellor Konrad Adenauer was responsible for increasing international friction; with 63 percent of the respondents answering, 59 percent considered Khrushchev a major contributor to world peace; and with 47 percent of the respondents answering, 43 percent considered President Kennedy to be a preserver of peace.[92]

Later, "world outlook" studies dealt with questions of war and peace and, particularly, disarmament. In 1952, according to the Western social scientists Kracauer and Berkman who interviewed Polish emigres, the Poles were eager for a war between the United States and the Soviet Union. Support for such a war, they said, stemmed from beliefs that defeat of the Soviet Union would mean the end of foreign domination over Poland, and that communism could not exist peacefully without world domination, and the "menace" should therefore be defeated before it grew in military strength. Victory for the United States was believed to be inevitable and destruction limited because of the war's necessarily short duration.[93] Whatever the validity or comparability of these findings, it is clear that Polish attitudes were of a much different character by the 1960s. By 1963, in fact, a survey indicated that the majority of the Polish population opposed even limited conventional warfare, and 68 percent rated atomic weapons

TABLE 2.7

On Justifications for War
(percent)

Can you imagine some value, reason, or ideal that could justify:	Yes	Could Be	No	Don't Know
Conventional war (without nuclear weapons)?	19	5	61	15
Nuclear war?	3	1	82	14

Source: Teresa Konwicka, Jacek Kurczewski, Aleksander Lutyk, Dorota Mycielska, Andrzej Sicinski, "Obraz swiata w roku 2000," Kultura i spoleczenstwo 12, no. 12 (1968): 119.

as the greatest threat to mankind.[94] By 1968, the pacifist inclination of the Polish population was clear, as indicated by the response to the question about war, shown in Table 2.7.

Beginning in 1964, the OBOP and the Center for Research on Contemporary Culture of the Polish Academy of Sciences participated in a series of cross-national studies on "Images of a Disarmed World," with the Institut Français d'Opinion Publique (Paris), and the International Peace Research Institute in Oslo. The project was sponsored by the European Coordination Center for Research and Documentation in Social Sciences.[95]

It is interesting to note that while the Poles were not particularly optimistic about prospects for disarmament, they were fairly confident in 1964 that world war would be avoided in the near future (though somewhat less so about the more distant future).

TABLE 2.8

On Future World Situation, 1964
(percent)

Expected Situation	In 5 Years			In 20 Years		
	France	Norway	Poland	France	Norway	Poland
World war	4	3	6	9	10	17
Increased armaments	25	16	23	11	10	4
About as now	31	49	29	9	16	4
Partial disarmament	22	20	15	18	23	13
Total disarmament	4	1	3	18	11	15
Don't know; no answer	14	11	24	35	30	47

Source: Andrzej Sicinski, " 'Don't Know' Answers in Cross-National Surveys," Public Opinion Quarterly 33, no. 1 (1970): 128.

(The large number of "don't know" or "no answer" responses here makes generalizations of these findings extremely risky.[96])

Optimism appears to have increased in all the areas in question by the time of a follow-up study in 1967, though, again, the number of nonresponses is too significant for comfortable generalization.

TABLE 2.9

On Future Situation, 1967
(percent)

Expected Situation	In 5 Years	In 20 Years
World war	1	8
Increased armaments	28	18
About as now	35	6
Partial disarmament	13	24
Total disarmament	5	14
Don't know, no answer	18	30

Source: Teresa Konwicka, Jacek Kurczewski, Aleksander Lutyk, Dorota Mycielska, Andrzej Sicinski, "Obraz swiata w roku 2000," Kultura i spoleczenstwo 12, no. 2 (1968): 118.

THE DECLINE OF OPINION POLLING

The period of the late 1950s and early 1960s was later referred to as the "renaissance of Polish sociology."[97] What followed, if we may strain the metaphor a bit, was not exactly a return to the "dark ages," but a "reformation," in which the new tools of empirical social science investigation were forced into the service of the modified orthodoxy of the stabilized Gomulka regime.

Public opinion polling was not without its detractors in Poland even in its heyday. The well-known journalist, novelist, and party apologist Jerzy Putrament, wrote in 1959:[98] "I am against such methods of investigating the human consciousness . . . against Gallupism. . . . Whether an interviewed group is large or small, the results of a poll are not treated as a scientific observation. They are a political act, acting *for* some or *against* others."

At that point, the defenders of public opinion polls still held sway—even those who granted some of the methodological imperfections and their political implications. Jan Szczepanski, a leading sociologist and also a Marxist theoretician, cautioned that the press polls had little scientific value, but noted that the polls were entirely appropriate to the new, post-October "sociopolitical" functions of the press as "reflectors of public opinion."[99] *Prasa Polska* warned, "It is worthwhile to remember the great role in Poland which these 'soundings' . . . have played in the achievement of a certain picture of the moods of the population."[100] Perhaps the most explicit acknowledgment of the legitimate political role of the polling activities was in an article on the establishment of the OBOP:[101]

Some said that since the majority of the population was ruled by an enlightened minority, knowledge of the views of the majority was in effect unimportant. Some people seemed to be afraid that the probing of public opinion could bring about a collision with certain requirements of a political nature. However, the view triumphed that for the democratic guidance of society it would be most useful to carry out public opinion surveys.

Political interests in this time, the heyday of anti-Stalinism, dictated support for polling.[102]

The triumph, however, of those who felt public opinion polls were useful for the democratic guidance of society was far from permanent. Events both inside and outside Poland eventually brought a half to the most significant polling activities.

The pioneering work of Polish survey researchers and sociologists had created unease, expressed in charges of revisionism, throughout the bloc from the very beginning. A lengthy debate was going on in the Soviet Union over the appropriateness, in the context of Marxist theory and socialist society, of empirical social science research, the methods and techniques of which had been developed in the capitalist West.

One of the first signs of the impact these developments would have on the future of Polish survey research came when Professor Jozef Chalasinski was removed from the editorship of two publications of the Polish Academy of Sciences, and the Institute of Social and Cultural History, which Chalasinski had headed, was closed, supposedly because of a "satirical" report on the "social transformation" in Poland that he had made at the International Sociological Congress at Stresa in 1959.

Emilia Wilder describes the "resolution" of the Soviet debate on empirical social science as follows:[103]

While "specialized social sciences" as developed in the West, with their advanced methods and techniques, should be adopted, Marxism must remain supreme as a general sociological theory to guide concrete research undertakings. The technical task of sociology in the context of socialist society is to provide expert support for the implementation of the leadership's organizational and planning tasks, and its ideological function is shaping of social consciousness of the people. The former can be greatly aided by the development of research along Western lines. The latter must be performed from an anti-capitalist and socialist position.

This understanding at hand, it remained to bring the revisionist Poles into line with the newly defined orthodoxy. Adam Schaff, the Marxist philosopher and theoretician, brought the issue to the fore in an article in which he attacked the "polling mania" of Polish sociology.[104] He was joined in the attack by another prominent Marxist sociologist, Jerzy Wiatr, who claimed that "inflation of the importance of surveys is always accompanied by the disparagement of the tried and tested methods: systematic observation of a selected group, and the method of historical and comparative analysis."

Empirical sociology still drew some staunch support. Wladyslaw Bienkowski, a politician as well as a social scientist, claimed that "results of admittedly imperfect surveys (could be put) to more fruitful uses than mere generalizations that are no more than inspired guesses." Stanislaw Ossowski, probably the most able of all postwar Polish sociologists, went further. He argued that " 'subjective consciousness,' once it has been rendered manifest, becomes a matter of social facts in terms of sociology" and that it ought to be "fundamentally possible to conduct research on the basis of homogeneous data."

But Schaff was clearly calling the tune. When he brought the debate to a close, for all practical purposes, in another article, he clearly stated the new line.[105] Sufficient knowledge of the subject matter, he said, "can only be obtained when surveys are based on other intensive research performed with the aid of a variety of methods."

This relegation of survey research to a subsidiary role within an all-embracing system of techniques—official reports, production statistics, autobiographies, correspondence, area monographs, and participant observation—has been a standard characteristic of social science research throughout the Soviet bloc (with the exceptions of Yugoslavia and Czechoslovakia in the 1968 period) since that time. As one leading Polish sociologist in the survey research field explains, "subjective views and beliefs" demand constant comparison with "objective descriptions of a given situation."[106]

Among other features of the new methodological approach noted by the same sociologist is that "emphasis lies on views and opinions expressed by selected social groups . . . rather than on the utilization of data averaged from national samples." As he further explains, "When the research is directed toward a correct assessment of current social needs, the significance of the opinions of the specific groups is not the same."[107]

The foregoing redefinition of the role and function of empirical social science research soon had visible effects both on the nature of research undertakings and on the institutions that performed them.

Much of the early post-October sociological work and the more amateur press polls came under severe attack. At the Party Plenum of July 1963, Gomulka charged that the work of several Polish sociologists in the area of social stratification was "tantamount to a revision of Leninist class theory."[108] Following this lead, party spokesman Andrzej Werblan, in an article in *Nowe Drogi* the same month, attacked several sociologists. These included Ossowski, criticized for "open revision of Marxist theory" in his important work on class structure and social consciousness, and Andrzej Malewski (a brilliant younger sociologist

who died in 1964) for "taking seriously the absurd theories of Milton Rokeach."
Werblan went on to attack the Warsaw University studies as follows:

> They were based on premises that would facilitate an interpretation
> of findings in a non-Marxist and politically harmful spirit. A number
> of questions in the poll had been developed under the influence of
> revisionist concepts and political assessments, a factor which favored
> truth-distorting conclusions as to the attitude of youth towards
> socialism, the Socialist Youth Union, its leadership, etc.

The Warsaw University youth studies, needless to say, were discontinued.
Though the 1961 study was supposed to be the first in a series of periodic fol-
lowups of the original study, no more were done. Sociological interest in the
area of youth attitudes, at least as reflected in empirical research undertakings,
dropped to zero. A summary of studies done by the OBOP, published in 1966,
lists no projects on that topic after 1959. An abstract on the reports of the
1959 "world-view" study concludes cryptically, and perhaps expediently:
"These findings are now in the nature of history."[109]
    A large portion of the work done after the early 1960s has been done at a
"local" level in response to "local" problems, rather than on problems of more
general interest. For example, approximately one-third of the projects undertaken by the OBOP are financed by it for their general theoretical interest.
The remaining two-thirds are commissioned by individual institutions, to help
solve a particular problem.[110] Examples of such studies would include reader-
ship studies for various periodicals, studies of plant organization or management
for an enterprise, marketing studies for an enterprise or industry, and surveys of
cultural needs for various cultural institutions.
    Many of the studies that are of a more general theoretical and social
importance are noticeably manipulative in their implications. Much of the work
on mass culture, for example, which constitutes approximately one-fourth of
all projects undertaken, is aimed at increasing the effectiveness of propaganda
and agitation activities. A few examples of specific projects may also serve as
illustration. The Chair of History of Social Thought, with the help of the OBOP,
carried out a major study in 1967 that cast light on the effectiveness of inculca-
tion of the official socialist view of Polish history. The study revealed that Poles
were most interested in the Polish role in World War II and in the interwar
period of Polish independence. They were least interested in the history of the
workers' movement and the creation and development of the Polish People's
Republic. In addition, the Poles revealed, by their choices of values to be emphasized in the teaching of Polish history, a persistent "romantic" as opposed
to the official "realist" view of history.[111] Another study conducted by the
Sociological Workshop of the Polish Army's Main Political Office (also with the
assistance of the OBOP), appears to be almost a "corrective," an example of

sociology's "ideological function of shaping the social consciousness of the people . . . from a . . . socialist position." This study, also conducted in 1967, purported to show the Poles' present evaluation of World War II, and it claimed to find that Poles now regard the People's Guard (Communist)* as the most important of the World War II underground organizations. A press report of the survey concluded: [112]

> The results of the survey show that there has been a further revaluation in the public mind of the rational and emotional attitudes to the various currents of armed struggle, conditioned by the existence and activity of various class groups in the area. The decisive majority of respondents fully approved the political line of the Polish Left, united under the Polish Workers' Party. It is possible to say that the old divisions are no longer reflected in the present-day evaluation. In this sense we can speak of the continuing process of socialist integration of society.

Institutions and personnel also felt the impact of the redefinition of the role of social science research. The OBOP, which had attained a considerable degree of methodological sophistication in many areas of survey research, including national sampling, was reorganized in the mid-1960s to act mainly as a local research institute for the Committee on Radio and Television.[113]

Wladyslaw Bienkowski, who opposed Schaff when the pendulum of official approbation began to swing away from the research activities, was purged in 1963. Many of the major researchers quietly survived for some time to come, but the purge of "revisionist intellectuals" that swept Poland in 1968 (along with an officially inspired wave of anti-Semitism and the exodus of much of Poland's minuscule remaining Jewish population) hit the social sciences particularly hard. In addition to the dismissal of many prominent sociologists from their academic and research positions, there was a substantial reorganization of social science activities, with a number of institutions being closed or merged with others.

The Ministry of Higher Education imposed a new, unified curriculum on all sociology departments in Polish universities. The new curriculum reduced the emphasis on theory in favor of applications and research, and eliminated, over the objection of an advisory committee of academic sociologists, a specialization in general sociological theory. Students may now choose to specialize in one of four applied areas.[114] A study by the ministry in 1967 found that the majority of sociology graduates were employed in industry and in cultural institutions.

---

*In actual fact, the Home Army (AK), dominated by four non-Communist parties, was a far larger and more effective resistance group than the People's Guard (GL).

To make sweeping generalizations about the character and quality of recent Polish sociology on the basis of the foregoing discussion would be unjustified, however. It has maintained a great deal of vigor and achieved increasing sophistication in some areas despite the difficult restrictions under which it has labored. Important long-range studies, some of them touched upon earlier in this chapter, are underway on such problems as the structural changes brought about by the war, urbanization, industrialization, migrations, the resettlement of the Western Territories, and the functions of law and motivations of public conformity to law.[115] In spite of the official disfavor in which the subject is held, problems of social stratification still evince much interest among Polish sociologists; and the "revisionist" works of Ossowski, who died in 1964, are frequently excerpted and reviewed in professional journals. A few Polish researchers were able to maintain contacts with Western sociology even during the mid-1960s (the significance of the disarmament studies conducted in cooperation with French and Norwegian institutes should not be overlooked in this regard), and the academic exchanges between Polish and Western social scientists have become increasingly frequent in more recent years.

There is evidence that the spirit of the idea of opinion polling has not been altogether abandoned. In an article written for *Nowe Drogi*, the Party's theoretical organ, in September 1971, Stefan Nowak,[116] one of the sociologists most closely identified with the Warsaw University studies, took the opportunity of Gomulka's removal from power to recall the "sociological renaissance" and describe in terms unmistakably reminiscent of the earlier period "the social usefulness of studies of public opinion and attitudes." Recalling the decisive attack led by Schaff on "polling mania," which rendered "difficult both research and the publication of findings," Nowak cited the dramatic events of the preceding December* as evidence of the shortsightedness and social harm of this approach . . . which expected every sociological study to be an anniversary panegyric praising socialist achievements." He continued,

> Those who held this view described as "negative thinking" the social commitment of researchers who believed that it is their scholarly and civic duty to reveal the problems and difficulties of social development, that it is also their duty to diagnose honestly the conflicts and complications coming to light in this development.

Nowak thereupon called for the creation of a new "research institute having at its disposal a national network of salaried poll-takers . . . [one that] would

---

*Riots and strikes by workers, which began in the Baltic coast cities of Gdansk and Gdynia, spread to other cities and led to the removal of Wladyslaw Gomulka as first secretary of the Party and his replacement by Edward Gierek.

try to conform to the highest organizational and methodological international standards." He noted the importance of who sponsors such work in obtaining sincere and complete answers and suggested that "the experience of many years in our country shows that a particularly propitious aura is created in such research by the authority of purely scholarly institutions." As final conditions for the success of the proposed new public opinion institute, he cited "a systematic and general method of keeping the public informed through mass communication media of the poll results" and of "showing to what extent the results of polls help guide decisions in matters of planning and social policy, i.e., to what extent each of the respondents, representing both himself and the society whose 'sample' he constituted, was instrumental in making such decisions ever better adapted to social needs."[117]

"Providing public opinion polls with the status of a consultation of the nation and keeping the public regularly informed of the results of this consultation," Nowak concluded, "may of itself become an important factor in satisfying social needs."[118]

The Gierek regime has not followed Nowak's advice, but it has dramatized the "consultations" by high Party leaders with miners, workers, and other citizens. This is said to be an effective way of ensuring that mass opinion is articulated to the political elite while, simultaneously, the elite has the opportunity to explain its policies to the citizenry. One may doubt the effectiveness of the "consultations," though their psychological value may be high, and it is known that opinion polls on sensitive political issues are still commissioned by the government. The results of these polls are "for internal use only," and it is therefore impossible to analyze them. However, after some personal and institutional rivalries were overcome, the OBOP was merged with another media organization and was reconstituted in the early 1970s. By 1976, three numbers of what is said to be its quarterly publication, *Przekazy i opinie*, had appeared. Mass media and youth seem to be the main concern of the opinion surveys reported in this journal, and it appears that polls with a more directly political relevance are simply not discussed outside restricted Party circles. Thus, Nowak's hope that the public would be kept "regularly informed of the results" of opinion polls has been realized only to a limited degree, and opinion polling in the 1970s seems to have lost the broad political significance that it had in the previous decade.

THE SIGNIFICANCE OF THE "RENAISSANCE"

One does not need to make the unwarranted identification of public opinion polling with such institutions as a multiparty system or free elections to see that Nowak accorded it considerably more significance than most of his Western counterparts, who have a great deal more experience with it but practice it in a much different context. From a somewhat different point of view, it might be said that the Gomulka regime was not incorrect in its assessment of the polling activities of the period 1956-63 as political acts.

Indeed, it is difficult to escape the conclusion that the polling activities in Poland during the period under discussion were at least as significant to "politics" as their findings were to sociology. One can take any number of different indicators to support this view—the sensitive political subject matter, dealt with in such a way as to permit "unorthodox findings"; the explicit statements of researchers; the response of the public; and the reverberations of survey findings in the developing policies of the Gomulka regime.

Most of the research studies examined in this chapter were highly political in the context of the October and post-October period—the youth studies, with their emphasis on attitudes to socialism and Marxism; the religiosity studies; agricultural problems, particularly those dealing with attitudes toward forms of land holding; the standard of living; social stratification in a supposedly "classless" society, and the like.

A comparison of the Polish youth studies and a poll on a similar topic conducted by the Public Opinion Institute of *Komsomol'skaia pravda*, the organ of the Young Communist League of the USSR, makes the difference between the political objectives of the Polish research and those of the traditional Soviet bloc propaganda techniques quite clear. The institute's third survey effort, in January 1961, asked the paper's readers between the ages of 15 and 28 to respond to 12 questions on the attitudes, ideas, and aspirations of their generation. In addition, they were asked to supply the following personal data: age, sex, education, employment or other activity, when they had started working regularly, address, and optionally, their names. The poll findings were, predictably, much different than the findings of the several studies of Polish youth. In contrast to the apparent apathy of the Poles, Soviet youth portrayed themselves as loyal, convinced, active, and enthusiastic "builders of communism." The responses to the survey questionnaire, many of them signed, were for the most part declarations of ideological loyalty and enthusiasm. Excerpts from the responses were widely published in *Komsomol'skaia pravda* and the rest of the Soviet press and hailed as "evidence of the true communist and patriotic spirit of Soviet youth."[119]

The Polish studies and the *Komosomol'skaia pravda* poll are hardly comparable from a technical standpoint, but this in itself is instructive. The carefully constructed and elaborate instrument (over 150 questions) employed in the Warsaw University studies, designed to reveal numerous shadings of opinion and to allow for in-depth analysis, contrasts sharply with the 12 general questions in the Soviet poll, as does the care taken in the Polish studies to achieve random samples of the population studied. This is not to deny the likelihood that Soviet youth were more ideologically orthodox or activist than their Polish counterparts, but only to point out that the *Komsomol'skaia pravda* poll was clearly neither constructed nor administered in such a way as to permit a scientific test of the proposition. Aside from the fact that the respondents had to be readers of the paper to know of the survey in the first place and had to fill out voluntarily and mail in the questionnaire—both factors that tend to bias the sample in favor of more activist elements of the population—the requiring of identifying data (address was sufficient, even if the respondent did not choose to give his name) encouraged precisely the kind of declamatory responses that were obtained, rather than expression of negative or even qualified opinions.

The Soviet poll might easily be placed in that category that Gitelman, in chapter 1, describes as "self-affirmation"—"carried out merely to confirm what the leadership wants to hear." The uses to which the results were put also clearly fall well within the orthodox propaganda framework of the Soviet-type regimes.

The purposes of the Polish studies, which also received a great deal of attention in the Polish press, must be explained differently. One does not have to look far to find explicit statements from Polish opinion researchers on the political motivations of the studies. Statements contemporary with the October and post-October studies are very similar to the views expressed by Nowak in the 1971 *Nowe Drogi* article. (Nowak himself was, of course, closely associated with the Warsaw University studies.) The statements by Jan Szczepanski or the unattributed statement from *Prasa Polska*, *Zycie Gospodarcze*, and *Polityka* cited earlier in this chapter, indicate the political motivations of the studies. Anna Pawelczynska, one of the most distinguished opinion researchers in post-October Poland and closely identified both with the Warsaw University studies and with the OBOP, is particularly clear: The functions of public opinion research, she says, are to provide:

> (1) a channel conveying important information in the form of objective and subjective observations of public life: a source of information, therefore, which provides a large number of political and social institutions with the basic premises for making decisions, and (2) a mouthpiece for democratic standards in public life, i.e., a research tool which conveys public views and opinions on a variety of subjects to those institutes responsible for social, political and economic activities.[120]

Andrzej Sicinski, director of the OBOP and a close colleague of Pawelczynska's, notes, in quoting her statement in a 1967 article in a Western journal, that "this definition of the function of social research in socialist countries would be acceptable to most Polish sociologists."[121]

The Polish press widely publicized both its own polling activities and those of the OBOP, urging public cooperation and emphasizing that this was a way of making views and needs known to the institutions that make policy.[122] The response of the Polish population to opinion research during the post-October period may suggest that is was persuaded by this viewpoint and took a much-desired opportunity to express its views. The overwhelming number of applications received by the OBOP after its request for volunteer interviewers (work that is paid in the West) is but one indication of the public enthusiasm. (The same phenomenon occurred in Yugoslavia and in Czechoslovakia.[123]) Perhaps even more interesting is the strikingly low rate of nonresponse encountered by the Polish poll-takers and the fact that "don't know," "no opinion," or "can't answer" responses on individual questions seldom constituted a significant proportion of the answers in most of the surveys conducted during the height of the post-October polling period.

A number of Western observers have speculated that people who have lived under conditions of totalitarianism and political terror may feel compelled to respond to "officially sanctioned" interviewers, that their responses may not be frank, and that survey results could therefore be seriously biased. In a personal interview early in 1969, OBOP Director Sicinski told this writer that the experience of the OBOP did not appear to bear out such theories and he did not personally believe them to be the case. Sicinski has stated in a journal article, however, that "even with the avoidance of 'delicate' questions, extensive press and radio propaganda explaining the survey technique was insufficient to eliminate resistance in the early stages."[124] A more recent work edited by Gostowski and Lutynski, also lends some credence to such a view. As a result of their investigation of research methods, these authors conclude that "the disparity is much greater in this country [Poland] than in the United States between private opinions and those disclosed to the interviewer."[125]

While these and other qualifications[126] certainly need to be kept in mind, another characteristic of the chronological development of response style in the Polish surveys seems to suggest that the public considered the polls as opportunity for introducing their views into policy-making process. At least in the surveys available to this writer, nonresponse, "don't know," and "no opinion" answers appear to have risen substantially from the initial striking lows and to have become significant in polls taken later, when it had become clear that, indeed, they were not (or were no longer) effective means of influencing policy.

The final question to be considered, then, is whether the public opinion research conducted during the 1956-63 period in Poland did, in fact, have any impact on the formulation of political policy, and if so, whether the impact was positive or negative.

No less an authority than Sicinski acknowledges the "lack of properly organized and institutionalized channels for conveying the data and conclusions from the research centers to the executive authorities. As yet, no satisfactory mechanism has been developed for introducing research data into the policy-making process"[127] (even though the OBOP itself had a policy of sending copies of every study conducted to all relevant government and Party organs). This failure formally to institutionalize channels of communication between opinion research centers and policy-making bodies may be taken as evidence that the governing bodies were not prepared to make a formal commitment to utilize "public opinion" as revealed by such research in the formulation of policy.

Nevertheless, the lack of such a formal commitment on the part of the governing institutions does not rule out the possibility that the information will influence them in other—more or less direct—ways. In the Polish case, several additional factors should be kept in mind.

First, it seems clear from many statements already quoted in this chapter that the regime for some time sanctioned and even encouraged the view that participation in surveys was a means of influencing policy—in direct statements to that effect, by its official support of the OBOP and other institutes engaged in such research, and by its permissiveness with regard to the widespread use and dissemination of survey results by the press. In countries where the means of mass communication are controlled by the government, such massive evidence of official approval is unlikely to occur by accident or without purpose.[128]

Second, we have already noted in the discussion of the youth and religiosity studies earlier in this chapter that the regime implemented a number of antireligious and ideological indoctrination measures when confronted with extensive survey evidence of widespread religiosity and lack of ideological orthodoxy. While this does not square with a theory of surveys as instruments for "the democratic guidance of society," it is evidence of information gathered through surveys being utilized in policy making. In fact, unlike the Warsaw University studies, later studies undertaken at the behest of the regime in these areas—such as the study of 12- and 13-year-olds designed to ferret out unorthodox "ritualistic attitudes" so they could be properly dealt with—appear to be directly manipulative in their ultimate intent.

Third, it can be argued that the findings of the Warsaw University studies, confirmed and elaborated in many of the other opinion polls and surveys undertaken during this period, did ultimately form the basis for the "Polish road to socialism," or, as it was more accurately called later, the "little stabilization." The main lines of the stabilization policy included the indefinite postponement of recollectivitzation in the countryside, aid to the spontaneously organized "agricultural circles," tolerance of private enterprise in handicrafts, retail trade, and light industry, more emphasis on consumer goods production, greater tolerance in the field of civil liberties, an attempt to present Marxist ideology in a low-keyed and more palatable manner, and most importantly, as it was put by Emilia Wilder, "the lures of more earthly advantages . . . in the pursuit of careers and pleasures."[129]

This program—if not always fully realized in practice—proved in its main outlines a lasting feature of the Gomulka regime.

The political context in which the opinion studies flourished must be kept in mind. The intellectual spirit of the Polish October—to which Gomulka owed his accession to power—was clearly revisionist, a revolt against the postwar decade of Soviet-imposed orthodoxy. And, while it seems apparent that the intellectual community, which spearheaded this revisionist revolt, and the general populace, too, understood the ultimate limits of Soviet tolerance, how much room for maneuver within that limit would be permitted remained to be determined.

Gomulka thus occupied a different position. He had to maintain a sufficient degree of orthodoxy to mollify the Soviet leadership, while at the same time accommodating to some degree the national aspirations that had brought him to power.

In retrospect, the revisionist intellectual and political community was clearly overoptimistic about where the borders of permissible deviation from Soviet orthodoxy would fall, and probably overestimated Gomulka's revisionist sympathies as well.

The flourishing of opinion studies in this context appears, then, to have two dimensions. On the one hand, the revisionist intellectual and political climate that fostered it predated and contributed to Gomulka's accession to power. In this sense, it may be said to have had something of a life of its own, and, in the beginning, the regime did not feel it had the power or the security to oppose such ventures, even though it might have wished to. It was not until Gomulka had achieved an effective compromise with the desires of the population in order to assure the peaceful continuation of Communist rule that he felt able to call a halt to these studies. On the other hand, whether he welcomed them or not, the survey results appear to have provided much information that was useful to the regime in establishing the modus vivendi, that is, the little stabilization.

We noted at the outset of this section that including opinion research in the category of pluralistic institutions was unjustified. Still, the Polish experience suggests that, under conditions of political instability, when the forms and content of a regime's legitimacy have not yet been firmly established, in the absence of other forms of political participation, public preferences may be ascertained through this kind of social science research to become real inputs in the policy-making process.

NOTES

1. Jozef Chalasinski, *Nauka Polska*, no. 2 (1955), quoted in *News from Behind the Iron Curtain* 5, no. 3 (March 1956).

2. Jozef Chalasinski, *Przeglad Kulturalny*, October 13-19, 1955, quoted in *News from Behind the Iron Curtain* 5, no. 3 (March 1956).

3. Andrzej Sicinski, ed., *Spoleczenstwo Polskie w Badaniach Ankietowych* (Warsaw: Committee for Research on Contemporary Culture, Polish Academy of Sciences, 1966), p. 37.

4. Andrzej Sicinski, "Public Opinion Surveys in Poland," *International Social Science Journal*, no. 1 (1963).

5. *Przeglad Kulturalny*, June 11 and August 1, 1959.

6. Hanna Malewska, "Z Badan nad zyciem seksualnym," *Kultura i spoleczenstwo* 6, no. 1 (January-March 1962): 89-101.

7. "Polish Opinion Polls," *East Europe* 9, no. 1 (January 1960): 5.

8. Zofia Jozefowicz, Stefan Nowak, and Anna Pawelczynska, "Students: Myth and Reality," *Polish Perspectives*, nos. 3-4 (1958), p. 21.

9. Z. Jozefowicz, S. Nowak, and A. Pawelczynska, "Students: Their Views of Society and Aspirations," *Polish Perspectives*, nos. 7-8 and 11-12 (1958), p. 33, reprinted from *Nowa Kultura*, October 12, 1958.

10. Z. Jozefowicz, S. Nowak, and A. Pawelczynska, "Students: Myth and Reality," *Polish Perspectives*, nos. 3-4 and 7-8 (1958), p. 27, reprinted from *Przeglad Kulturalny*, July 17, 1958.

11. Ibid., p. 27.

12. W. Wisniewski, "Tolerance and Egalitarianism," *Polish Sociological Bulletin*, no. 1 (1963), p. 23.

13. Jozefowicz et al., in *Nowa Kultura*, op. cit., p. 42.

14. Ibid., p. 43.

15. Sicinski, ed., *Spoleczenstwo*, op. cit., p. 37.

16. Emilia Wilder, "Impact of Poland's 'Stabilization' on Youth," *Public Opinion Quarterly* 28, no. 1 (Summer 1964): 449.

17. Stefan Nowak, "Correlational Control of Meaning of Attitudinal Variables," *Polish Sociological Bulletin*, nos. 3-4 (1962), pp. 19-25.

18. Tadeusz Jaroszewski, "Dynamika praktyk religijnych i postaw swiatopogladowych w Polsce w swietle badan socjologicznych, *Kultura i spoleczenstwo* 10, no. 1 (January-March 1966): 135.

19. Among the more interesting reports on these studies are Anna Pawelczynska's "Dynamika i Funkcje Postaw Wobec Religii" (Dynamics and Functions of Religious Attitudes), *Studia socjologiczno-polityczne*, no. 10 (1961); Tadeusz Jaroszewski's "Dynamika Praktyk Religijnych i Postaw Swiatopogladowych w Polsce w Swietle Badan Socjologicznych" (Dynamics of the Practice of Religion and Attitudes Toward the World in Poland in Light of Sociological Research), *Kultura i spoleczenstwo* 10, no. 1 (January-March 1966); and Czeslaw Staciwa's "Spoleczne Aspekty Religijnosci Mlodziezy Poborowej" (Social Aspects of Religiosity Among Drafted Youths), *Studia socjologiczno-polityczne*, no. 24.

20. Ibid., pp. 141-42.

21. Anna Pawelczynska, "Dynamika i funkcje postaw wobec religii," *Studia socjologiczno-polityczne*, no. 10 (1961), p. 93.

22. Ibid., p. 91.

23. Ibid., p. 72.

24. Ibid., pp. 75-76.

25. M. Kozakiewicz, "Swiatopoglad 1,000 nauczycieli," cited by Jaroszewski, op. cit., p. 137.

26. Irene Nowakowska, "Z Badan nad typologia postaw spolecznych Polskiego uczonego," cited by Jaroszewski, op. cit., p. 137.

27. Czeslaw Staciwa, "Spoleczne aspekty religijnosci mlodziezy poborowej," *Studia socjologiczno-polityczne*, no. 24 (1968), pp. 76-80.

28. Jaroszewski, op. cit., p. 139.

29. Pawelczynska, op. cit., pp. 83-86.

30. Izabela Wiatr, "Opinie o zaspokojeniu potrzeb materialnych ludnosci miejskiej," in Sicinski, ed., *Spoleczenstwo*, op. cit., p. 84.

31. Zygmunt Zekonski, "Wstepne informacje o strukturze zywienia ludnosci miast," in Sicinski, ed., *Spoleczenstwo*, op. cit., p. 75.

32. Ibid., p. 76.

33. Ibid., p. 75.

34. Roman Peretiatkowicz, "Zakupy w Warszawie," in Sicinski, ed., *Spoleczenstwo*, op. cit., p. 79.

35. Central Statistical Office, *Concise Statistical Yearbook of Poland, 1969* (Warsaw, 1970).

36. Boguslaw Galeski, "Farmers' Attitudes to Their Occupation," *Polish Sociological Bulletin*, no. 1 (1963), pp. 58-60.

37. Ibid., p. 59.

38. Zdzislaw Szpakowski, "Potrzeby spoleczno-kulturalne wsi," in Sicinski, ed., *Spoleczenstwo*, op. cit., p. 74.

39. Galeski, op. cit., p. 64.

40. Waclaw Makarczyk, "Stosunki spoleczno-gospodarcze na wsi," in Sicinski, ed., *Spoleczenstwo*, op. cit., p. 26.

41. Waclaw Makarczyk and Danuta Markowska, "Opinie chlopow o niektorych sprawach uregulowanych ostatnie aktami ustawodawczmi," in Sicinski, ed., *Spoleczenstwo*, op. cit., p. 28.

42. Ibid., pp. 28-29.

43. Ibid., p. 29.

44. Makarczyk, op. cit., p. 26.

45. Galeski, op. cit., p. 67.

46. Leszek Kacmarczyk, "Problemy gospodarstw zaniedbanych w opinii mieszkancow 6 wsi," in Sicinski, ed., *Spoleczenstwo*, op. cit., p. 29-30.

47. Leszek Kaczmarczyk, "Problemy gospodarstw zaniedbanych w opinii mieszkancow wsi Polckiej," in Sicinski, ed., *Spoleczenstwo*, op. cit., p. 29.

48. Ibid.

49. Dyzma Galaj, "Attitude of the Rural Population to Part-Time Farmers," *Polish Sociological Bulletin*, no. 1 (1965), p. 117.

50. Ibid., p. 70.

51. Ibid., pp. 118-19.

52. Ibid., p. 119 (data for Plock region only).

53. Zdislaw Szpakowski, "Potrzeby spoleczno-kulturalne wsi," in Sicinski, ed., *Spoleczenstwo*, op. cit., p. 32.

54. Waclaw Makarczyk, "Stabilnosc zawodowa i aktywnosc gospodarska rolnikow," in Sicinski, ed., *Spoleczenstwo*, op. cit., p. 33.

55. Waclaw Makarczyk, "Tendencje migracijne mieszkancow wsi," in Sicinski, ed., *Spoleczenstwo*, op. cit., p. 33.

56. Franciszek Adamski, "The Steel Workers' Occupation and Family," *Polish Sociological Bulletin*, no. 1 (1965), p. 104.

57. Aleksander Matejko, "Steel Workers' Attitudes to Their Occupation," *Polish Sociological Bulletin*, no. 1 (1965), p. 99.

58. Ibid., p. 98.

59. Ibid., p. 99.

60. Ibid., p. 101.

61. Zofia Jozefowicz and Zbigniew Sufin, "Moralnosc pracy i zjawiska w zakladzie przemyslowym," in Sicinski, ed., *Spoleczenstwo*, op. cit., p. 11.

62. Danuta Markowska and Zbigniew Sufin, "Moralnosc pracy i zjawiska z nia zwiazane w zakladzie przemyslowym," in Sicinski, ed., *Spoleczenstwo*, op. cit., p. 11.

63. Krystyna Lutynska, "Office Workers' Views on Their Social Position," *Polish Sociological Bulletin*, no. 1 (1964), p. 80.

64. Ibid., p. 81.

65. Ibid., p. 82.

66. Jan Woskowski, "Primary School Teachers and Their Social Position in People's Poland," *Polish Sociological Bulletin*, no. 1 (1964), p. 89.

67. Ibid., p. 88. An extensive study of teachers and their outlooks is Joseph Fiszman's *Revolution and Tradition in People's Poland* (Princeton, N.J.: Princeton University Press, 1972).

68. Zygmunt Drodzek and Anna Preiss-Zajdowa, "Kobiety wobec pracy zawodowej," in Sicinski, ed., *Spoleczenstwo*, op. cit., p. 15.

69. Ibid.

70. Ibid., p. 16.

71. Adam Sarapata, "Poglady mieszkancow Warszawy na strukturze spoleczna," *Studia socjologiczno-polityczne* 6 (1960): 93-148.

72. Adam Sarapata, "Iustum Pretium," *Polish Sociological Bulletin*, no. 1 (1963), pp. 41-56.

73. Stefan Nowak, "Changes of Social Structure in Social Consciousness," *Polish Sociological Bulletin*, no. 2 (1964), pp. 34-53.

74. Nowak, op. cit., p. 35.

75. Andrzej Sicinski, "Rozwoj miasta a swiadomosc jego obywateli," *Kultura i spoleczenstwo* 6, no. 1 (1961): 165. See also Z. Dulczewski, *Spoleczne Aspekty Migracji na Ziemiach Zachodnich* (Poznan, 1964); and W. Markiewicz and P. Rybicki, *Przemiany Spoleczne na Ziemiach Zachodnich* (Poznan, 1967) for studies of the adaptation and integration of settlers in the Western Territories. A recent study of the Western Territories is Z. Anthony Kruszewski, *The Oder-Neisse Boundary and Poland's Modernization* (New York: Praeger 1972).

76. Wieslaw Wisniewski, "Mieszkancy Pulaw o sobie i swoim miescie," in Sicinski, ed., *Spoleczenstwo*, op. cit., p. 19.

77. Andrzej Sicinski, "Mieszkancy Slupska o zyciu swoim i swego miasta," in Sicinski, ed., *Spoleczenstwo*, op. cit., p. 20.

78. Irena Nowakowska, "Szczecinek: ludzie i problemy powiatowego miasta," in Sicinski, ed., *Spoleczenstwo*, op. cit., p. 17.

79. Sicinski, "Rozwoj," op. cit., p. 166.

80. Jan Weglenski, "Dynamika procesu stabilizacji mieszkancow Swinoujscia," in Sicinski, ed., *Spoleczenstwo*, op. cit., p. 17.

81. Anna Pawelczynska and Miroslawa Jastrzab, "Zlocieniec i jego mieszkancy," in Sicinski, ed., *Spoleczenstwo*, op. cit., p. 18.

82. Sicinski, "Rozwoj," op. cit., p. 166.

83. Anna Pawelczynska, "Przyczynek do problematyki stabilizacji na Ziemiach Zachodnich," *Studia Socjologiczno-Polityczne*, no. 8 (1961), p. 173.

84. Sicinski, "Rozwoj," op. cit., p. 170.

85. Ibid., p. 171.

86. Ibid., p. 169.

87. Pawelczynska and Jastrzab, op. cit., p. 18.

88. Sicinski, ed., *Spoleczenstwo*, op. cit.

89. Andrzej Sicinski, "Stereotypes of Countries and Nations," *Polish Sociological Bulletin*, no. 1 (1968), p. 82.

90. Ibid., p. 83.

91. Ibid.

92. Johan Galtung and Andrzej Sicinski, "Public Opinion and Disarmament" (unpublished manuscript).

93. Siegfried Kracauer and Paul Berkman, *Satellite Mentality* (New York: Praeger, 1956), p. 152.

94. Andrzej Sicinski, "Peace and War in Polish Public Opinion," *Polish Sociological Bulletin*, no. 2 (1967), p. 34.

95. Andrzej Sicinski, " 'Don't Know' Answers in Cross-National Surveys," *Public Opinion Quarterly* 33, no. 1 (1970): 126-27, n. 4.

96. Ibid., p. 128.

97. Stefan Nowak, "The Social Usefulness of Studies of Public Opinion and Attitudes," Radio Free Europe (RFE) Polish Press Survey, no. 2333, p. 2, translated from *Nowe Drogi*, September 1971.

98. In *Przeglad Kulturalny*, August 20, 1959.

99. In *Polityka*, October 11, 1958.

100. *Prasa Polska*, October 1958.

101. In *Zycie Gospodarcze*, September 13, 1959.

102. See the discussion in Emilia Wilder, "Poland: Sociology in Eastern Europe," *Problems of Communism* 14, no. 1 (January-February 1965), pp. 58-62.

103. Ibid., p. 60.

104. In *Polityka*, April 21, 1961.

105. In *Polityka*, July 27, 1962.

106. Andrzej Sincinski, "Developments in East European Public Opinion Research," *Polls* 3, no. 1 (Autumn 1967): 5.

107. Ibid.

108. *Trybuna Ludu*, July 6, 1963.

109. Sicinski, ed., *Spoleczenstwo*, op. cit., p. 58.

110. Ibid., p. 3.

111. W. Wernic, "Has the Great Teacher Been Forgotten?", *Tygodnik Demokraticzny*, September 10, 1967, translated in RFE Polish Press Survey, no. 2099, October 16, 1967.

112. "World War II as Evaluated by a Pole in 1966," *Zycie Literackie*, January 29, 1967, translated in RFE Polish Press Survey, no. 2041, February 16, 1967.

113. Nowak, "The Social Usefulness . . . ," op. cit., p. 13.

114. Jan Lutynski, "The New Unified Sociology Curriculum in Poland," *Polish Sociological Bulletin*, no. 1 (1969).

115. See Adam Podgorecki, "Law and Morals in Theory and Operation," *Polish Sociological Bulletin*, no. 1 (1969).

116. Nowak, "Social Usefulness," op. cit.

117. Ibid.

118. Ibid.

119. *Komsomol'skaia pravda*, July 21 and 22, 1961. For a more detailed discussion of the results, see chap. 4 in this volume.

120. Anna Pawelczynska, "Zalozenia i problemy badan opinii publicznej w Polsce," *Kultura i spoleczenstwo* 10, no. 1 (1966).

121. Sicinski, "Developments," op. cit., pp. 3 and 8.

122. Ibid., pp. 5-6.

123. F. Dzinic, "Opinion Surveys in a Federal Republic," *Polls* 3, no. 3 (1968): 5; and chap. 3 of this volume on Czechoslovakia.

124. Sicinski, "Developments," op. cit., p. 9.

125. See a review of Gostowski and Lutynski's book, *Analizy i proby technik badawczych w sociologii*, in *Polish Sociological Bulletin*, no. 1 (1969), p. 91.

126. See chap. 1 for a more extensive treatment of the problems of response-style in Soviet bloc countries. For a treatment of a different aspect of the question, see Sicinski, " 'Don't Know,' " op. cit.

127. Sicinski, "Developments," op. cit., p. 9.

128. For an interesting discussion of how the channels of mass communication in totalitarian societies serve to inform the public of expected norms of behavior, see Paul Keckskemeti, "Totalitarian Communications as a Means of Control: A Note on the Sociology of Propaganda," *Public Opinion Quarterly* (Summer 1950), op. cit., pp. 224-34.

129. Wilder, "Impact of Poland's 'Stabilization' on Youth," op. cit.

3

PUBLIC OPINION
IN CZECHOSLOVAKIA
Zvi Y. Gitelman

Before World War II, Czechoslovakia had the highest literacy rate, numerically smallest peasantry, and generally most educated population in Eastern Europe. It could be expected that, especially under the democratic conditions that prevailed in Czechoslovakia between 1918 and 1938, there would be informed and articulate public opinion on political issues. Nevertheless, despite the fact that empirical sociology had developed in interwar Czechoslovakia, it was only after the war that a public opinion research institute was established in Prague. Public opinion certainly played a role in the political life of the Czechoslovak republic, with its free and lively press, democratic electoral system, many parties, and generally civil libertarian atmosphere, despite authoritarian features in the nationality and political spheres.

But opinion polls were not a regular or important feature of Czechoslovak democracy. Only in 1946 did the newly founded Czechoslovak Institute for Public Opinion Research begin conducting surveys on a national scale. The institute was attached to the Ministry of Information, and its directors conceived of it as a "tool for democracy."[1] The institute conducted electoral surveys, investigated attitudes on international and domestic political questions, and surveyed citizens' opinions on some of the difficult economic problems faced by the Czechoslovaks after the war.

In general, one gets the impression from several of the surveys that the years of Nazi occupation were not without their impact and that there was a somewhat authoritarian mood among the populace immediately after the war. Seventy-six percent of respondents, asked whether the government should have the right forcibly to shift manpower from one place to another responded in the affirmative, 39 percent giving an unqualified "yes," and 37 percent "yes, in case it is necessary." Research on attitudes toward child rearing also showed authoritarian outlooks, and more people suggested force than any other means to get badly needed labor into the coal-mining industry.

Interestingly, when in May 1947, Czechoslovaks were asked, "The Italian parliament has abolished the death penalty; do you think Czechoslovakia should do the same?" 25 percent of the respondents were in favor of abolition and 54 percent were not, with 21 percent answering "don't know." Two months later, the question was asked again, but this time the USSR's abolition of the death penalty was substituted for Italy's. Thirty-six percent now expressed the opinion that Czechoslovakia should abolish it, 44 percent were still opposed to abolition, and 20 percent "didn't know." Since only a short time had elapsed between the two questions, presumably the greater popularity of the USSR served to alter the response structure.[2] In its electoral survey of 1946, the institute predicted the results with great accuracy[3] and was complimented by Klement Gottwald.[4]

The Czechoslovak Institute for Public Opinion Research conducted its surveys only in the Czech lands, worked with a small staff, and generally employed two survey methods: the Gallup variation, using a quota sample, and the mass observation technique. Sixteen issues of its journal appeared between 1946 and 1948, and the results of surveys were made available to the mass media, which reported them frequently and often prominently. Social scientists not connected with the institute also published in the institute's journal, *Public Opinion*, and the tone of the journal was characterized by "antifascism, the construction of socialism, and the spirit of the Kosice program." Despite the socialist outlook of the journal, two of its employees accepted a Rockefeller Foundation grant that enabled them to spend three months in the United States studying opinion research methods.

The apparent accuracy and reliability of the institute's findings led indirectly to its downfall. In the fall of 1947, the institute conducted an electoral survey that showed that the popularity of the Communist Party had declined considerably. Several observers have concluded that this hastened the decision of the Communist Party to seize power by any means, rather than rely on a steady accretion of parliamentary and electoral strength to bring it to power. Writing in 1966, one of the leading figures in the institute, Cenek Adamec, cautiously raised the question,[5]

> Why did the journal *Public Opinion* cease publication on 1948? Why did the opinion research institute cease its activity later on? The author does not consider himself competent to answer the question but will try to formulate it generally. The criticism and rejection of sociology undoubtedly was linked to public opinion research as well. In the last period of its activity, which lasted until 1950, the public opinion institute was connected with the Masaryk Institute for National Education . . . where for a short time it conducted research on educational themes and in the field of the book trade. . . . The

February events caused a great upheaval in social psychology, changes for which the institute was not methodologically prepared.

As in Poland, the seizure of total power by the Communist Party meant the replacement of "bourgeois" sociology by the "science" of Marxism-Leninism. As part of this change, opinion research was halted, the public opinion institute was dissolved, and the orthodox doctrine of the "identification premise" was imposed. For the entire Stalinist period, which lasted longer in Czechoslovakia than in most other socialist countries, social science was thoroughly "Bolshevized," with the repression of Western methods and the elevation of Stalin's pronouncements to the last word in all fields. Obviously, public opinion research could not be carried out under such conditions. It was simply postulated that the masses dutifully and enthusiastically followed whatever line the possessors of superior historical consciousness declared as the policy and thought of the moment. The events of 1968 dramatically demonstrated that a public opinion sharply at variance with the official line continued to exist throughout the post-1948 period. But it lay dormant and invisible until conditions changed and allowed it to surface once again.

Under pressure from elements within Czechoslovakia and from the Soviet Party leadership, the Czechoslovak Party began to take the first meaningful steps away from Stalinist orthodoxies in various areas. In the 1960s, the flowering of empirical sociological research ("concrete research") in the USSR legitimized Czechoslovak efforts in this area, and the disciplines of sociology, psychology, and even, later on, political science (*politologie*) were revived. Departments of sociology were opened in several universities and in the academies of science in Bohemia and Slovakia. Even more government ministries opened departments for sociological research related to their functional responsibilities. The emphasis was on those areas wherein research could provide quick and visible "practical" results and payoffs. Thus, industrial sociology developed as a field that could improve the Czechoslovak economy by making industrial production more efficient, raising the morale and efficiency of the workers, providing managers with information that they could use in increasing production. At the same time, studies of students and youth were launched with the declared purpose of simultaneously serving the needs of the younger generation and providing the Party with the kind of information it could use to make more attractive political appeals to the younger generation, an area that was clearly a trouble spot for the regime, as the declining membership in the Communist youth organization indicated. A study done in 1966 showed that only 11.3 percent of the students who were members of the Party "joined out of conviction." Only 2 percent thought Czechoslovakia had gotten full advantage out of socialism, and only 7 percent of the students said the Party influenced the majority of students either consistently or even from time to time.[6]

The revival of Czechoslovak social science was made possible politically by social science development in the Soviet Union; it was greatly helped intellectually by the flowering of Polish sociology after 1956. An examination of Czechoslovak journals reveals that scholars in Prague, Brno, Bratislava, and elsewhere had carefully studied the works of such outstanding Polish scholars as Jan Szczepanski, Stanislaw Ossowski, Adam Sarapata, and Jerzy Wiatr, thus reestablishing indirect links to Western scholarship. Many conferences were held to which Polish, Hungarian, East German, Soviet, and even Yugoslav scholars were invited, and such journals as *Sociologicky casopis* featured articles by sociologists, philosophers, and psychologists from these countries. From "concrete research," the Czechoslovaks gradually and cautiously moved toward sociological theory, studies of social stratification in a socialist society, and attempts to introduce such concepts as systems analysis to the new field of political science. A major project, directed by Pavel Machonin, attempted comprehensively, systematically, and thoroughly to analyze contemporary Czechoslovak society from a sociological standpoint.[7] Social science succeeded in attracting a young cadre of talented scholars, some of whom had tried to do social scientific work under various guises in earlier years and were now eager to exploit the new, if limited, opportunities that presented themselves.

In March 1966 the Czechoslovak Academy of Sciences sponsored a two-day seminar on public opinion research wherein recommendations were made to establish a public opinion section of the Czechoslovak Sociological Association. Cenek Adamec, now employed in the Central Institute for Health Education, launched what seemed to be a trial balloon by publishing his paper given at the seminar on "The Beginnings of Public Opinion Research Among Us." The activities of the postwar research institute were described at some length, along with a general description of some types of opinion polling in the United States.[8] Both the title and Adamec's concluding remarks made clear that a revival, or continuation, of opinion research was being proposed. Public opinion research had not been included in the 20 areas of sociological research listed in the landmark resolution of the Party Central Committee, "Report on the Problems of Development of Sociology in the Czechoslovak Socialist Republic," taken on March 17, 1965.[9] Nevertheless, it was being discussed in the scholarly journals. One lengthy review of American and Soviet writings on public opinion went so far as to criticize a book by Soviet scholar A. K. Uledov as simplistic and conservative and pointed out that the socialist approach to the study of public opinion had much to learn from Western work in the field.[10]

After a hiatus of nearly 20 years, an Institute for Research on Public Opinion was once again established in Prague, on January 1, 1967. It was an autonomous institute attached to the Czechoslovak Academy of Sciences. At the same time, a "Cabinet" of Public Opinion and Cultural Research was established in Bratislava in order to research those problems pertaining specifically to Slovakia, whereas the Prague institute, unlike its postwar predecessor, would take the whole country within its purview. The budget of the institute came from the Academy of Sciences with partial funding of commissioned projects coming from the commissioners. The director of the institute was Dr. Jaroslava Zapletalova, and a small professional staff was recruited. The mandate of the presidium of the Academy of Sciences to the new institute stressed theoretical and social scientific tasks heavily, paying little attention to practical uses of the institute's work.

Staffing and planning the institute were completed in the winter of 1967, and in the summer of that year advertisements were placed in the newspapers inviting people to apply for jobs as interviewers. About 4,000 applications were received, and two networks of interviewers, each consisting of 250 people, were selected. No people with official or political jobs were selected as interviewers, and university students were by and large excluded as well. The aim of the institute was to recruit networks of interviewers that in their own composition would approach the demographic composition of the population as a whole, with the exceptions noted. In early 1968, the first training surveys were launched, research being done "in keeping with the still valid rule that all research and its results must be approved by the high Party organs."[11] In only one survey conducted by the institute was probability sampling used. In all others, despite the fact that the Czechoslovaks were aware of its shortcomings, quota sampling was employed, with attention paid to region and six types of community according to size, sex, age groups, and social groups.

Quota sampling was used rather than probability sampling because it guaranteed the anonymity of respondents, which, as Cenek Adamec said in 1968, "is still important in our country." Moreover, the accurate residence lists needed for probability sampling were not available. The size of the sample was normally between 1,500 and 2,000, with interviewers using the Czech, Slovak, and Hungarian languages. Some 18 surveys were conducted, of which 11 concerned political subjects.

The sympathies of the institute staff, like that of the Czechoslovak intelligentsia as a whole, were generally with the political reformers, and they believed that, as Adamec put it in an interview in *Reporter*, "our research will aid in the process of democratization." While the institute paid a great deal of attention to methodological questions, constantly revising its own procedures, it made a direct and regular input into the political process. First, results of opinion surveys were sent to leading political personalities and institutions with the express intention of having these influence policy formulation. This had a particularly great impact in 1968 when the questions of power, personalities, and policies were so much alive. Second, the results of surveys were made available to the general public through the press conferences called by the institute. The liberal media especially—*Literarni Listy*, *Reporter*, and the newspaper of the People's Party, *Kidova Demokracie*—featured the results of surveys taken by the institute and by other bodies. References made to the findings of these surveys in speeches by politicians such as Josef Smrkovsky, Alexander Dubcek, and others attest to the attention paid them in the highest circles. In fact, reliable sources indicated that leading politicians would frequently call the institute to inquire about the results of the latest survey, particularly those that measured the relative popularity of public figures. Finally, the results of opinion surveys, which almost always supported liberalizing trends, were seized upon eagerly by a population that had been forced for so long to maintain a dual consciousness, with private conviction hidden under outward conformity to an unpopular Party line.

Now, for the first time in 20 years, Czechoslovaks could have more confidence in the veracity and genuineness of what they were told was the way most people felt, and they were able to strengthen their own convictions when they realized that these were widely shared. As journalist Helena Klimova put it, "For twenty years the citizens' consciousness suffered from a sort of schizophrenia, conducting two monologues: a monologue of genuine, but not public opinion."[12] Now the private monologue and the public one were merged into sincere dialogues on the great political issues of the day.

Public opinion research was an important element in stirring up the refreshing winds of the Prague Spring, and aside from its importance in shaping the atmospherics of the period, it was also a direct, powerful, and effective input into the policy-making process. In fact, some would argue that the very one-sidedness of public opinion and its high visibility made it more difficult for the Dubcek leadership to rein in the unbridled enthusiasms of the day, and this, in turn, convinced the Soviets that the Party had lost control over the masses, and that spontaneity was winning out over consciousness. Be that as it may, there is no doubt that the results of the opinion surveys dramatized the bankruptcy of traditional communism in Czechoslovakia and indicated the depth and breadth of desire for reform. Especially because the new leadership adopted a democratic, consultative style, mass opinion and behavior became all the more important in the total political picture.

PUBLIC OPINION IN A REFORMED COMMUNIST POLITICAL SYSTEM

In the 1960s, as Czechoslovakia began to emerge from under the suffocating blanket of Stalinism, the role and nature of public opinion in a socialist system were reexamined. One writer, in his call for the discovery of true public opinion, reminded his readers of the prevailing orthodoxies of Stalinism.

In the 1950s the conclusion was arrived at that unanimity of opinion prevailed among all the people, that the interests of the Party and those of the people were absolutely identical, and that therefore it was not necessary to examine public opinion. Hence, individual divergent opinions were not "bruited about," we hid our heads in the sand, and we preferred to conceal real problems. We were guided, almost to a pathological degree, by the proverb "Don't wash your dirty linen in public."[13]

In 1966 Miroslav Galuska also criticized the "identification premise" and suggested that the media were not allowing "sufficient room to the voice of public opinion." For this reason, he argued, an underground public opinion, at variance with what was publicly represented as public opinion, was created.[14]

Throughout the Prague Spring, the intelligentsia and reformist politicians emphasized the need to involve the citizenry in decision making in a meaningful way and to keep them truly informed on the issues of the day. To take just one example of many, the Slovak jurist and political theorist Michal Lakatos emphasized that "One can govern only in the name of the citizens. . . . A socialist democracy quite definitely cannot exist if the community of citizens is deprived of influence on political direction, if all power does not derive from it. . . . The issue is to increase the influence of the community of citizens on politics."[15] Dr. Zapletalova, explaining the mission of the Institute for Research on Public Opinion, emphasized the importance of opinion research as an input into decision making and governance:

Democratic socialism, when understood as real participation of citizens in social decisions, cannot be imagined without public opinion research. . . . Public opinion research can become an effective instrument for the democratization of our life. It is able to find by objective methods, very quickly and in a reliable way, what problems the public has, what are its fundamental needs, interests and desires. The organs of the social system gain from this research one of the safest supports for their decisions, and they can confront their intentions with the existing state of the social psyche and find to what degree the measures are acceptable to society.

She then expressed the hope that "in the future each significant action in the political sphere, in economics, education, and the health services, that has consequences for the whole of society will be connected with public opinion research. Only in this way is it possible to compensate for uncertainty, often even subjectivism and illusions, and avoid bad, sometimes tragic consequences."[16] Adamec pointed out that elections are not a perfect instrument for uncovering public opinion because of their infrequency, the possibility of fraud, expense, and degree of abstention. Furthermore, he implicitly criticized the contention of the "monist-traditionalist" school of socialist public opinion by pointing to the inadequacies of analysis of reports, discussions at political meetings, and the like as gauges of opinion: Not all people are represented in such forums, reports from meetings are subjective and purposely distorted to protect the rapporteurs, and such expressions of opinion as letters to editors may not be representative of a large number of people.[17]

The importance of genuine public opinion, and hence of scientific opinion research, was acknowledged by the highest political authorities. Reformers such as Smrkovsky emphasized the importance of involving citizens in decision making and encouraged the polling activity that various organizations were engaged in. In his speech to the Central Committee on April 1, Alexander Dubcek cited public opinion polls as confirming the idea that the citizenry would welcome the chance to influence the political bodies and the Party in particular. He stressed that[18]

> We are more and more confirming that social movement cannot be simply decreed, that reason cannot be imposed on it from the outside, but that under our conditions this reason lies first of all in the knowledge, interests, and movements of the broad masses, and that it is the task of the Party to discover this reason, to give it final shape, to improve it, to emphasize progressive thinking and deeds. . . . This difficult task must be borne by the whole Party.

The Action Program of the Czechoslovak Communist Party addressed itself specifically to the question of public opinion and supported the legitimacy of opinion pluralism. The program also upheld the abandonment of preliminary censorship and stated that the working class could no longer be denied information, nor be told "which of their opinions can or cannot be expressed publicly, where public opinion may play a role and where not. *Public opinion polls must be systematically used in preparing important decisions, and the main results of the research should be made public.*"[19] Even after the invasion of Czechoslovakia by the Warsaw Pact Allies, political reformers continued to speak out for the importance of opinion research and stressed the need for the free expression of political opinion.[20]

While opinion surveys were conducted by various organizations even after the August invasion, the invasion had a major impact on this activity. The Prague institute announced that in 1969 it would no longer conduct surveys on political matters but would concentrate on economic, health, social, and cultural questions. Desirous of establishing international contacts, the Prague institute had earlier approached Soviet scholars to gain their cooperation in a joint project but had received no reply to repeated inquiries. After the invasion, the institute remained hopeful that it could participate in the American-Yugoslav "Opinion Makers" project, but this was not to be. By late 1970, the institute seems to have ceased functioning altogether, a fate suffered by almost all Czechoslovak sociological and political research institutes and organizations. It seems to have been reestablished as part of the reorganization of the Czechoslovak Academy of Sciences, and it conducted a poll in June 1971, and again in September.

OPINION POLLS AND SOCIAL ISSUES

In the late 1960s, a few individual and institutional efforts were made to conduct opinion polls on a small scale, investigating a variety of social questions, some of which had clear political implications. As early as 1965 Slovak scholars conducted a survey on questions of war and peace and used the experience to refine their techniques and suggest improvements.[21] A study of attitudes of army recruits yielded some ideologically disquieting results, and studies of attitudes toward religion revealed the persistence of religious belief, at least in Slovakia.[22] The Communist Party sponsored a comprehensive study of religiosity in North Moravia, conducted by Erika Kadlecova, and the monograph that resulted proved to be a major contribution to the sociology of religion in Communist countries, and served as a model for other Czechoslovak scholars.[23] Comparisons with studies done in 1946 and in 1963 showed that religious belief and formal affiliation were declining, but not at a very precipitous rate, and that the Catholic Church was suffering a greater defection of communicants than was the Protestant. Kadlecova's study also showed that formal affiliation with the church and self-identification as a believer persisted after faith had been lost in essential doctrines of the religion.

Building on Kadlecova's study, the Sociological Institute of the Slovak Academy of Sciences surveyed the Slovak population in the fall of 1968 in order to answer a complex of questions concerning religious belief and practice. Quota sampling was used to construct a sample of 1,400 adults in the first survey of its kind in Slovakia. As a Slovak scholar stated with some justification, "It is the first step on the road from the former general approach to a differentiated approach to the problems of religion and atheism."[24] The results of the Kadlecova study were compared to the findings in Slovakia, and the following general picture of religious belief and atheism emerged:

(in percent)

(N = 1,265)	Slovakia	North Moravian Region	Slovaks in Ostrava District
Atheists	14.1	30.0	13
Believers	70.7	30.0	30
Undetermined	15.2	40.0	57

The very high percentage of adult believers in Slovakia obviously called for a great deal of explanation, and this was essayed in terms of Slovakia's history, her relative backwardness, and the heritage of "the clerico-fascist, so-called Slovak state" of World War II. It was acknowledged, however, that "Religion is not yet a matter of the past and it is still potent enough to remain a great *Weltanschauung* and a politico-ideological force (*28.2 percent of the sample expressed the opinion that priests should also exercise a politico-public function*)."[25]

The structure of belief by denominations was found to be as follows:*

(in percent)

	Total Sample (N = 1,265)	Of This, Believers (N = 894)
Catholic (Roman and Greek)	81.6	57.63
Protestant	18.0	12.72
Greek Orthodox	0.1	0.08
Jewish	0.1	0.08
Small denominations and sects	0.2	0.15

As expected, there were twice as many atheists among men as among women, and the largest percentage of atheists was found in the age group 25-39, with the next highest percentage of atheists among those between 18 and 24 years old. It was also discovered that there was no clear inverse relationship between religiosity and atheism. While it is true that religiosity continuously declines as one moves down the age categories, atheism does not show a proportionate rise. "In other words, the decline of religion does not lead automatically to the rise of atheism," but to a mixture of atheism, partial belief, and indifference.

In an attempt to understand the relation of religious belief to various age cohorts, the Slovak scholars drew an interesting "profile" of two generations. The 25-39 age group, among whom the highest proportion of atheists had been found, was the generation that had emerged from World War II to participate in the

> national-democratic revolution of 1945, and the victory of the socialist revolution in 1948. . . . It is a generation of revolutionary enthusiasm, ardent building of socialism, youth activity, acceptance of Marxism-Leninism, and mass exodus from the churches. Its world is primarily a world of ideology, its interests are concentrated chiefly upon ideological values. . . . Therefore, it has adopted an active, and above all, an ideological attitude toward religion as an ideology of the bourgeois society with which it had its own social experience.[26]

The younger generation, by contrast, already born and bred under conditions of socialism,

> has had a new social experience. It was educated toward the acceptance of ideals and their further development and realization.

---

*The two columns are mistakenly reversed in the original.

It began to compare these ideals with reality. The system of values, established and passed on to it by the older generation began to appear problematical. Gradually this age group is becoming a generation of lost illusions—the disillusioned generation. Disillusionment gives birth to skepticism, to lack of faith in official ideals, to lack of faith in any ideology.

Therefore, the values of the younger generation are "concrete":[27]

Its political ideals are subordinated to the present. . . . Compared with the preceding generation, it sees the purpose of life in the satisfaction of immediate individual needs and interests, and this results, in some respects, in a consumer style of life. The younger generation has a less intense interest in the values and problems of a whole-social nature, especially in the political-ideological ones.

Finally, it was shown that religion was strongest in smaller communities, among those with only an elementary education, and among the peasantry. While those findings were expected, the low percentage of atheists among the working class was not.

(in percent)

	Atheists	Believers	Undecided
Workers (N = 732)	10.0	73.4	16.5
Employees (N = 350)	28.0	54.3	17.7
Peasants (N = 183)	3.3	91.2	5.5

The surprising attachment to the church evidenced by the workers was explained by the fact that they had only recently arrived from the countryside, that they had not been reached by the atheist movement, and by the fact that the "most progressive" among them had been recruited into Party and state administration. Among Slovaks living in Moravia, the proportion of believers was about the same as in the overall population, but the proportion of atheists was much lower. The largest group was the "undecided," constituting 57 percent of those surveyed. The conclusion was that[28]

Religiousness among the Slovaks living in the Ostrava region is vague. . . . On the other hand, it has not been replaced by any other, consistently materialistic *Weltanschauung.* . . . This situation is not changed by the fact that these people, when they return to their villages, again start participating in church rites. This is only evidence that religious belief is to a large degree, a matter of tradition, habit, public opinion, etc.

By carefully examining the distribution, depth, and nature of religious belief, and controlling for a number of important variables, the Slovak study provided a valuable insight into the nature of Slovak society, the successes and failures of Communist socialization in Slovakia, and the interaction between Slovak tradition and engineered social change.

A more delicate and more politically relevant social issue is the relationship between Czechs and Slovaks, a problem that has been an important part of Czechoslovak politics since 1918. In October 1968, approximately six weeks after the Warsaw Pact invasion, the Prague institute conducted a survey of Czech and Slovak attitudes toward history. Using mostly open questions, the survey team asked respondents to express opinions on various historical questions. When asked which epoch in their respective histories Czechs and Slovaks considered "most glorious, ascendant, progressive," Czechs most frequently mentioned the First (interwar) Republic, the Hussite period, and the age of Charles IV, with only 3 percent of the respondents mentioning the post-1948 period, but 21 percent mentioning the Prague Spring period. Among Slovaks, who had felt themselves under a Czech yoke in the interwar republic, only 17 percent mentioned it as a glorious historical period, but the most frequently mentioned periods (both by 36 percent of the respondents) were the age of Ludovit Stur, the moving spirit of the Slovak national renaissance, and the Prague Spring period. Thus, a greater proportion of Slovaks than Czechs rated the Prague Spring as a glorious historical epoch, undoubtedly because one of its features was the federalization of the republic. Interestingly, 17 percent of the Slovaks mentioned the post-1948 period as a glorious one. In general, almost 90 percent of the Slovak answers referred to contemporary or recent periods, whereas Czechs mentioned eras further back in history.[29] Both Czechs and Slovaks most frequently mentioned the Nazi occupation as "the most unfortunate" period for the nation. More Czechs (31 percent) than Slovaks (25 percent) mentioned the Soviet-led invasion in this context, and Slovaks (31 percent) more frequently mentioned the 1950s than Czechs (20 percent) in this regard.

When asked, "Whom do you consider the greatest personages in our history?", Czechs most frequently mentioned Tomas Masaryk and Jan Hus, while Slovaks mentioned Ludovit Stur and Alexander Dubcek, the latter being mentioned by only 20 percent of the Czech respondents. Eight percent of the Slovaks mentioned Klement Gottwald and four percent mentioned Gustav Husak, while the Czechs did not mention them or any other figures from the pre-1968 Communist era. Interestingly, when compared to the results of a similar survey taken in 1946, it was seen that Masaryk had held the esteem of the population, while Eduard Benes, second only to Masaryk in 1946, fell to 7 percent of the mentions among Czechs and was not mentioned by Slovaks.[30]

Czechs and Slovaks displayed markedly different literary preferences, but agreed that France and Germany had most influenced Czech and Slovak cultures, and that Yugoslavs were most similar to Czechs and Slovaks in their character and culture. Slovaks mentioned Poles after Yugoslavs, and the nations of the USSR in third place, while Czechs placed Austrians second and Poles third. When asked what tied Czechs and slovaks to each other more than anything else, both nations mentioned similarity of language and origin most frequently. Both mentioned a common state and geographical propinquity, as well as a common tradition as other important bonds between the two.[31]

Reforms in the relationship between Czechs and Slovaks were extremely important to the latter, as can be seen from a poll conducted by the Bratislava Education Institute. In a survey of 918 Slovaks, 93.6 percent expressed the opinion that the relationship between the two nations must be put on a new basis, while only 1.1 percent said this was not necessary, 2.1 percent expressed no interest in the problem, and 3.2 percent expressed no opinion. Over three-quarters of the respondents favored a federal structure, while 17.4 percent would have been satisfied with the "improvement of our present system."[32]

PUBLIC OPINION AND THE POLITICAL ISSUES OF THE PRAGUE SPRING

The most dramatic and important activity in opinion research concerned the major political issues of the day, issues that were being aired and debated with unprecedented frankness, vigor, and sincerity. The change in Party leadership that took place in January 1968 was at first greeted with only mild interest and some skepticism on the part of the population, which was not yet able to determine its significance. In a survey conducted by the Prague institute in mid-February, only half of the 1,444 respondents claimed to have read or heard about the Central Committee meetings of December and January, though, as might be expected, almost three-quarters of the 381 Party members surveyed had been aware of the meetings. Nearly half of those who had been aware of the meetings attached "great" importance to them, while over 30 percent could not say what significance the meetings had. Again, over half of those aware of the sessions believed that the results "would influence our society favorably," and only 1.2 percent thought their effect would be unfavorable, with 20 percent believing that no change would come about, and another 20 percent answering "don't know." Interestingly, Slovaks (Dubcek was the first Slovak ever to be the leading political personage of the state), those with higher education, males, and Party members evaluated the results of the Central Committee sessions more favorably than the sample as a whole. Information about the sessions and optimism about them were highly correlated.[33]

Optimism about the political changes taking place grew rapidly. By March, over 70 percent of a much smaller sample (N = 268) than had been taken in February evaluated the January plenum of the Central Committee positively. The same survey indicated that some of the most important ideas of the reformers had wide support in the population. The Prague institute asked, "Do you think that at present there is too much, too little, or enough freedom of speech?" Fifty-two percent believed there was enough, 26 percent thought there was too much, and only 18 percent thought there was too little. Yet, 70 percent rejected the notion that radio and television had been taking up matters that were not their proper concern, and over 80 percent agreed that Antonin Novotny should resign his post as president of the republic—which he soon did.[34] In July a national sample was asked to express its opinion on the abolition of censorship. The question was put as follows: "Recently the national assembly approved the abolition of censorship. Do you consider this new law to be right or not right?"[35]

(in percent)

Region	Right	Not Right	No Opinion Don't Know
Czechoslovakia (N = 1,772)	86	5	9
Czech regions (N = 1,306)	91	3	6
Slovak regions (N = 466)	74	8	18

As in the cases of Hungary and Poland, in 1956, the terror and injustices of the Stalinist period were in Czechoslovakia the most important moral issues of the day, with far-reaching implications for personnel and policy even in the late 1960s. Revelations about miscarriages of justice, torture, false accusations, and the like discredited a number of important officials still occupying high posts in 1968. Judges, lawyers, and secret police officials who had been accomplices to the acts of the 1950s suddenly found their activities of those years being publicly scrutinized and criticized. Resignations, dismissals, and even suicides followed in the aftermath of the investigations conducted by the new minister of the interior and by other organs of the reformist government.

A "Club 231," whose membership consisted of those sentenced under the infamous paragraph 231 for crimes against the state, became one of the most vocal and important new pressure groups to appear on the Czechoslovak scene. It had branches all over the country, a testimony to the scope of the terror, and pressed for the exoneration and rehabilitation of the victims of the "cult of personality." This effort was strongly supported by the population as a whole. In March 1968, a sample of 1,476 was asked to agree or disagree with the decision to rehabilitate people illegally prosecuted in the 1950s or later. Fully 91 percent agreed to the rehabilitations, 7 percent said it was better to "forget it all," and the rest expressed no opinion. Concerning those guilty of abuses during the terror, 58 percent thought they should be put on trial, 37 percent said they should be dismissed from all posts, 3 percent "asked that the past be forgotten," and 2 percent had no opinion.[36] Perhaps on no other issue was there such widespread consensus as on the need for rehabilitation of purge victims, and by implication, on the desire to avoid any repetition of the terror. This may be one of the reasons that Gustav Husak, despite the pressures exerted by antireform elements in the Party, has been able to keep his pledge that whatever the fate of reformist programs and of the reformist leadership, there will be no trials and purges such as took place in the early 1950s.

The impression one gets from all the surveys undertaken by various bodies is of overwhelming, generalized support for the policies, for the Dubcek leadership, and for the continued democratization of political life. Asked in March, "Do you believe present developments will strengthen or weaken democracy?", 76 percent of the respondents thought socialism would be strengthened, 6 percent thought it would be weakened, and 18 percent could not answer. Ninety percent thought that democracy would be strengthened.[37]

In July, respondents were asked by the Institute of Sociology at Charles University, "Do you wish us to return to capitalism?" Only 5 percent answered in the affirmative, with 89 percent saying no, and 6 percent expressing no opinion.[38] Naturally, the results of this poll were frequently cited in refutation of Soviet charges that there was a great danger of a capitalist restoration in Czechoslovakia. The Soviets also charged, perhaps with greater plausibility, that the Communist Party was abandoning its traditional commanding role and was losing control over Czechoslovak politics and society. Be that as it may, opinion polls vividly illustrated the great improvement in the Party's popularity and, hence, authority. In June-July 1968, the following question was posed: "When you evaluate the political events in our republic, can you say whether you have confidence in the Communist Party of Czechoslovakia?" While only 11 percent expressed "complete confidence," 40 percent expressed qualified confidence, 33 percent were indifferent, and only 16 percent expressed no confidence at all. The same respondents were asked "What confidence did you have in the Party before January 1968," and only 6 percent expressed complete confidence, 17 percent qualified confidence, and fully 48 percent no confidence whatsoever.[39] Granting that the latter results may have been affected by problems of recall and response set, nevertheless the one-sidedness of the results is impressive. Eighty-seven percent of the respondents in the same survey declared themselves satisfied or partly satisfied with the Dubcek regime, while only 7 percent said they were dissatisfied.[40]

Popular support for political reform naturally extended to support for the reformist politicians as well. In four surveys during 1968 and in one carried out in March 1969, respondents were asked to mention the names of political personages whom they trusted the most. The results show the consistent and great trust accorded to President Ludviic Svoboda and to Party Secretary Alexander Dubcek, though in the aftermath of the invasion, support for Dubcek declined somewhat. All the names mentioned were in one way or another connected with the reformist wing of the Party, with none of the conservatives, such as Vasil

Bilak, Alois Indra, Drahomir Kolder, or Oldrich Svestka mentioned a significant number of times. The third-ranking name was that of Josef Smrkovsky, one of the most outspokenly liberal of the reformers and a frequent target of Soviet criticism even before the invasion. Gustav Husak, favored in March by over 50 percent of the Slovak population to become chairman of the Slovak National Council,[41] never achieved national popularity either before or after the invasion, and one would assume that trust in Husak has not greatly increased since he replaced Dubcek in April 1969.

The Czechoslovak public strongly supported the unfettered activities of the mass media during most of 1968. A study in March by the Czechoslovak radio revealed that of 1,614 respondents, 97 percent considered it correct to inform the public of all important events, whether pleasant or not, and two-thirds of the respondents did not mind the fact that contradictory opinions were expressed on the radio and television.[42] A variety of surveys reinforced the notion that the population was pleased with the greater openness and general performance of the media since censorship had been abolished.[43] In early 1969 the Prague institute conducted a national survey, asking when, during recent years, the various mass media most closely reflected the respondents' views. Over 80 percent named some time after January 1968.[44]

For about seven months after the invasion, the Prague institute and some other organizations were able to continue surveying attitudes on political issues. The Prague institute was understandably unable to mount a nationwide survey immediately after the invasion and sampled the Prague population alone. Ninety-nine percent of the respondents declared that they trusted Alexander Dubcek "as the leading personality of our life." Reacting to the Soviet rationale for the invasion, the institute asked, "Do you think that before the entrance of foreign armies there was or was not a danger of counterrevolution?" Only 2 percent of the over 200 respondents responded in the affirmative, with 93 percent denying the existence of a counterrevolutionary danger. Great confidence was expressed in Dubcek, in the National Assembly headed by Smrkovsky, and in the government of Oldrich Cernik, as well as in the journalists who continued as before during and even after the invasion. Ninety-five percent expressed willingness to continue supporting the Action Program of the Party, and not a single respondent answered in the negative.[45] In mid-September, when a bit more distance had been gained from the invasion and some changes had been made in Party personnel, a national survey was conducted and the following question was posed:[46] "When you evaluate political developments in our republic, do you or do you not have trust in the new leadership of the Party headed by Alexander Dubcek?"

(in percent)

	Have Trust	Have Trust with Reservations	No Trust	Don't Know; No Opinion
Total Respondents (N = 1,873)	85	13	1	1
Czech lands (N = 1,318)	83	15	1	1
Slovakia (N = 555)	91	7	0	2

It was reported that many respondents who answered that they had reservations had such about certain individuals and that, furthermore, "the Communist Party is now under the pressure of foreign forces and is not operating under normal conditions."

The picture that emerges, then, is of a nation uniting in hope for a better political future, trusting its reformist leadership, and welcoming the democratization of Czechoslovak life through the program of "socialism with a human face." Hope and trust were dealt a severe blow by the "fraternal assistance" rendered to Czechoslovakia by her Warsaw Pact allies. In December 1968, a national survey by the Prague institute asked, "When you consider the present situation in Czechoslovakia, what is your most frequent feeling?" (open question). Coding the responses into several categories, the institute presented the following results: [47]

(in percent)

Most Frequent Feeling	Czech Lands	Slovakia	Czechoslovakia
Oppression and helplessness	20	25	22
Insecurity and lack of information	19	24	20
Disappointment and betrayal	15	9	13
Depression, anxiety, fear	10	17	12
Pessimism and skepticism	14	5	12
Trust and hope	4	7	5

In several surveys the desire for the withdrawal of foreign troops, continuation of "post-January policies," and the like were most often mentioned as the foremost wishes of the population.

These moods and desires were reflected in surveys conducted in Moravia and in Slovakia. Social scientists in Brno surveyed Moravian youth and found that more than half their respondents declared themselves generally dissatisfied with life. The political situation, the inability to travel abroad, and the limited use one could make of one's talents were cited as the primary reasons for this dissatisfaction.

> Asked about their political views and attitudes, 43.1 percent of the younger generation declared that they are not interested in politics at the moment but that they were interested in the period between January and August 1968; 33.8 percent are interested in politics in a passive way. . . . An absolute majority of the young people said that the socialist system was good but that some aspects, including some of a fundamental nature, must be changed. Of the total number of the young people among whom the poll was carried out 18.2 percent favored the capitalist system. This would be viewed as a warning.[48]

Nearly 70 percent of those interviewed did not believe that the post-January policies could be realized under the circumstances—among university students the figure was 83 percent—and nearly 60 percent expressed no confidence in the political leadership of Husak. In all, 70 percent of the youth were said to have taken a pessimistic view of the future development of Czechoslovak society. A survey of 1,200 people in Slovakia made in June 1969 showed similar moods. The loaded questions of this survey showed how the political situation had negatively affected the entire enterprise of opinion surveying. For example, the phrasing of the following question could hardly be said to be unbiased: "At the Party Central Committee session Gustav Husak emphasized the desire of the majority of our people to be able to live in a calm atmosphere, and their demand that the activities of those people who spread chaos and intensify the social disintegration should cease. Is this also your view?"[49] Despite the heavily loaded nature of the question and the likelihood that respondents were by now afraid to give the "wrong" answer, only 58.9 percent were affirmative, 20.3 percent partly affirmative, 14.6 did not know or refused to answer, and 5.5 percent answered no. Fear and hesitation are probably reflected in the responses to a question, "Are you in favor of the efforts to intensify the leading role of the Party in public life?" ("Intensifying the role of the Party" was one of the slogans of Dubcek's critics and was proclaimed a major task of the postinvasion period.) While half responded "yes," and 14 percent responded "no," fully 37 percent either refused to answer or said they did not know, a very high nonresponse rate for Czechoslovakia.[50]

Under the postinvasion conditions prevailing in the country, public opinion itself as well as opinion surveying could not possibly play the role they had during the heady days of the Prague Spring. The Soviet occupiers paid the opinion surveyors a left-handed compliment by attacking them as accomplices in the criminal attempt to reform communism in Czechoslovakia. The pamphlet *On Events in Czechoslovakia*,a Soviet whitewash of the invasion that showed that the art of historical falsification was not yet lost in the USSR, railed against "Trumped-up 'public opinion polls' which were made such broad use of by the reactionary forces . . . precisely at the time when a sizable portion of the population was misinformed no doubt due to the absence of censorship" and which "also served the goal of generating an atmosphere of instability and confusion."[51] Little wonder that the media now selectively and tendentiously reported the results of those polls that were still being conducted.[52] In December 1968, polls showed that there was widespread support for the student strike protesting the invasion and calling for further reform, and in March 1969 a poll showed that most people believed Jan Palach's self-immolation had helped the national cause.[53] But by the middle of 1969, surveys on political topics seem to have ceased altogether, and the process of "normalization" was in full swing. During the spring and summer of 1970, the Czechoslovak Sociological Society was purged, and all of its sections were closed down and then selectively reopened.[54] The Institute for Research on Public Opinion was reopened under new direction, and by September 1971 it had conducted at least four studies, none on political topics.[55]

The Czechoslovak experience with public opinion polling points out many lessons for the student of Communist political systems. The very introduction and withdrawal of opinion surveys were in themselves symbols or indicators of the larger changes that were taking place in the political style of the leadership and in the nature of the political system as a whole. The officials of the Prague Institute for Research on Public Opinion were not being boastful when they claimed that their activities were a part of the democratization process and contributed to its further development. Opinion surveys pulled aside the veil of official myths and dogmas and permitted both the Czechoslovak population and the outside world a rare glimpse into the true thinking of large numbers of citizens. It became clear to all that 20 years of Communist socialization had not extinguished some of the traditions of Czechoslovak political culture, and that the gap between state and society was indeed large until the reformist leadership took over. The results of the surveys undoubtedly gave the population a "sense of statistical community," which increased their confidence in the correctness of the path they had chosen. The leadership, too, operating in an atmosphere of great uncertainty and high risk, was clearly encouraged that for the first time in a long time political integration seemed possible of achievement in Czechoslovakia. Conversely, the dramatic, vivid, and unambiguous nature of most of the polls may have increased the disquietude of those, inside and outside of the country, who saw in "socialism with a human face" an alternative, challenging the fundamentals of the political model developed in the Soviet Union. Opinion polls allowed "spontaneity" a much larger role than the Leninists, who always place "consciousness" ahead of spontaneity, could tolerate. Thus, the polling of opinion on important and controversial political issues had many consequences, especially because of the empirical results of the polls. The surveys meant different things to different people, but all seemed to agree that they had injected a new element, new concepts, and a new spirit, into a political system that was desperately trying to save itself but was destroyed by those who claimed that by destroying it they were saving it.

NOTES

1. Cenek Adamec and Ivan Viden, "Polls Come to Czechoslovakia," *Public Opinion Quarterly* 11 (Winter 1947): 550. See more extensively Cenek Adamec, "Pocatky vyzkum verejneho mineni u nas," *Sociologicky casopis* 2, nos. 1 and 3 (1966).

2. From surveys reported in the institute's journal, *Verejne mineni*, 1946-47. For a list of topics included in the institute's surveys, see Adamec, op. cit., Part 2, p. 393.

3. See the comparison of institute survey results with those of the actual elections in Adamec, op. cit.

4. Ibid., Part 1, p. 2.

5. Ibid., Part 2, p. 398.

6. See "Studenti o sobe," *Student*, March 27, 1968, p. 11; and Galia Golan, "Youth in Czechoslovakia," *Journal of Contemporary History* 5, no. 1 (1970).

7. After delays caused mainly by political considerations, the findings of this project were published in Pavel Machonin, ed., *Ceskoslovenska spolecnost* (Prague, 1969).

8. See Adamec, op. cit. For a report on the seminar, see V. Kalivoda, "Seminar o sociologii verejneho mineni," *Sociologicky casopis* 2, no. 5 (1966): 624-26.

9. See "Z jednani stranickych organu ustredniho vyboru komunisticke strany Ceskoslovenska o sociologii v CSSR," *Sociologicky casopis* 1, no. 4 (1965).

10. Hanus Steiner, "Americky a sovetsky pohled na teorii verejneho mineni," *Sociologicky casopis* 1, no. 2 (1965): 162-65.

11. "Verejne mineni v objektach vyzkumu," *Reporter* 3, no. 14 (April 3-10, 1968): 8.

12. "Co si myslime u nas doma?," *Listy*, no. 6 (1969), p. 3.

13. "−sky/sal−," "Don't Lie, Don't Sigh," *Obrana Lidu*, February 25, 1967, Radio Free Europe Czechoslovak Press Survey (RFE-CPS), no. 1898.

14. Miroslav Galuska, "Are We Sufficiently Informed?," *Kulturni tvorba*, December 1, 1966, RFE-CPS, no. 1875.

15. M. Lakatos, "The Citizens Try to Find Their Place," *Kulturni noviny*, February 24, 1968, RFE-CPS, no. 2024.

16. "Rozhovor o verejnem mineni," *Nova mysl* 12, no. 12 (December 1968): 1511 (Interview by Jan Hysek of three members of the Institute of Public Opinion Research: Jaroslava Zapletalova, Milan Benes, and Cenek Adamec).

17. Ibid., pp. 1519-20.

18. Speech at the Plenary Session of the Central Committee of the Communist Party of Czechoslovakia, April 1, 1968, in Paul Ello, ed., *Czechoslovakia's Blueprint for "Freedom"* (Washington, D.C.: Acropolis Books, 1968), p. 35.

19. *Akcni program komunisticke strany Ceskoslovenska* (Prague, 1968), p. 23. Emphasis added.

20. See, for example, Venek Silhan, "Politics and Politicians," *Prace*, December 12, 1968, RFE-CPS, no. 2162.

21. Alexander Fazik, "O niektorych metodologickych skusenostiach jedneho konkretneho vyzkumu," *Sociologicky casopis* 3, no. 2 (1967).

22. On the army recruits, see Jaromir Dedek, "Nektera pouceni z vyzkumu postoju mezi vojaku zakladni sluzby," *Sociologicky casopis* 4, no. 6 (1968).

23. Kadlecova's study is entitled *Sociologicky vyzkum religiozity Severo/Moravskeho kraje* (Prague: Academia, 1967) and contains an English summary.

24. P. Prusak, "Some Results of a Survey on Religiousness in Slovakia," *Sociologia*, no. 1 (1970), RFE-CPS, no. 2308, p. 5.

25. Ibid., p. 7. Emphasis added.

26. Ibid., pp. 12 and 13.

27. Ibid., p. 14.

28. Ibid., pp. 18-19.

29. Ustav pro vyzkum verejneho mineni CSAV, *Vztah Cechu a Slovaku k dejinam* (Prague, 1968), pp. 7-9.

30. Ibid., pp. 15-17.

31. Ibid., p. 36.

32. CTK International Service, March 27, 1968.

33. Ustav pro vyzkum verejneho mineni, *Verejne mineni o zasedani UV-KSC v prosinci 1967 a lednu 1968*, pp. 4, 7, 11-12. See also "Verejne mineni v objektach vyzkumu," *Reporter* 3, no. 14 (April 3-10, 1968): 9.

34. UVVM, "Rychly pruzkum verejneho mineni," March 25, 1968. For somewhat different figures, see Jaroslaw Piekalkiewicz, *Public Opinion Polling in Czechoslovakia*,

1968-69 (New York: Praeger, 1972), p. 83. This is a compendium of polls conducted in 1968-69. The author cites no sources for any of the polls "in order to protect the original sources," though quite a few were reported in the press.

35. Reported in Ithiel de Sola Pool, "Public Opinion in Czechoslovakia," *Public Opinion Quarterly* 34, no. 1 (Spring 1970): 20, and in Piekalkiewicz, op. cit., p. 84.

36. Ibid., and "Jak je verejne mineni: Devet z deseti pro rehabilitaci," *Lidova Demokracie*, May 4, 1968, p. 5.

37. "Rozhovor," op. cit., p. 1521. For slightly different figures, see *Lidova Demokracie*, May 4, 1968, p. 5. See also Piekalkiewicz, op. cit., p. 27 ff.

38. Helena Klimova, "Co si myslime u nas doma?," *Listy*, no. 6 (1969). See also *Polls* 3, no. 4 (1968): 17; and Jaroslaw Piekalkiewicz, "What the Czechoslovaks Want," *East Europe* 20, no. 5 (May 1971): 4. See also Piekalkiewicz, op. cit., pp. 3-12.

39. "Rozhovor," op. cit., p. 1521, and Piekalkiewicz, op. cit., p. 143.

40. *Polls* 3, no. 4 (1968): 17.

41. CTK International Service, March 27, 1968.

42. Jiri Hudecek, "Co si mysli lide o sdelovacich prostredcich," *Reporter* 4, no. 14.

43. See the several surveys listed in ibid.

44. Ibid., p. 14. See also Piekalkiewicz, op. cit., pp. 35-42.

45. "Co si lid mysli," *Reporter* 3, no. 36 (September 18-25, 1968): 8, translation in RFE-CPS, no. 2130.

46. "Rozhovor," op. cit., p. 1521.

47. Reported by Vladimir Nepras,"Nachazi lid slyseni?," *Reporter* 4, no. 6 (February 13, 1969): 12.

48. F. Motycka, "Notes on a Public Opinion Poll," *Tribuna*, August 6, 1969, RFE-CPS, no. 2249, p. 5.

49. M. Mitosinka, "Verejna mienka ako sockologicka snimka," *Nove slovo*, August 14, 1969, p. 9, English translation in RFE-CPS, no. 2254.

50. Ibid.

51. English-language version, p. 22. For the comments of the Czechoslovak Institute of Public Opinion, see "Scientists Talk about the 'White Book,'" *Reporter*, no. 42 (November 30, 1968), RFE-CPS, no. 2132.

52. See, for example, "Jak vidi na Slovensku soucasnou politickou situaci," *Lidova Demokracie* July 31, 1969, p. 3.

53. Piekalkiewicz, op. cit., pp. 62-63.

54. *Sociologicky casopis*, no. 1 (1972): 98-102.

55. A study of consumer satisfaction is reported in "Results of a Public Opinion Poll," *Lidova Demokracie*, December 11, 1971, RFE-CPS, no. 2410; see also J. Becvar, "The Results of an Opinion Poll on the Employment and Household Duties of Women," *Odborar*, no. 12 (October 1972), RFE-CPS, no. 2462. For a poll conducted by the Czech Ministry of Education, see J. Jelinek and A. Fazik, "What Do the Young Think About War, Peace, and the Army," *Tribuna*, no. 33 (August 16, 1972), RFE-CPS, no. 2450.

4

PUBLIC OPINION
IN THE SOVIET UNION
Walter D. Connor

Systematic study of public opinion, like many other areas of social research, remains shallowly rooted in Soviet soil. Aside from several interesting studies conducted in the 1920s (in the context of a freer atmosphere for social investigation than any that has existed in the USSR since), public opinion research must be regarded as a child of the 1960s, born in a period that saw the transfer of power from Khrushchev to an impressively enduring "collective leadership," and perhaps never to emerge, in sophistication of technique and employment of data collected, from the adolescence in which it still remains. Certainly, as foregoing and succeeding chapters in this volume indicate, the enterprise of public opinion research has been of modest scale and impact in the USSR, compared to its history in some of the East European states.

Yet even the halting beginnings of empirical inquiry into public opinion, coming on the heels of the literary "thaw" of the late 1950s, which saw the publication of artistic attempts to express contemporary Soviet realities, such as Vladimir Dudintsev's *Not By Bread Alone*, could not but have drawn attention. What could have been more in contrast to the Stalinst system of manufactured consensus, undergirded by terror and threat, than an attempt, however modest, to investigate, rather than assert, the content of Soviet "public" attitudes toward different topics and issues? The very fact that polls began to be reported in 1960 quickly caught the attention of at least one student of Soviet affairs;[1] the fact that the first half of the 1960s saw a growth both in the polling trend and in the dissemination of poll results to mass audiences prompted another to observe in 1965 that the introduction of polling represented "one of the most striking departures from the climate of Stalinism."[2] It is now almost 20 years since polls emerged in the USSR—and also some time since the deemphasis of their early "mass" aspect: A sufficient period, one hopes, to permit an examination of the rationale of their development, of the information some, at least, have yielded, of their impact, and of how public opinion, thus revealed, has interacted with Soviet reality.

INFORMATION AND CONTROL: THE POST-STALIN DILEMMA

The Stalinist polity, in David Apter's terminology, was one of low information and high coercion.[3] The military and political context of the Soviet state's birth probably sufficed to guarantee a large role to terror and coercion in the Bolsheviks' attempts to maintain control, achieve stability, and move forward in realization of their designs. Stepping forward, in wartime, into the vacuum left by the collapse of Czarism, the Bolsheviks possessed little by way of normative or material resources to ensure compliance with their line—hence they mobilized the coercive resources they possessed,[4] which held the promise of at least short-run effectiveness. Force and violence accompanied the early phases of their assumption of power.

In this, of course, the Bolsheviks were little different from other revolutionary elites in their seizure-of-power phases. But the transformational goals of the Bolsheviks, as they emerged after the reconstruction period of the New Economic Policy (NEP)—the commitments to industrialization, collectivization, and a restructuring of social relations—heralded a "mobilizational" or "system-building" phase in which, once more, coercive resources were to be intensively employed. The very rapidity and intensity of the forced-draft industrialization and the collectivization of agriculture that took place under the first two five-year plans guaranteed that some emergent normative resources would be squandered, due to the immense sacrifices the population, both urban and rural, was called upon to make, and indicated that once more coercive resources would be the only ones readily available.

What emerged from Stalinist modernization was, indeed, a more modern society, but one with some special structural characteristics that distinguished it clearly from the modern societies of the West. In a general way, they might be summarized in terms of two concepts: differentiation and integration.[5] The USSR, like other modern societies, had a high degree of differentiation—that is, it was marked by structural complexity and a diversity of specialized sectors— economic, military, scientific, educational, and others—typically present only in mixed or nonspecialized forms in more traditional, primitive societies. As a complex society, it presented the problem of coordination, or integration, of these diverse sectors into a working whole.

Strategies of integration, however, show more diversity than do the challenges of complexity that call them forth. History, political culture, the level of

societal complexity reached prior to the campaign for modernization, all influence the choice of strategy (or reduce the range of choices available). Low on
normative and material resources, the Stalinist elite chose a "command," rather
than a "contractual," mode of integration.[6] The differentiated sectors of the
Soviet system, rather than developing the relative autonomy that characterized
their counterparts in Western societies, remained under the domination of the
polity—the Soviet government and Communist Party apparatus. In the politicized Soviet system, the polity and other sectors were not coordinated by an
exchange of outputs, by negotiation on a quid pro quo basis, as in those Western
systems where interest articulation is a complex process, bringing many parties
to the bargaining table, but by the fiat of the polity itself, in whose hands
critical coercive (and, gradually accumulating, material) resources were lodged.[7]

The system that had developed, then, to return to Apter's terminology,
was one of high coercion and correspondingly low information. In the system-
building phase, with ideologically determined and set goals shared among the
elite, and the masses either consenting reluctantly or opposing such goals,[8] but
in any case going unconsulted, information mattered little. The elite knew where
it was going and saw that it was good. As repository and custodian of a "scientific" understanding of historical process and social change, the elite felt it had
the need not to consult the masses but only to drive them in the proper direction. Embodying the tendency to exaggerate the degree to which ambitious
objectives had already been attained, this attitude amounted to an affirmation of
the "identification" thesis noted earlier by Gitelman, wherein a population already imbued with the scientific ideology and world view of the leadership held
a monolithic, homogeneous public opinion fully in support of that leadership
and its policies. Insofar as the leaders, in Stalin's time and for a few years thereafter, doubted the total validity of the identification thesis, they utilized the by
now familiar "open" channels (letters to the daily press, questions from the
floor at Party, trade union, and other meetings) and their closed counterparts
(the intelligence network of the secret police), as well as the ex post facto results of their own policies, insofar as these could be determined.

As an instance of ambitious national development, the USSR was, by
the mid-1950s, a success—and success itself was the creator of problems its
leadership faced. The high-coercion/low-information pattern no longer fit as the
agenda of the post-Stalin elite shifted from system building to system management. The highly developed industrial base, the relatively high level of mass
education, and the increasing institutional maturity of Soviet society in general
called for a new approach to the society's management, one that would increase
the flow of information about the moods and thoughts of the citizenry reaching
the elite. The polity had, through the years of privation, war, and postwar reconstruction, accumulated normative and material resources sufficient to permit
a shift away from the earlier primary reliance on coercive resources. By the
late 1950s, in other words, the Soviet system had attained a substantial legiti-

macy in the eyes of the masses, and thus the rulers recognized the level of political consciousness the masses had attained under their tutelage. New departures in the gathering of information were now conceivable.

The initial importance of the turn to opinion polling in 1960, whatever the fate of the enterprise later, can be appreciated best when one understands that, though the Stalinist system made use of secret informers and other channels mentioned earlier to gauge opinion and reaction, on many of the critically important policy initiatives of the whole period, the Stalinist system generated most of its information through what Apter has termed the "feedback of decision, that is, knowledge of the consequences of actions taken."[9] A prime example here is the "information" generated about peasant attitudes toward collectivization: The attitudes, negative in the extreme, became evident only in massive resistance to the process of rapid and forcible collectivization as it was being carried out. Dallin and Breslauer summarize the process:

> Charged with destroying the kulaks and simultaneously with setting up cooperatives and collectives, local cadres typically vied with each other in forcing peasants into higher-level organizations. As a result, foot-dragging and sabotage on the part of the peasants lowered the productivity of established cooperatives, thus further lowering the economic inducement for other peasants to join voluntarily. And so the cycle of stagnation and repression went on, until the regime had either to slow down the transformation or opt for more coercion. At the same time, liquidating the kulaks meant eliminating those most vigorously opposed to giving up their farms and produce— namely, the most skilled and productive farmers. This, of course, could only contribute further to general economic stagnation in the countryside.[10]

Such a mode of information-gathering is a costly one. The commitment to a fundamentally unviable policy or strategy—to one so dysfunctional in consequences that its implementation may represent a net loss in terms of objectives sought—may be made before its nature is recognized. Further, the commitment itself may be of such a nature that the path, once embarked upon, cannot be abandoned: "The regime had either to slow down the transformation or opt for more coercion," and it did the latter, because the "information" was not enough to counteract Stalin's determination to collectivize. The information was ignored, thus necessitating the use of more coercion in the pursuit of the objective.[11]

However costly such a system, many had grown used to working within its premises and were ready to shun innovation of any sort. Thus, it is interesting to note that the first, amateurish, but widely publicized poll evoked some extremely negative reactions, simply because it indicated such a shift from the practice of so many years. The basic question—"Will mankind succeed in averting war?"—was an expressive one, and it is not surprising that of the 1,000 respondents whose opinions were published in *Komsomol'skaia pravda* on May 19, 1960[12] only 21 answered "no," with 11 "indefinite." B. A. Grushin, reminiscing in a book seven years later, notes the reaction of some to the study he had conducted:[13]

> Some comrades objected to such a posing of the question: they said that it was both practically useless and, as a matter of principle, impermissible "to place in doubt a truth established by Marxist-Leninist theory and written down in the resolutions of the Twentieth Congress of the CPSU."

Though the poll may indeed have been "practically useless," such objections did not stem the tide of polls that emerged in the 1960s.

As the trend toward more polling developed in the years after 1960, another potential problem—the quality of information and the growing quantity that to some threatened overload—arose, though in a lesser sense than that which Adam Schaff had called in the Polish context a "polling mania." What, after all, are the capacities of a system like the Soviet for utilizing information? It was not admirably equipped to absorb and process information in the Stalinist period. Coercion itself tended to maximize distortion in the upward flow of information, as well as limiting the amount of such information. Apter sees dangers of "overload" and evaluational difficulties as potential problems for high-information systems:[14] one might anticipate that a system in transition from low to high information, somewhere along the way, is even more likely to encounter such problems.[15] Whether polling led in this direction or not, however, is a question to be resolved only later, in the context of what we know of the history of the opinion research enterprise as it developed later.

Thus far, we have taken a loose, systemic view—that the maturing, and increasingly complex, Soviet system needed, or could readily benefit from, better and more information on public attitudes and potential responses in the business of day-to-day administration and in the process whereby choices were made between different courses of governmental action—realizing fully that public opinion would be only one, and not necessarily a very important factor, in certain types of decision. Did those Soviet researchers and others who favored public opinion research and sought state support for its expansion take the same tack in their arguments? It is an interesting question, and the evidence of their writings (though these, understandably, are not couched in such terms as "high coercion"), indicates that the answer is positive on the whole. Soviet writers, apparently, perceived the situation in a way not very dissimilar from Western diagnoses. Writing from the perspective of the early 1960s, A. K. Uledov reminded readers that in "the period of Stalin's personality cult public opinion was often ignored and decisions on important questions of policy were adopted without the necessary attention to the objective demands of practical life."[16]

Others made the same point as Uledov and broadened the discussion at times to include more general proposals concerning the increased efficiency of governmental administration to be gained from better public intelligence. But there was another function that public opinion studies, and the use of their results, were seen as performing, one quite relevant in a system that, neither in rhetoric nor in reality, had given up its claim to lead the masses, rather than to follow their opinions. This was the business of education, or better socialization (*vospitanie*). In this connection, one should note that the years of emergence of public opinion studies—roughly, 1960-63—were years when great emphasis was laid by the Khrushchev leadership on new modes of propagandizing, new ways of enlisting the public in a broader range of social participation and experience, in the "state of the entire people" (*obshchenarodnoe gosudarstvo*). In such a context, Grushin's words take on added meaning.[17]

> The fact of a person's participation in a survey . . . the necessity that he express his opinion on important questions of social life, facilitate the person's general development as a citizen; strengthen in the person a feeling of active interest in general affairs, develop a consciousness of his own role and importance in the mechanism of social management, broaden his perspective, his ability to view things not from the "mound" of his narrow "I" but from the viewpoint of public interest, [and] finally, strengthen his understanding of the unity of views of all members of society.

Uledov sees, in the "struggle" of different opinions, a somewhat similar "educative" outcome: For him, there are clearly right and wrong opinions.[18]

> Differences in views and the struggle of opinions in our society are linked with the struggle of the new with the old, behind which stand leading people and lagging people. The peculiar quality of the struggle of opinions, expressing the confrontation of the new and the old in the life of socialist society, consists in the fact that there develops on the side of the new, the leading, a majority of the people, and public opinion is formed, as a rule, in support of it.
>
> Differences in opinion and the struggle of opinions in socialist society are also conditioned by the action of a number of other causes. Among them are causes connected with *different levels of consciousness* upon which opinion is formed. It is evident that opinion is formed both on the level of ordinary consciousness and on the level of theoretical consciousness. Far from always does ordinary consciousness make it possible to examine correctly phenomena of social life, which leads to a struggle of [these] opinions with views on the very same phenomena expressed on the level of theoretical consciousness. For example, in judging Dudintsev's novel

> *Not by Bread Alone* . . . two opinions confronted each other,
> formed on different levels. Certain segments of youth, especially
> from among the students, greeted the novel enthusiastically. The
> insufficient ideological training of this segment of youth, [its] in-
> comprehension of the principle of Party-mindedness (*partiinost'*)
> in literature, did not permit it to understand the viciousness of the
> very idea of the novel, running down the socialist structure. But
> the opinion formed from the position of Marxist-Leninist ideology
> correctly judged the novel of Dudintsev as weak in both ideological
> and artistic aspects.

Most revealing is the way in which Uledov finally translates "public opinion"
into one of the controlling elements of individual behavior, flowing from a
"public" whom he views as a large "reference group."[19]

> *Public opinion serves for the person as a criterion for the judgment
> of his acts.* The person judges his own acts in correspondence with
> the demands of the *Kollektiv*, expressed through the general opin-
> ion. The higher the demands presented to the person, the higher also
> his responsibility for his behavior and the greater the correspondence
> between his behavior and social norms. And conversely, lesser de-
> mands, a weakening on the part of opinion of moral control over the
> behavior of the person opens the possibility of a person's incorrect
> judgment of his own deeds and a falling away from a strict ob-
> servance of social norms. Arising for the person as a "measure of
> himself," public opinion plays also the role of guiding force in
> socialization.

Even with the strictures implied here on the uses to which public opinion
might be put, with a line of reasoning suggesting that control, as well as information, might be a beneficiary of a growth in research, the spirits of many who
found the prospects of participating in empirical social investigation attractive
were undampened. The lid was off, it seemed, and as Grushin wrote in a 1967
book (by which time, in fact, some of the early enthusiasm may have worn
off):[20]

> Literally every person who has once thought of conducting an
> inquiry announces that he has become a sociologist. . . . Journalists
> and managers, Party and Komsomol workers, directors of movie
> theaters and policemen—all as one are now busy with questionnaires.
> Of course, the causes of this phenomenon are complex. It is not
> only because of the fact that sociology has become fashionable. The
> main thing is that people are trying to satisfy the long hunger for
> knowledge of the concrete processes going on in society, to fill in
> the vacuum which has existed for a long time in this regard.

On what sort of food was the hunger satisfied, if at all? It is time to look at some of the major subjects of public opinion research in the USSR, from which some answers should emerge.

YOUTH: UNDER THE MAGNIFYING GLASS

Though *Komsomol'skaia pravda*, the official organ of the youth organizations, was the cradle of public opinion studies, it was not until almost a year after the birth of the paper's Public Opinion Institute that the pollsters finally turned their attention directly to youth—with a 12-item questionnaire in the January 6, 1961 *Komsomol'skaia pravda*, "What do you think of your generation?"[21]

The questionnaire itself presented an interesting combination of investigatory and celebratory elements: One question asked the respondents' opinions about the strongest (positive) characteristics of Soviet youth, while another asked if there were any negative characteristics of a widespread nature. In addition to these inquiries, youth were asked whether a presence or lack of goals characterized their generation, and whether they, personally, had goals in life, what they had done about achieving them, and their degree of confidence that the goals would be attained.

The form of the poll had both pluses and minuses. For those who sought it, it provided anonymity and allowed a reader to formulate his responses without "an interested party interposed between the respondent's innermost thoughts and his blank questionnaire"[22] —something the earlier polls had included. On the negative side, however, the poll was based on a "convenience" sample of the crudest sort. *Komsomol'skaia pravda*, though a mass medium, was scarcely the food and drink of all Soviet youth.

Most evident was an underrepresentation of collective-farm youth—even if one adds half of the number of those in military service to the total of 601 identified *kolkhozniki*, one arrives at a total of 2,645, or 15 percent of the number of respondents—small indeed given the number of Soviet youth on farms in 1961.

As might be expected, the bias was also heavily urban: 4,105 respondents lived in cities of over 500,000 persons, 11,407 in smaller cities, workers' settlements and railroad centers, and only 1,933 in villages.[23]

The results of the poll were viewed, with pride, as Soviet youth's endorsement of itself. Of the 17,446 respondents, 83.4 percent replied that they were pleased with their generation, 11.1 percent that they were not, and 5.5 percent could give no definite answer.[24] These figures, however, fail to reflect some substantial differences among subgroups. Some of these may be seen by noting the range of negative answers. Among occupational groups, displeasure was lowest among school children (6 percent) but rose to a high in what was probably the best-educated group, engineers—25 percent.[25] Displeasure increased with age, from 6.1 percent for respondents under 17, to 14.8 percent for those 23-30 years of age, and with urban quality of residence—of the 1,214 Moscow respondents, 19.2 percent were displeased with their generation, while 15.2 percent of those in other large (over 500,000) cities were—in the villages, the figure declined to 6 percent.[26]

Space considerations limit any detailed treatment of the other poll results, but it is worthwhile to consider the responses to two other items. When asked what qualities were strongest among Soviet youth, the respondents listed qualities overwhelmingly positive, in line with what seemed to be the thrust of the questions. The ten most frequently cited qualities, with the numbers citing them, follow (many respondents named more than one quality):

Patriotism, love for the socialist Motherland	5,592
Determination, steadfastness, courage, etc.	5,411
Devotion to the party, to Communist ideas	3,865
Striving for knowledge	3,548
Love of work	3,460
Collectivism	2,598
Liveliness, enthusiasm	2,103
Striving for the "new"	1,089
Love of peace	1,042
Internationalism, lack of national prejudices	535

If these open-end responses[27] represent a tendency to verbalize sentiments in much the same way as agit-prop handbooks do, they still no doubt reflect some real conviction, as well as the conventionalization of Soviet political language. The same may also be true of those who responded to the question by citing negative qualities: self-interest (330); nihilism (188); religious beliefs (152); desire to lead a life of pleasure (76); even nationalism (28).[28]

Some, however, turned a positive answer to the initial question into a deviant credo they projected onto Soviet youth as a whole (thus, perhaps, grasping the opportunity to assert an anonymous nonconformity).[29]

> The generation pleases me, because contemporary youth loves money, wine, women, freedom of speech and action. Their strongest characteristics: egoism, egocentrism, thirst for profit and power over plebeians.

To the question about negative qualities widespread among their peers, respondents gave varying and interesting answers. A list of the ten most frequently cited negative qualities, and the number citing each, follows.[30]

Drinking	4,093
Imitation of Western styles, *stiliazhnichestvo*	2,900

Crudity of ethical and esthetic feelings	2,564
Lack of culture in behavior	1,587
Passivity	1,496
Disrespect for work	883
Dependence	791
Vulgar narrowness of interests	417
Striving for material wealth	406
Disrespect for elders	355

The book-length presentation of the results, B. Grushin and V. V. Chikin's *Confession of a Generation*, devoted considerable space to discussion of the negative qualities cited. The authors seemed little surprised that nomination of drinking as the worst problem was shared by virtually all groups, independent of education or occupation.[31] The strongest response here came from rural residents—27.5 percent mentioned drinking as a widespread problem (as opposed to 19.9 percent of those from large cities).[32] The widespread nature of Soviet alcohol problems, affecting youth as well as those of middle age, is too clear for even conformist and "positive" respondents to ignore.[33]

More interesting was the author's response to the large vote for imitation of the West, for *stiliazhnichestvo*. Most groups agreed in placing it second, with unusually high scores from some unexpected sources—school children, for instance, led among groups by occupation, with 27.9 percent mentioning it, and while *kolkhozniki* scored lowest (8.9 percent—only 0.6 percent less than engineers), on a residential basis, village dwellers nominated it in the same proportions (13.4 percent) as Muscovites![34] The tendency to nominate aping Western styles declined with age (from 26.4 percent for those under 17 to 13.6 percent for those 23-30)[35] and with education (from 18.7 percent for those with less than secondary education to 9.5 percent for those with higher education).

In explaining the substantial agreement on the widespread nature of a phenomenon that was mainly connected with large cities (yet was at the "center of attention . . . of rural dwellers also"),[36] the authors rather frankly addressed two of the main sources of opinion molding and formation—Komsomol organizations and the mass media. Komsomol workers, they argued, had lacked a sense of scale (*chuvstvo mery*) in launching their campaigns against *stiliagi*.[37] Any symptom—tight pants, colorful shirts, pointed shoes—was presented as an indicator of a corrupt consciousness, which led to "taking narrow trousers for a narrow spirit." Thus, the label *stiliaga* took upon itself an expanded meaning, getting further away from its original behavioral referents (*tuneiadets, fartsovshchik*), and evoked a public response that also indicated the lack of a sense of scale.

Mass media, especially the press, had drawn great attention to the problem and also, through a lack of analysis, promoted the overreactions (sending squads of activists out to cut long hair, tear "mod" shirts off the wearers, and so on) that they were later forced to decry. As Grushin noted in a later book, the "sensationalist" approach had created an atmosphere in which the *stiliaga* appeared in everyone's mind (even those who had never seen a large city), wherein almost "every city and settlement began to 'create' their 'own' object for criticism—their own 'stiliagi,' " the final result being "a mistaken overestimation by public opinion of the actual boundaries of the 'problem of *stiliazhnichestvo*.' "[38]

Such, then, were some of the findings and results of the first youth poll. It is interesting to note that, with minor exceptions,[39] subsequent large-scale studies of youth opinion focused on more instrumental and less "expressive" topics: how youth spent its leisure time,[40] the attitudes and problems that led rural youth to abandon the villages in increasing numbers,* and other topics more closely related, it seems, to real social and economic problems.

One interesting exception, however, was a study conducted among Leningrad youth, emphasizing young workers, in 1963-64 and in 1966,[41] which, in a general way, replicated some of the inquiries of the *Komsomol'skaia pravda* poll—although with a sample of smaller size, and somewhat different characteristics.[42] While some other results of this poll will be discussed in a later section, here we will limit ourselves to the responses of Leningrad youth to the question of their pleasure or displeasure with their generation. In 1963-64, of 2,035 asked, 86.4 percent replied that they were pleased, 12.5 percent indicated displeasure, and 1.1 percent gave no answer:[43] figures rather similar to the earlier poll of 17,446 respondents. Also, as in the earlier study, frequency of negative answers tended to increase with age and education: 9.8 percent of those up to 19 responded negatively; 13.4 percent of those 19-25; and 17.8 percent of those 26-30.[44] By education levels, 10.9 percent of those with less than secondary education gave negative responses;[45] this increased to 14.6 percent for those with secondary, and 25 percent for those with higher education.[46] The "stormy 1960s," to judge from the polls, had little effect on the youth of the USSR, and the regime could comfort itself with the results.

LAW AND SOCIAL CONTROL

Access to information about popular attitudes in another area was sought through opinion-polling techniques in the later 1960s—the area of law, citizens' knowledge of, and response to it. Such studies were a natural development of the rebirth of empirical research in law—especially in the criminal law/criminology areas—which began in the later 1950s. The main focus of criminological research in the rebirth period was straightforward investigation of the social backgrounds

---

*This, of course, has been a continuing preoccupation of Soviet social science and applied research and is not limited to opinion polling as a method of data gathering.

of criminals and juvenile delinquents, studies of sentencing and disposition patterns in People's Courts and Commissions on Juvenile Affairs, and various treatments of crime-prevention programs and techniques. While the role of the public in crime prevention and in the rehabilitation of wrongdoers was often alluded to,[47] much of the discussion took place within a programmatic framework: praise for the work of the *druzhiny*, the comrades' courts, and the *kollektivs* that rehabilitated straying members released to them by the courts, and frequent criticisms of "some citizens" who showed insufficient intolerance toward criminal behavior, drunkenness, and the like. But no serious attempt was made to investigate, in an empirical way,[48] knowledge or attitudes of the public toward the law, toward their own presumptive role as enforcers thereof, or the degree to which they readily assumed the burdens of being their brothers' keepers.

An early and modest attempt at getting some notion of public knowledge of legal provisions was a poll of 218 Muscovites in 1968.[49] Of this group, none of whom had any connection with the criminal justice system, 31 persons had higher education, 31 were students in higher educational institutions, 36 were pupils in the ninth and tenth grades; the remaining 120 "other citizens" included a "substantial number of students in schools for working youth." The poll, administered by staff members of the All-Union Institute for the Study of the Causes and Elaboration of Preventive Measures of Crime (under the USSR *Prokuratura*), posed a number of "example" cases and asked respondents to interpret the law's demands. The answers showed fairly notable gaps in public legal knowledge, which increased as the subjects grew more complex. The following are some examples of responses to questions on whether one is or is not criminally liable for:

- keeping a pistol with a permit: 22 percent wrong (half of whom said "not liable")

- having a dagger at home without a permit: 79 percent did not realize that criminal liability attached to this

- killing a criminal whom he sees is about to stab a person observer does not know: 32 percent answered (incorrectly) "liable" or "don't know"

More demanding questions elicited even fewer correct responses. To a question about what constituted illegal private enterprise activity and activity of a "commercial middleman," only 4.5 percent answered correctly—56.3 percent responded "don't know." Only 0.4 percent correctly named "prohibited business activities," while 83 percent answered "don't know."

While this study focused primarily on knowledge, rather than attitudes, such was not the case with a somewhat more interesting (and revealing) study conducted among "827 male employees at plants and offices" in Saratov by anonymous questionnaire.[50] Asked whether a crime had ever been committed in their presence, 34.4 percent of the respondents responded yes—of these, 45 percent had witnessed "hooliganism" or a crime against the person, while for the remainder, the offense witnessed was directed against public or private property. Of the 285 who had witnessed a crime, 80.7 percent claimed they had tried to stop it. For these, the outcomes of their interventions had varied: 26.5 percent had received injuries, 29.5 percent had inflicted them, and 2.1 had been sued for damages—the remainder had been "rewarded" in one way or another.

What of the motivations of the nonintervening 19.7 percent? Of this group, 30.5 percent replied that they feared being held liable themselves, 21 percent cited physical handicap, and 11.5 percent admitted "indifference."[51]

Though the Saratov study did not give separate figures for nonintervention in crimes against the person and in crimes against property, the sizable place the latter occupy in Soviet criminal statistics[52] makes public attitudes toward property offenses a matter of special interest. Of the greatest interest are the attitudes toward that large number of property offenses involving stealing from the factory where one works—how do workers view the pilferage of their co-workers, a practice that accounts for a good deal of "inventory shrinkage" in Soviet plants?

An attempt to provide some answers was made by two Leningrad legal specialists connected with police schools, through an investigation of the attitudes and suggestions of 600 employees of a rubber footwear plant of the Red Triangle combine in Leningrad.[53] Red Triangle was an enterprise heavily hit by thievery; for the three years preceding the investigation (which took place, apparently in 1968 or 1969), thefts in the plant had accounted for 51.3 percent of all thefts, and petty thefts for 70.07 percent of all offenses in that category, tried in the court of the *raion* where the plant was located.[54]

The 600-person sample broke down as follows: workers, 67 percent; foremen, 11 percent; administrative personnel 7.4 percent; security personnel, 6 percent; auxiliary workers (such as chauffeurs), 4.4 percent; accountants and "materially responsible" persons, 4.2 percent. Little other information is given about the sample, and only one item in the questionnaire is dealt with: one asking respondents' opinions as to causes for the widespread theft in the plant. The responses, in order of declining frequency, are listed below. Though their direct informational value is, perhaps, limited, they afford an interesting look into the feelings of employees about the world of work they inhabit, expressed in response to an open-ended question.

- Poor security: over 50 percent
- Low level of labor discipline: about 50 percent
- Lack of punishment for thieves: 35 percent
- Drunkenness (on job, and as factor causing drinkers to steal items to obtain money for drink): about 30 percent

- Attitude that socialist property is "no one's," "up for grabs": 25 percent
- Indifference of workers to instances of theft they witness: 15 percent
- Poor accounting: 11 percent
- Retail shortages of "stylish" rubber overshoes (causing thefts for own use or for sale to others): 10 percent

These are, of course, only opinions, and the question is basically one of fact: What are the causes? In a more perfect world (in the sense of being more easily accessible, in all its complexity, to techniques that might measure and accurately assign relative weights to different factors), such opinions would be unnecessary. But in the here and now, they do reveal the world of the factory as it appears to insiders. There is a good deal of independent evidence to confirm that all the factors mentioned are very much a part of Soviet plants[55]—from drunkenness on the job to workers' winking at the thievery of their comrades—and there can be little doubt that such pilferage is, for its volume, one of the most underreported offenses against Soviet criminal law. (This is, of course, also true of many other countries.) While such a poll may tell the MVD little that is new, it does tend to confirm the thoughts of professionals in crime prevention about the factors that make theft so much a part of the Soviet factory's day-to-day operations.

POLITICS: PROPAGANDA, INTEREST, PARTICIPATION

Since public opinion is viewed by Party and state not so much as a "given," a force to which policy need be accommodated, as it is seen as a force to be molded, to be channeled in support of policies and programs (though such of course does not preclude, but indeed requires, "discovering" it), it is not surprising that polling techniques have also been utilized to gather information about popular responses to political messages as transmitted through mass media and the agit-prop system, about interest manifested in political events both domestic and foreign, and about participation in "public work"—the various voluntary activities many Soviet citizens are called upon to perform, in their capacities as Party, Komsomol, or trade union members. The results of such studies published in the late 1960s indicated a modest scope of inquiry, but the indication is deceptive. In the 1960s, and into the 1970s, many polls were not published. To the degree that the political-institutional vicissitudes of public opinion research permit its continuance today, polls touching on sensitive topics yield up their results almost exclusively "for internal use only."

Two studies conducted in the Baltic area, although reported only partially, contain some noteworthy observations. Estonian research on responses of students in the (part-time) system of political education (*politicheskoe prosveshchenie*) established that reactions (to the same mode of presentation) varied with educational level—those of low education were more "reachable" through an "emotional-obvious" approach, while those with higher education proved more responsive to a "debatable-rational" one (those of medium education seemed to require a combination of the two).[56] Such findings have clear implications for the frequently criticized uniformity and lack of inventiveness in presenting political material to audiences of varying composition.

The Agit-Prop Department of the Lithuanian Party Central Committee directed a study in April-June 1965 in three districts of that republic, focusing on the effectiveness of ideological work among the rural population. The findings of this and other studies in rural Lithuania were not such as to generate confidence that "messages" were reaching the villagers. Concentrating on the printed word, researchers found a set of factors that were turning villagers away from political reading.[57]

> How is this explained? The causes here are many. First, the insufficient network of libraries and their base. Librarians are often changed, and in their work there is not the necessary continuity. Political books are propagandized weakly and get lost amid the well-printed and nicely manufactured creative literature. Second, the consequences of the cult of personality and subjectivism have had an influence on the lowering of interest in political books. Third, our publishing houses infrequently release political books written in a language comprehensible to the most general reader. The published books, as a rule, are very bulky and overloaded with allegedly learned turns of phrase.

A study in Uzbekistan drew attention to dissatisfaction with political studies within a rather special group—Party members. Many expressed dissatisfaction with the form of study, and those with higher educations often found themselves, to their dismay, exposed to rather elementary forms of presentation in beginning political schools (*nachal'nye*) *politshkoly*.[58] Evaluations of mastery of subject material given students in the beginning political schools and in the next-step "schools of the fundamentals of Marxism-Leninism" showed unsatisfactory performance in many cases—fully 31.8 percent of one group was rated unsatisfactory in knowledge of a very fundamental topic—the biography of Lenin![59]

The troubles indicated in this underperforming system of intra-Party education was clearly connected to a longer-term problem—the degeneration of what are supposed to be deep discussions, with a certain long-range perspective, into shallow exchanges about current Party and state decrees. In April 1965, before the studies just cited were conducted,[60]

> a poll was taken of 13,000 communists in order to ascertain what they had studied in the system of political education since 1956 and what questions of Marxist-Leninist theory they would like to study further. It turned out that in the course of ten years 29 per-

cent of those questioned had not studied the history of the CPSU,
73 percent—political economy, 87 percent—philosophy. In the
system of political education, there were studied, basically [only]
current Party and state documents.

TABLE 4.1

Levels of Interest in Politics
(percent)

	Constant Interest	Intermittent Interest	No Interest	No Answer
Domestic Politics				
All	67.5	14.5	5.9	12.1
By age				
up to 19				
20-22				
23-25				
26-28				
29-30				
By sex				
male	70.0	9.6	5.9	14.5
female	61.8	18.1	5.6	14.1
By marital status				
married	71.5	11.2	4.9	12.4
unmarried	60.6	20.2	5.7	13.5
Foreign Politics				
All	65.0	13.8	3.7	17.5
By age				
up to 19	57.3			
20-22	62.1			
23-25	68.2			
26-28	69.7			
29-30	68.4			
By sex				
male	73.5	7.9	3.6	15.0
female	71.1	18.1	3.0	7.8
By marital status				
married	68.8	11.1	2.9	17.2
unmarried	59.0	13.5	3.4	24.1

Source: S. N. Ikonnikova and V. T. Lisovskii, *Molodezh: O sebe, o svoich sverstnikakh* (Leningrad: Lenizdat, 1969), pp. 57-59.

Soviet sensitivity to Western observations and predictions that youth were growing, and would continue to become, apolitical and the desire to refute these assertions of *apolitichnost'* seem to be behind an inquiry into interest in politics contained in the Leningrad youth poll referred to earlier.[61] Table 4.1 summarizes the data for the total group (N = 2,204) and subgroups therein. Response to these findings was, not unexpectedly, somewhat self-congratulatory. The small differences between sexes were taken not as an indication that women were basically less interested in politics than men but only as demonstrating women's daily overload in housework and marketing, which reduces their free time in the USSR.[62] Similarly, in response to the asserted convictions of "bourgeois sociologists" that family responsibilities limit political interest, the authors referred in rebuttal to the figures showing the reverse—asserted interest is greater among the married than among the unmarried.[63] Only two points seemed to disturb the investigators—the lower level of interest among the younger cohorts of the sample (which was viewed as demonstrating a need for differentiated forms of "political upbringing" by age),[64] and the (relatively) large combined totals of "not interested" and "no answer" on many items.[65]

When the Leningrad poll turned to actual "behavior," with the question "Do you participate in public work (*obshchestvennaia rabota*)?" the findings were not so satisfactory. This question was posed both in the 1963-64 study (N = 2,035) and in 1966. Table 4.2 presents the results in summary form.

TABLE 4.2

Question: "Do You Participate in Public Work?"

Participation in Public Work	1963-64 Amount	1963-64 Percent	1966 Amount	1966 Percent
Yes	952	(46.7)	979	(44.4)
No	365	(18.1)	876	(39.7)
Would like to but have not been asked	539	(26.4)	221	(10.1)
No answer	179	(8.8)	129	(5.8)

Source: S. N. Ikonnikova and V. T. Lisovskii, *Molodezh: O sebe, o svoich sverstnikakh* (Leningrad: Lenizdat, 1969), p. 59.

The decline in participation between the first and second study may, indeed, as the authors claim,[66] be due to a sampling problem: But they are silent on the marked increase of simple "no" answers and the concomitant large drop in answers expressing the desire to participate.

More disquieting were responses when account was taken of membership in the Party and Komsomol. As Table 4.3 shows, less than half of Komsomol members are active participants. While members of the CPSU itself may be expected to respond overwhelmingly yes (since such activity is a virtual sine qua non of rank-and-file membership), the youth organization members scarcely rise above the average for the whole 1966 sample. To some degree, this may be explained by large proportions of students in higher educational institutions among

TABLE 4.3

Party and Komsomol Participation in Public Work
(percent)

Participation in Public Work	Party Member	Komsomol Member	Unaffiliated
Yes	82.3	46.5	23.8
No	7.5	37.1	41.0
Would like to but not asked	2.1	9.7	10.2
No answer	8.1	6.7	25.0

Source: S. N. Ikonnlkova and V. T. Lisovskii, Molodezh: O sebe, o svoich sverstnikakh (Leningrad: Lenizdat, 1969), p. 61.

the Komsomol members (these, especially in final years of study, are low participators).[67] But the study's authors also see in the figures testimony to organizational and administrative problems in the Komsomol that make many youth resistant to anything beyond pro forma membership.[68] The afflictions of Soviet youth organizations, given a good deal of attention by domestic and foreign observers in the past, seem to be enduring.

The record of research into the sensitive area of the political convictions of the Soviet citizenry is, on the whole, unimpressive. Questions have not been sharply posed; inquiry has nibbled at the edges of political attitudes, rather than getting at the center. In this respect, Soviet public opinion research, at least such of it as has been published, has lagged behind, and in many cases quite far behind, the sort of inquiry attempted in some of the East European states. It may well be that, with some exceptions of potential significance, Soviet political opinion is of the "mass" variety—that a "public" or publics in the sense commonly understood does not exist in the USSR. But the nature of the research that has been made openly accessible in the Soviet Union would not allow us to make a firm judgment, and insofar as this is a question of concern to Soviet leaders, they must perforce rely on other, nonpublic information to answer it.

LABOR AND PRODUCTIVITY

A final object of public opinion research worth our notice is an area that lies at the heart of Soviet concerns—the productivity and efficiency of the economy, and ways to increase them. Here, public opinion research studies overlap substantially with more professional sociological investigations of work satisfaction, labor mobility, and other topics related to the Soviet world of work and the individual's place within it. They may in fact have been largely superseded by the latter.[69]

Still, one venture by *Komsomol'skaia pravda*'s pollsters into the area deserves attention: a 1961 study of attitudes toward, and ideas about, the "movement for Communist labor."[70] The movement, one of the characteristic phenomena of the Khruschev years (though it has continued under his successors), included at the time of the study, about 20 million persons competing singly for the title of "Shock-Worker of Communist Labor," or jointly for similar brigade titles. The criteria went beyond simple productivity, toward interworker relations, conduct in daily life, and other areas—but it was unclear exactly how all these criteria were being implemented, and indeed on what bases the many titles (by the end of 1961, about 800 to factories and enterprises, 187,000 to brigades, and over 3 million to individuals) were being awarded. Information about these questions was among the data sought by the study.

The design of the study illustrated again the peculiarities and difficulties of Soviet polling in its early years. The first questionnaire, as with some other studies, was a clip-out published in *Komsomol'skaia pravda*. The response rate was rather low—1,295 questionnaires were returned, 834 from persons not participating in the movement, and 461 from current participants.[71] For deeper and more authoritative comments on the patterns and problems of the movement, the opinions of 367 collectives that had been awarded titles were sought via a mailed questionnaire. The latter was a diverse group, including small (two persons) and huge (2,000 to 3,000 persons) collectives in different branches of the economy and geographical areas (each collective, apparently, submitted one completed questionnaire—the implications of a single set of anawers summarizing the opinion of a large collective are disturbing, to say the least).

In their report of the poll results, B. A. Grushin and V. V. Chikin highlighted some of the problems and abuses that, in the opinions of the respondents, had developed in the movement. With productivity a major concern, a tendency developed toward the conferral of titles exclusively on productivity criteria—a violation of the official spirit of the movement.[72]

The fact that frequently, in the awarding of titles, production indicators rule exclusively, was noted by 24.2 percent of the [nonparticipants], 25.3 percent of the [participants] and 27.2 percent of [those already awarded titles]. Here people spoke often about violations of the principle of complexity not by way of any "evil" intent, but due to the absence of clear criteria allowing one to subject easily to analysis those aspects of the life of the *kollektiv* (person) which lie outside the sphere of work.

Other respondents touched upon another difficulty inherent in the effective tying of performance criteria to productivity. While the "movement" was presumably for all, the nature of work outside material production (for example, accounting and other white-collar specialties), hard to quantify in terms of output, made it difficult for incumbents of such positions to compete for titles with any hope of success.[73]

The authors were understandably reluctant to minimize the importance of productivity as a mark of "Communist labor," as were the respondents, who presumably understood quite well that the main aim, at least, of the whole movement was productivity, and nothing else. Almost two-thirds of those holding titles nominated productivity as the most important characteristic, and Grushin and Chikin saw productivity's preeminent status as "the result of the dialectical union of conscious discipline and the newest technique, creativity, and interestedness (*zainteresovannost'*) in the general task."[74]

Emerging also from the responses were some revealing highlights of "simulation" and subversion of even the productivity focus of the movement, as local enterprise directors felt themselves compelled to show that they and their subordinates were not laggards. A young machinist recounted how the principle of voluntarism was violated in his own plant.[75]

> We learned almost accidentally that our shift had been included in the struggle for the title. ... They didn't ask our opinion, explained nothing, though the majority of us didn't know, and in fact we don't know now, what Communist labor is. The "struggle" for the title came down to the assembling of data: how do you fulfill the norm, do you help the police, where do you study? If you don't study, start studying—or get transferred to a lesser job. Then the factory committee . . . held a meeting right in the shop and without wasted words gave us the honorary title.

A far cry from the "formula"—a brigade's members gathering and convincing one another of the need for, and desirability of, entering the competition, and exerting both one's labor powers and rationalization techniques, as well as developing new modes of mutual aid and interpersonal relations in the shop! A Kiev construction worker provided a more generalized scenario of the birth of a (not atypical) "brigade of Communist labor."[76]

The question is posed thus: "Why, comrade construction supervisor, have you no brigade of Communist labor? And in Ivanovo they've got . . . two! You're working very badly." The construction supervisor goes to the public organizations: "Understand, something no good is happening—at the other [construction sites] they've got brigades of Communist labor, and we haven't." They propose a solution—let's go and give a title to Petrov's brigade. They decide. And there in Petrov's brigade they don't fulfill the plan, they do low-quality work, they drink vodka and curse. . . . But now the supervisor and the heads of the public organizations are praised for it—in fact we've already got five brigades of Communist labor and all the others are struggling for the title!

The *Komsomol'skaia pravda* poll was hardly systematic, and some of the questionnaire items were loosely formulated,[77] yet these results are interesting in their indication of two separate stages of modification the movement tended to undergo in practice: the first, concentrating the evaluative focus on strictly quantitative productivity indicators, to the detriment of less measurable indices such as interpersonal relations in the collective, mutual help, systematic upgrading of qualifications, and so on. In the second stage, as some of the responses indicate, productivity gives place to its simulation, and, due to the decentralized nature of the award process, awards are made in order that an enterprise should have its own outstanding brigades and not "look bad." Whether an opinion poll was necessary to inform responsible officials that such avoidances were occurring is perhaps questionable, but surely it was in the interest of many middle-level officials to restrict the upward flow of information about how so many brigades of Communist labor were born, and the poll made it more difficult for them to do so.

Other areas of public opinion research could be discussed—areas such as leisure time,[78] marriage,[79] and responses to the press by readers[80]—into which inquiries have been numerous. But considerations of space, as well as the difficulty of sustaining readers' attention through what threatens to grow into an overlong catalogue of findings (many of which, at least, are of questionable validity), suggest that we now examine the development, and assess the significance and implications, of the research enterprise described in the preceding sections.

OPINION RESEARCH: FUNCTIONS AND FULFILLMENT

On balance, the achievements of Soviet public opinion research—as measured by methodological development, institutional sponsorship, and the scope and depth of topics subjected to investigation—seem quite modest. From the first approach to the public in 1960 with the rather general (though not unimportant) question "Will mankind succeed in averting war," it is hard to find evidence of any thoroughgoing professionalization in sampling, in averting the problems linked to eliciting expected or approved (but not necessarily real) opinions, or in other areas where the flawed procedures of many of the polls reported earlier give good reason to question their validity.

This was not, however, simply a problem of professionalization and resource allocation for an infant and unfamiliar subdiscipline. True, in its first manifestation (the Public Opinion Institute of *Komsomol'skaia pravda*), the infant was, as Grushin observed, regarded as "illegitimate"[81] —probably as much for its amateurism and lack of staff and general academic status as for its halting attempts to open new areas for inquiry. But the institute lasted barely five years before it was laid to rest.

Its demise could not be interpreted as a signal that opinion research had as yet gone too far for some in the regime. As Ellen Mickiewicz observed,[82] based on some Soviet comments, the installation of Leonid Brezhnev and Alexei Kosygin apparently coincided with moves forward in general sociological investigation and in opinion research. Studies of various sorts continued and grew. Though it is going too far to consider the majority of them as public opinion studies (as one recent observer does),[83] the middle to late 1960s were scarcely a time of wholesale reversal.

In 1967, the Soviet scholar R. A. Safarov called for the establishment of a legitimate opinion research institute, under the wing of the Academy of Sciences.[84] And, in 1969, the call was answered, with Grushin (whose own intelligence and expertise were only palely reflected in the books and articles of the *Komsomol'skaia pravda* period) named as director of the Center for the Study of Public Opinion in the Academy of Sciences' Institute for Concrete Social Research.[85] We are, however, fated to know little of the output of this presumably better-supported operation for, as Gitelman noted earlier, its life was a short one. Engaged to a large extent in work classified as secret, it operated under close surveillance. Either because of its personnel's political inclinations, or because of the explosive quality of some of the data it collected, or both, if failed to survive 1971.

That opinion research of some sort survives in the USSR we need not doubt, but aside from occasional rather innocuous poll reports, and intermittent calls for greater attention to opinion research in the pursuit of more effective administration and management, it is, by and large, invisible.

Safarov, in a 1975 book,[86] makes a seemingly strong case for the importance of learning "what the public thinks" and taking it into account. But, despite a style that goes rather far by the restrictive standards of Soviet public discourse (implying that state officials who willfully disregard public opinion should face criminal responsibility, and arguing that the Soviets are, after all responsible to the electors), he limits his scope to state administration, and never

PUBLIC OPINION IN RETROSPECT

On the basis of the fate of public opinion research alone, it would be hard to argue that the USSR has moved very far from the low-information phase. But opinion polling cannot be viewed outside the broader context of the development of social research in the USSR in general—and here the picture, if not clear, suggests something different. Though public opinion studies have failed to flower, empirical social research has advanced in the years discussed here on several fronts. If the researches of economists, sociologists, criminologists, and manpower specialists have often seemed safe and noncontroversial, it should be remembered that they were not meant to be otherwise; nothing more than better information—better appreciations of social and economic reality—has been the goal of the regime in fostering a good deal of research. The regime has benefited, to some degree, from the results of such research—it could scarcely fail to do so, though a system with a different political structure might have made better use of information. (Still, it must be emphasized that, insofar as the important decisions are always political, no amount of information will point unambiguously to their rational formulation.)

In recent times, social research has evidently seen some hard times (especially manifest in the Rutkevich purge of the staff of the Academy of Sciences' institute in Moscow), but in other centers, work continues, even if failing to address the topics most of interest to Western observers of the Soviet political system. That system, in fact, probably depends on empirical social research to a greater degree in the late 1970s than ever before. It has not liberalized in any significant measure—the rise of political dissidence in the late 1960s, indeed, probably cast a good deal of suspicion on researchers in less legitimate, more exposed areas such as public opinion, and partly led to the tightening—but, to emphasize the point, there was no reason to expect political liberalization from an increased emphasis on, and tolerance of, "establishment" social research. The failure of public opinion research to reach a takeoff point in the USSR and turn into a "growth industry" is not the failure of some shakily sponsored official program of reform and renewal in borad areas of political and social life, for it never had such a programmatic underpinning. Opinion research, insofar as one can fix the causes of its fate at all, is a casualty of a decision that the USSR needs to have other kinds of information about the lives of its citizens more than it needs to know about their convictions about issues.

What seems essential here is a measured appreciation of the role public opinion can play in the Soviet political system, which in turn conditions what might have been expected of public opinion research in the past, and what we can expect of it, should support be generated for its revival in the near-term future.

In more than half a century of Soviet rule, public opinion has been little consulted by the leadership, for reasons that are rather clear. Certain policies, whether dictated by ideology or simply by deep-rooted, "arational" convictions shared by sufficient numbers of the elite, have neither been submissible to plebiscitarian approval, nor popular enough to win it had they been. Opinion here has been irrelevant; coercion has made up the distance between official commitment and mass opinion, with the results, whether collectivized agriculture or the nature of the political system itself, left to acquire the mass legitimacy that comes with time and a lack of perceived alternatives. In other areas, such as foreign policy and defense, the leadership has been able, generally without coercion, to rely on a public opinion ranging from permissive to supportive, guaranteed to some degree by control of mass communications, but genuine nonetheless.

Thus, major political questions have not been submitted to public discussion, and, for the most part, it may be argued, the public is not equipped to submit them to discussion. To the degree that, as I have argued elsewhere, the Soviet mass is apolitical, conceives of itself as impotent to initiate change (alternatively, lacks convictions of efficacy), and expects the state to provide certain goods and services in about the measure that the state has managed to provide, it is more subject than participant in political-culture terms. Untutored and inexperienced in even the inattentive and generalized consideration of political issues characteristic of Western publics, the Soviet mass might have little to say that, formulated in opinion-poll terms, could guide policy matters.

Thus, both the priorities and practice of the regime, and the qualities of the mass, limit the role public opinion can play in the USSR. Those, a small minority, who articulate personal opinion and conviction in the political realm, as soon as it falls outside the confines of the permissible range of variation, become dissidents—their harsh treatment as much a result of their attempt to participate in politics without official license as it is a result of the particular nature of those convictions.

In such a system, public opinion can influence state decisions, but mainly in areas less sensitive than politics. The sphere of consumer goods and services is a likely area and has provided the focus of some research. Yet here, research is really necessary more on specifics and details than on the big picture: the phenomena of growing inventories, of unsold, shoddy goods piling up on the shelves of unattractive and poorly managed retail outlets are sufficient, without recourse to polls, to tell planners that the masses are "voting with their feet," or with their increased recourse to savings accounts. The same, all things being equal, might be said about other areas that fall within the sphere of everyday state and economic administration: a regime responsive to public opinion in such areas, possessed of the material and organizational resources to respond, could do much to alleviate the lot of the Soviet citizen without changing in any critical ways.

Research of this sort has gone on, of course, and some still probably is occurring, if only for the internal consumption of economic planners and ministry officials. Such research need not be published or be called opinion research. That it is not is a measure of the general sensitivity such research, and even the name, acquired as the leadership apparently became concerned that opinion polls were straying too far into the realm of political convictions. Though such polls were largely secret, and though the demand for such information came from the state, some of the answers, however conformist the majority of the Soviet public, were evidently disquieting enough to limit research to politically innocuous areas, where it is likely to remain for some time to come.

NOTES

1. See, for example, Allen Kassof,"Moscow Discovers Public Opinion Polls," *Problems of Communism* 10, no. 3 (May-June 1961): 52-55.

2. Paul Hollander, "The Dilemmas of Soviet Sociology," *Problems of Communism* 14, no. 6 (November-December 1965): 43.

3. David E. Apter, *The Politics of Modernization* (Chicago: University of Chicago Press, 1965), p. 40.

4. The terms normative, material, and coercive resources are drawn from Alexander Dallin and George Breslauer, *Political Terror in Communist Systems* (Stanford: Stanford University Press, 1970), p. 2.

5. The discussion that follows is drawn in part from the present author's"Societal Complexity and Political Dissent: Five Soviet Themes," paper presented at Fifth National Convention, American Association for the Advancement of Slavic Studies, Dallas, March 15-18, 1972.

6. See T. H. Rigby, "Traditional, Market, and Organizational Societies and the USSR," *World Politics* 14, no. 4 (July 1964): 539-57.

7. This, at least, represents one of the "models" of Soviet integration. See Mark G. Field, "Soviet Society and Communist Party Controls: A Case of 'Constricted' Development," in Donald W. Treadgold, ed., *Soviet and Chinese Communism: Similarities and Differences* (Seattle: University of Washington Press, 1967), pp. 185-211.

8. See Barrington Moore, *Social Origins of Dictatorship and Democracy* (Boston: Beacon Press, 1967), p. 506.

9. Apter, op. cit., p. 239. This is not to overlook the vast network of informers and other auxiliaries to the already large secret police intelligence system during the Stalin years, but only to assert that at critical junctures, such as the forced collectivization, information was primarily of a "feedback-of-decision" variety. It was indeed the informer network itself that sometimes provided the conduit for such information.

10. Dallin and Breslauer, op. cit., pp. 72-73.

11. Ibid.

12. Translated in *Current Digest of the Soviet Press* (CDSP), June 15, 1960, pp. 24-29.

13. B. A. Grushin, *Mneniia o mire i mir mnenii* (Moscow: Izdatel'stvo politicheskoi literatury, 1967), p. 140.

14. Apter, op. cit., p. 41.

15. See Lewis S. Feuer, "Problems and Unproblems in Soviet Social Theory," *Slavic Review* 23, no. 1 (March 1964) (also cited by Apter, op. cit., p. 239); and Zygmunt Baumann, "Eastern European and Soviet Social Science: A Case Study in Stimulus Diffusion," paper presented at the Conference on the Influence of Eastern Europe and the Western

Territories of the USSR on Soviet Society, University of Michigan, Ann Arbor, May 14-16, 1970.

16. A. K. Uledov, *Obshchestvennoe mnenie sovetskogo obshchestva* (Moscow: Izdatel'stvo sotsial'no-ekonomicheskoi literatury, 1963), p. 323.

17. Grushin, op. cit., p. 315.

18. Uledov, op. cit., pp. 159-60.

19. Ibid., pp. 353-54.

20. Grushin, op. cit., p. 345.

21. The results were published first in *Komsomol'skaia pravda*, July 21, 1961, pp. 1-4, and July 22, 1961, pp. 3-4, translated, respectively, in *CDSP*, September 20, 1961, pp. 3-8, and September 27, 1961, pp. 11-15. The fullest report of the results (and the source we shall refer to here) is the book-length study, B. A. Grushin and V. V. Chikin, *Ispoved' pokoleniia* (Moscow: Molodaia gvardiia, 1962).

22. Kassof, op. cit., p. 52.

23. Grushin and Chikin, op. cit., p. 22.

24. Ibid., p. 38.

25. Ibid., p. 39.

26. Ibid., p. 40.

27. For these "positive" qualities, see ibid., p. 64.

28. See note 21.

29. Grushin and Chikin, op. cit., p. 204.

30. Ibid., p. 154.

31. Ibid., pp. 154 ff., 244.

32. Ibid., p. 244.

33. On alcohol problems, see the present author's "Alcohol and Soviet Society," *Slavic Review* 30, no. 3 (September 1971): 570-88; and, for greater detail, *Deviance in Soviet Society: Crime, Delinquency, and Alcoholism* (New York: Columbia University Press, 1972), pp. 35-79.

34. Grushin and Chikin, op. cit., p. 245.

35. Table 10, p. 245 of ibid., which lists the 13.6 percent against an age category of 30 to 43 years (!) is in error.

36. Grushin, op. cit., p. 241.

37. See Grushin and Chikin, op. cit., pp. 201-2.

38. Grushin, op. cit., p. 243.

39. Such was the poll addressed to youth on what items they would place in a rocket being sent to Mars, to reflect the times. *Komsomol'skaia pravda*, October 20, 1963, pp. 1-3; October 22, 1963, pp. 2-4; October 23, 1963, pp. 2-3; and October 24, 1963, pp. 3-4, translated in *CDSP*, December 4, 1963.

40. *Komsomol'skaia pravda*, December 27, 1963, pp. 2-3, translated in CDSP March 11, 1964, pp. 39-30. See also *Komsomol'skaia pravda*, June 16, 1965, pp. 2-3, translated in CDSP, August 25, 1965, pp. 13-15.

41. S. N. Ikonnikova, V. T. Lisovskii, *Molodezh: o sebe, o svoikh sverstnikakh* (Leningrad: Lenizdat, 1969).

42. Ikonnikova and Lisovskii's sample was designed to make it, apparently, more representative of the Leningrad population in its composition than that of the USSR as a whole, and aimed mainly at securing the views of working youth. The composition of the sample is described in detail in ibid., pp. 12-19.

43. Ibid., p. 36.

44. Ibid., p. 38.

45. This figure is based on a combination of two categories—"primary through 5-6 years" and "7-9 years"—due to the very small N of the former category, though Ikonnikova and Lisovskii report them separately (ibid., p. 17, table 1).

46 Ibid., p. 39.

47. See Connor, *Deviance in Soviet Society*, op. cit., pp. 194-98.

48. See, for example, the exchange of views between two jurists in *Izvestiia* (April 17, and June 30, 1966), translated in *Soviet Review* 8, no. 1 (Spring 1967).

49. *Izvestiia*, October 24, 1968, p. 5, translated in CDSP, November 13, 1968, pp. 24-25.

50. V. Kozak, "Chto znaiut grazhdane o neobkhodimoi oborone," *Sovetskaia iustitsiia*, no. 18 (1968), pp. 12-13, summarized in *Current Abstracts of the Soviet Press*, November, 1968, p. 4.

51. See ibid., p. 13.

52. See Connor, *Deviance in Soviet Society*, op. cit., pp. 149-50.

53. L. A. Andreeva and G. A. Levitskii, "Obstoiatel'stva, sposobstvuiushchie khishcheniiam (Opyt vyiavleniia obshchestvennogo mneniia)," *Sovetskoe gosudarstvo i pravo*, no. 11 (1969), pp. 104-6.

54. The notion of the public opinion of a smaller "universe," such as the factory, is discussed in Grushin, pp. 197-98.

55. See Andreeva and Levitskii, op. cit.; and also Connor, *Deviance in Soviet Society*, op. cit., pp. 48-49 and 102-6.

56. L. N. Lentsman, "Konkretnye sotsiologicheskie issledovaniia partiino-ideologicheskoi raboty v Estonskoi SSR," in *Problemy nauchnogo kommunizma*, vol. 2 (Moscow: Mysl', 1968), p. 73, citing a study by M. I. Fedorova, "Sistema politicheskogo prosveshcheniia na zavode (opyt knokretnogo sotsiologicheskogo issledovaniia)," in ibid., pp. 209-23.

57. A. S. Barkauskas, "Rukovodit'–znachit gluboko izuchat' zhizn'," in *Problemy nauchnogo kommunizma*, op. cit., p. 89.

58. V. T. Syzrantsev, "O konkretnykh sotsiologicheskikh issledovaniiakh v partiino-ideologicheskoi rabote," in *Problemy nauchnogo kommunizma*, op. cit., pp. 116-17.

59. Ibid., pp. 118-19.

60. Ibid., p. 115.

61. See Ikonnikova and Lisovskii, op. cit., pp. 55-56, for the authors' "ideological" introduction to the data on apoliticality.

62. Ibid., p. 58.

63. Ibid., p. 59.

64. Ibid., p. 57.

65. Ibid.

66. Ibid., pp. 59-60.

67. See ibid., pp. 64-65.

68. See ibid., pp. 61-63.

69. See, for example, A. G. Zdravomyslov, V. P. Rozhin, and V. A. Iadov, eds., *Man and His Work*, trans. and ed. by Stephen P. Dunn (White Plains, N.Y.: International Arts and Sciences Press, 1970); originally published as *Chelovek i ego rabota* (Moscow: Mysl', 1967).

70. The study is reported in B. A. Grushin and V. V. Chikin, "Problemy dvizheniia za kommunisticheskii trud v SSSR," *Istoriia SSSR*, no. 5 (1962), pp. 17-44.

71. Ibid., p. 19.

72. Ibid., p. 20.

73. Ibid., p. 21.

74. Ibid., p. 25.

75. Ibid., p. 38.

76. Ibid., pp. 36-37.

77. The questionnaire items are reprinted in ibid., pp. 18-19.

78. See note 40, and also B. A. Grushin, *Svobodnoe vremia: aktual'nye problemy* (Moscow: Mysl', 1967).

79. See B. A. Grushin, " 'Slushaetsia delo o razvode . . .': o tak nazyvaemykh 'leg-komyslennykh brakakh'," *Molodaia gvardiia*, June 1964, pp. 164-91, and July 1964, pp. 255-82.

80. For a review of research on newspaper readers' attitudes, see Ellen Mickiewicz, "Policy Applications of Public Opinion Research in the Soviet Union," *Public Opinion Quarterly* 36 (Winter 1972-73): 566-78.

81. Grushin, *Mneniia*, op. cit., p. 12.

82. Mickiewicz, op. cit., p. 566.

83. See the compilation by Sergei Voronitsyn, "A Compendium of Public Opinion Polls Conducted in the USSR From 1960 to 1975," *Radio Liberty Research Supplement*, May 2, 1975.

84. R. A. Safarov, "Vyiavlenie obshchestvennogo mneniia v gosudarstvenno-pravovoi praktike," *Sovetskoe gosudarstvo i pravo*, no. 10 (1967), pp. 49-53.

85. See the brief announcement by Grushin in Andras Sekfiu, ed., *Obshchestvennoe mnenie i massovaia kommunikatsiia—Rabochee soveshchanie v Budapesht 1971* (Budapest: Hungarian Radio and Television, Scientific Center for Research on Mass Communications, 1972), pp. 205-6.

86. R. A. Safarov, *Obshchestvennoe mnenie i gosudarstvennoe upravlenie* (Moscow: Iuridicheskaia literatura, 1975).

5

PUBLIC OPINION
IN HUNGARY
Robert Blumstock

An account of Hungarian history during this century would show a long series of political misadventures and economic cataclysms aggravated by a disingenuous racism and a class structure second to none in its energetic repression of the basic elements of social justice. The chronology of regimes begins with the remnants of an autocratic feudalism under a decaying, moribund empire; a short-lived republic led by a reformist nobleman who was given the task of extricating the nation from a disastrous war; a revolutionary Councils Republic, engineered by an ill-prepared vanguard that could neither understand nor obtain the support of the peasantry; a counterrevolutionary despotism under the guidance of an admiral of a nonexistent navy acting as regent for a king whose return was neither desired nor sought; a Stalinist regime that attempted to impose a fundamentalist catechism of modernity modeled on the Soviet Union; a short-lived revolutionary outbreak directed against this counterfeit tyranny, which, although a failure, did set the stage for what is currently regarded as the most politically generous and economically adventurous system in Eastern Europe.

The consequent development of sociology, and social research in general, in this environment exhibits a spasmodic and convulsive character in which creative amateurs, lacking formal training in sociology, alternate between feverish activity and hopefulness and passive and enforced quiescence. These vacillations of mood and direction are inextricably linked with the political definition and acceptance or rejection of the nature and consequences of research on the social order. Out of this flux, prior to World War II, three relatively distinct social research paths were initiated:[1] (1) an urban radical tradition drawing inspiration from both Marxism and German political and ideological currents;

132

(2) a rural-populist tradition whose major emphasis centered on the problems of the peasantry; and (3) the beginnings of the study of social issues and problems related to urbanization and industrialization.

While all three styles coexisted to some extent, the radical group was largely dissipated as a consequence of the involvement of several of their number in the unsuccessful Councils Republic in 1919. Exile was, for many, a preferred alternative to the anticipated punishments of the counterrevolutionary tribunals. The populists were the most vital center of social concern during the interwar years when the depression wreaked havoc with agricultural prices and the plight of the peasantry, under these circumstances, deteriorated. The third active cohort consisted of a group of intellectuals who did not share a uniform perspective, ideological or procedural, but who laid the groundwork for a rigorous empirical examination of social processes.

The initiation of discussion on social issues at the turn of the twentieth century was dominated by a radical and largely, although not exclusively, Jewish middle-class intellectual coterie, who were involved in the discovery of both their own marginality and the contradictions of a semifeudal industrializing nation. Out of this ferment an organization, the Social-Scientific Society, and a journal, *Huszadik Szazad* (The Twentieth Century), were founded. Hungary at this juncture exhibited few of the characteristics of industrial and urban development that had already exerted its influence on Western Europe. With a politically disenfranchised peasantry, a small and poorly organized proletariat, and a gentry intent on maintaining its political dominance, only this small interstitial urban collectivity was available to pose questions concerning the nature and organization of the society in which it lived. The members of this group were by no means dispassionate analysts, and, when the opportunity to create a better society on the ruins of the old order presented itself in 1919 with the establishment of the Councils Republic, a goodly number were recruited from this alienated, yet optimistic, cadre. The active involvement of these "social scientists" in this revolutionary regime did not augur well for the future development of the nascent science of society. The autocratic, legitimist regime that followed the demise of the republic defined sociology as a potential threat to its stability and proscribed the future possibility of its development.* In effect, further opportunity for critical discussions on the nature of the social order were foreclosed from this quarter, and such men as Karl Mannheim, Oscar Jaszi, and Gyorgy Lukacs, among others, went on to develop their interests and careers away from the limitations imposed by Hungarian reaction, in Europe and the United States.

---

* A Chair of Social Philosophy was established in 1940 with Istvan Dekany as the first and only incumbent. Courses in social philosophy were offered during the interwar period, with the main emphasis being on legal and juridical studies. In 1920 the Hungarian So-

With the decline of this perspective on social issues, a group of writers arose, known variously as "village researchers" or "populists," who began to focus attention on the problems of the peasantry. Those who were directly involved in the awakening of this concern were not drawn from the marginal urban sectors of the country but were in most cases of peasant or rural origins. The resulting work was largely literary and descriptive. The major emphasis was the imprinting of a deeply personal style of analysis and criticism of the human costs involved in the destruction of a traditional life style. The work of this group is usually subsumed under the term "sociography" to distinguish it stylistically from more procedurally rigorous analyses.[4] Yet, whatever weaknesses it may have had, it remained a major avenue for the exposure of life among a depressed and abandoned population.

The third development in the growth of social research during the period under review involved a continuation of the earlier urban radical tradition combined with a more rigorous and analytic approach to the data of the Hungarian experience. In a recently published autobiographical account, Gyula Rezler, one of the leading figures behind much of the investigative effort that took place during the years 1933-43, reviews both the literature published and the difficulties involved in attempting research at this time.[5] His own interest in research began while he was still a university student. Against the advice of his academic advisers, who thought the topic too politically sensitive, he began to gather material for his first published work, *The Development of a Working Class in Large-Scale Industry in Hungary, 1848-1914.*[6] He quickly discovered that there was a dearth of material available on this topic and that whatever did exist, such as journals published by labor organizations as well as secret police reports on their activities, was located in the basements and storerooms of libraries. After completing this work, which was subsequently brought out by a sympathetic

---

ciological Society was formed and the review *Tarsadalomtudomany* (Social Science Review) was founded replacing *Huszadik Szaszad*, which ceased publication in 1918. Another journal, *Szazadunk* (Our Century) was founded in 1926, which published articles focusing on social criticism.[2]

The first Chair of Sociology was established after the war in 1946. The first and only incumbent of this Chair, Alexander Szalai, was one of the central figures in the organization of the Hungarian Institute of Public Opinion. Szalai only held the Chair for one year, and then it was absorbed into a university institute. This move restrained the possibility of the development of a training center for sociologists and was one of the indications of the resurgence of the political suspicion that surrounded sociology prior to the dissolution of the coalition government and the coming to power of Matyas Rakosi. A Chair of Sociology has now once again been established, at Eotvos Lorand University, but the delay in providing training facilities for sociologists has been general in Eastern Europe, with the possible exception of Poland. One reason offered for this is that the research function of sociologists could be more easily controlled and directed than teaching, which could develop a more autonomous oppositional stance.[3]

publisher, Rezler obtained a position with the Hungarian Price Commission, which allowed him access to company records and other data on the general working conditions prevalent in industry. Without this official position within the state bureaucracy, he would have been unable to collect essential data.[7] One of the real fruits of his perseverance was that he was able to recruit a small group who together collected data on labor conditions in the major industrial enterprises. Subsequent to this, the group of researchers recruited for this work became, under Rezler's direction, the core of the Hungarian Institute for Labor Studies, which was founded in the summer of 1943. The conditions in Hungary at that time, with the Russian Army approaching the frontier and the Germans preparing for the occupation of the nation, were hardly propitious for a full-scale development of research, and the work of the institute terminated in 1944.

After the war, Rezler, following a by-now traditional Hungarian pattern of those involved in social inquiry, left the country to begin a new career in North America. The continuation of his work was delayed nearly two decades until political considerations allowed for the establishment of the Sociology Research Group in 1963 under Andras Hegedus, who had been prime minister during the last days of the Rakosi regime.

This short summary of a half-century's development hardly does justice to all the personalities, issues, and problems that characterize the activities of these pioneering efforts in social inquiry and research.[8] Yet in light of the disparate character of the groups involved, there are at least two common themes that appear throughout this developmental period. First, since a paucity of information existed on the actual workings of Hungarian society, one of the underlying motives behind the initiation of much of the work done was to discover and announce the nature and extent of injustice. Second, and complementarily, although there was never any general agreement on either ideology or research procedures, there existed an overriding commitment to the transformation of the system into one that controlled and eliminated problems in inequity.

The programs of action that arose from these groups were displayed and reiterated in a vacuum, as these critics functioned without the power or influence to effect change.[9] Had history followed a different course, there is no saying what might have been, but this kind of questioning of the foibles of the past is a fruitless and unrewarding task. What we can see is that recent developments, as we shall discuss later, have markedly changed the definition, nature, and position of the social sciences in Hungary. No longer is social research viewed as a potentially subversive element undermining the political legitimacy of the state. Rather the major political and economic emphases now center on the cooptation of social scientists into advisory and consultative capacities, in which their work is defined as a resource in the effort to control, manage, and direct the issues that arise in a modernizing state, for the achievement of the predetermined goals set by the Communist Party.

EARLY PUBLIC OPINION STUDIES

Given the diffuse nature of the progress of social research in Hungary, it is difficult to locate a fixed historical point from which public opinion studies commence. Several starting points are possible—for example, as early as 1912, Robert Braun,[10] with the encouragement of W. I. Thomas, initiated a study of the inhabitants of a village in southeastern Hungary, the purpose of which was to analyze the life-style and attitudes of Hungarian peasants. The work of the sociographers may also be seen as a beginning of the quest for discovering opinions, attitudes, and values of selected samples of the population. The introduction of Western sociological writings by the Social-Scientific Society and the formation of the Galileo circle by university students in 1909, may also be seen as precursors of social analysis. In addition, Rezler's work provides a bench mark in the development of a concern for the interaction between the conditions of, and responses to, the industrial work situation. Yet another source coincident with the introduction of the radio is the radio listener surveys that began in 1927, with additional surveys conducted on popular and classical music tastes in 1933-34 and 1941. Additional consumer research was begun in the years just prior to World War II, with studies done on wine tastes and consumption, smoking habits, and fruit-eating patterns.[11]

The war years did not enhance the prospects for the development of free inquiry, although at several points attempts were made to gauge opinions on a variety of topics, ranging from ethical and legal matters to the popularity of political figures and newspapers.[12] Approximately one year before the end of the war in March 1944, Professor Paul H. Schiller, of the Department of Psychology of Pazmany University (now Eotvos Lorand University) in Budapest, organized a small research team of staff and students and posed some questions to the population of the city about their sentiments toward continuing the war.[13] Almost at the same time as the interviewers were directing questions, the German occupation of the country took place.

A quarter-century had passed since Nicholas Horthy, as regent, triumphantly entered the city. The policies followed by the various governments that led the nation during this era were motivated by a virulent irredentism for the territories lost after World War I, and by a noxious anti-Semitism, which placed the blame for the predicament of the country at the doorstep of the handiest, and most visibly identifiable, enemy, the Jew.[14] As a consequence of German support, some territory was regained from Czechoslovakia, Romania, and Yugoslavia. The price demanded from Hungary by Germany for these concessions to its territorial ambitions was an even closer submission to Germany's resolve to eliminate the Jews from Europe. The full horror of the German plans altogether exceeded the more limited and opportunistic Hungarian design to regain ancestral lands and control and degrade but not eliminate its Jews. Hungary's Jewish population suffered innumerable indignities, yet there were no mass deportations, as had occurred in the rest of Europe, until the German occupation.[15] Hungary's limited ability to maintain autonomy in internal policy was thus at an end, as was the relative safety of its Jewish population.

While these subsequent events were not unknown at the time of Schiller's survey, there must have been some foreboding about the future on the part of those questioned. Unfortunately, no details are available on how the study was conducted, the number interviewed, or the sampling procedures followed. Despite these obvious shortcomings, both the questions and responses indicate the temper of the population at this crucial historical juncture.[16]

Do you think it would be advantageous for Hungary to follow Finland's lead in seeking a separate peace?

Yes	82%
No	11
Don't know/no answer	7

Do you think it would be advantageous or disadvantageous to Hungary's interest to seek a separate peace?

Advantageous	79%
Disadvantageous	16
Don't know/no answer	5

Another question directed to the population by Professor Schiller suggests that many in the capital maintained their optimism about the possibility of Budapest's escaping destruction. Just three weeks prior to the first bombing of the city, the question was asked: "Do you think Budapest will be bombed?" Fifty-three percent replied no, while 24 percent said yes, with 23 percent undecided.[17]

While the questions and the direction of the responses are intriguing, these data remain solely as an artifact of the last attempt, prior to the end of the war, to gauge opinions on issues of public concern. Almost immediately after the war, in August 1945, the Hungarian Institute of Public Opinion was founded by the Hungarian Press Agency. Professor Schiller was named director of this, the first institute of public opinion in Central Europe. Modeled upon the American Institute of Public Opinion, it operated autonomously without subvention by the state, its sole source of financial support coming from subscriptions and fees charged to clients.[18] The range of investigations undertaken reached broadly into a variety of areas, and of the 140 known studies completed during the nearly four years of its existence, the 120 studies still available may be grouped into the following categories.[19]

Economic and national politics	62
Foreign politics	10
Cultural, social, and miscellaneous	36
Reports on surveys completed elsewhere	12

The measurement of public opinion in Hungary was on a far firmer footing than ever before in that there now existed a recognized group devoting its energies to investigating a broad range of issues with relatively large population samples. Initially, the staff of the institute numbered eight, but even at the best of times the total number of people employed was only about 20.[20] The collecting, coding, and reproducing of material was performed with the aid of part-time help. The interviewing staff, almost all of whom were students, totaled approximately 30 in Budapest, with an additional five to six in each of the larger centers outside the capital. For each national survey, there were 2,000 respondents drawn from Budapest with another 5,000 to 8,000 selected from the other centers. The active engagement of the staff in its work is attested to by the fact that during the first 18 months of its existence approximately 150,000 people were interviewed and they provided over 1 million responses that were then organized and coded.[21]

Methodological sophistication was not one of the strong points of the studies undertaken, and with few exceptions the cross-tabulations rarely mention the social sources of the population interviewed. Improvisation was clearly the order of the day in drawing samples. Several reasons for this procedural drawback are given in the August 1947 report of the institute. The first major difficulty in delimiting population parameters was a result of the shifts that had taken place in the nation's boundaries as a consequence of the war. The last censuses were taken in 1938 and 1941, and, at both of these times, the nation's borders were markedly different from what they were to become after the war. Second, significant population changes and shifts had taken place. In addition to the military losses suffered, the Jewish population, numbering close to 800,000 before the war, was decimated and reduced to approximately 200,000. Third, the problem of representativeness was further compounded by changes in the nature, organization, and composition of the labor force. New occupations were continually appearing for which categorization was difficult, while many prewar occupations had disappeared. The organizational problem of discovering and codifying a new slate of occupations was a near Herculean but necessary task if sample selection was to be in any way representative of the new social structure. Just as this problem was nearing solution in the late summer of 1948, the institute began to be subject to political pressures, with many of the staff either jailed or forced to seek exile. While the political turmoil of this period in Hungary is not our direct concern, the demise of the institute coincides with the consolidation of power that took place under the aegis of the Communist Party, under the leadership of Matyas Rakosi. The atmosphere generated during the next several years was not conducive to unrestrained inquiry into attitudes and opinions. The whole tone of this period was one in which the questioning of policy was not tolerated and the institute as well as other sources of potential or real criticism were once again silenced.

The war had wrought considerable physical destruction to the country.[22] Industrial capacity was 46 percent less than it had been at the beginning of the war, agricultural livestock was reduced to 30-40 percent of its prewar level; 85 percent of vehicular rolling stock (railroad cars) was destroyed; 83 percent of the nation's bridges were gone; 75 percent of the housing in Budapest was damaged. In addition to the decimation of the Jewish population, military losses combined with the emigration of thousands reduced the population 4-5 percent below its prewar level. The country had reached a point from which any change was an improvement over the present circumstances.

It was during this initial period of reconstruction that the institute began and ended its work, and a review of some of the completed studies may give insight into the nature of the problems and issues in the immediate postwar period.

SOME RESULTS

One early and significant result of the institute's work was the accurate prediction of the results of the first postwar election held in November 1945.[23]

Party	Public Opinion Institute Projection	Actual Result
	(percent)	
Social Democrats	17.6	18.0
Communist	19.9	17.5
Small Holders	53.2	56.0
Peasant Party	7.2	7.0
Democrats	2.1	1.5

Given the less-than-perfect circumstances under which the polls were conducted, the above results indicate that the work of the institute was fair and unbiased. This was the first election in six years, and the nature of the political changes that took place is manifested if these results are compared to the previous election held in May 1939. At that time the votes cast were shared by the political parties as follows:[24]

MEP (Party of Hungarian Life) (the government party)	50%
Christian Party	3
National Socialists	25

Liberals	2
Small Holders Party	15
Social Democratic Party	4

The Small Holders Party was in direct competition with the Arrow Cross Party (the National Socialist Party), "in the constituencies where the Arrow-Cross had as a rule not set up candidates, the Small Holders remained the strongest oppositionist party . . . , but where the Arrow-Cross were competing with the Small Holders Party, the former scored second behind the government party."[25] It is difficult to contrast the figures and to show from them the social sources on which the parties drew. One interpretation, current after results were known, was that the leftists moved en masse to the extreme right. A contrasting interpretation given at the same time was that the vast majority of supporters for the fascist parties were drawn from the middle classes, from those with German origins, as well as from the working-class sectors of society.[26] In the 1945 election, the Small Holders Party may have offered a haven for these sectors along with the vast majority of peasants. A significant proportion, however, of the middle and working classes aligned with the left-wing parties, the Social Democrats, and the Communists. These parties formed, along with the Small Holders, the backbone of the coalition government.

On three occasions in 1946, the institute surveyed the mood of the population with the question, "Will the coalition government continue?" The responses were as follows:

	March	September	December
Yes	64%	48%	33%
No	34	50	52
Unsure	2	2	15

Future events proved that the apparent uncertainty of the population in the coalition government's viability was well founded. This, however, is not to say that major changes in the economic structure found no support in the population. In an early study completed in December 1945, opinions were asked about the policy of nationalizing factories and banks, and the following table shows that the dominant opinion favored such action.

	Factories	Banks
Support nationalization	67%	75%
Oppose nationalization	32	23
Don't know/no answer	1	1

Further, in March 1947, of those questioned 54 percent were of the view that Hungary was clearly moving in the direction of socialist development, while 45 percent disagreed. From these sparse data, it seems fair to conclude that the events occurring in the two intervening years between these studies may have cooled some of the ardor for a total reorganization of the nation's economy but that socialism was perceived for most as the only clear alternative for the future.

As a check on the population's perception of progress in the rebuilding and reorganization of essential services in 1946 and for two subsequent years, a sample of the residents of Budapest were asked to evaluate changes in the standard of living during the year. The scale used defined January 1945 as 0, while the ideal state was 100. Table 5.1 shows the average scores for a variety of items.

TABLE 5.1

Budapest Residents on Rebuilding of Hungary
(year 1945 is 0; ideal state is 100)

		1946	1947	1948
1.	Changes in one's own level of living	19	39	42
2.	The rebuilding of the country and the increase in productivity (from the perspective of the increase in productivity)	24	46	55
3.	... from the perspective of socialist development	27	40	47
4.	... from the perspective of the economic situation	22	46	57
5.	... from the perspective of the development of cultural life	23	47	57
6.	... from the perspective of obtaining food	20	49	56
7.	... from the perspective of obtaining clothing	10	25	30
8.	... from every standpoint	21	46	48

Source: Compiled by the author from mimeographed data consulted at Parliamentary Library, Budapest, Hungary, 1972.

The perception of improvement was general, with somewhat more progress visible in the economic and cultural areas. The alleviation of food shortages proceeded somewhat more quickly than the solution to clothing insufficiencies. Part of the explanation for this lies in the policy of land distribution effected almost immediately after the war, which was an inducement to the peasantry to begin production. The making of clothing and other durable goods was dependent on the capacities of plants to acquire raw material and facilities and was hampered by the physical destruction of the means of production and the rampant inflation that followed the end of the war, which made the procurement of appropriate machinery difficult.

These surveys did not continue after 1948, and, if these averages are any guide in evaluating changes, it appears that the perception of "progress" was slowing down at about the same time as coercion in the political structure was increasing.

The institute's scope was wide, and among other topics investigated were opinions on the use of the radio as a medium for political broadcasts, awareness of and attitudes toward the United Nations, the disposition to the idea of a Danubian confederation, educational reform, and tastes in books and music. One study with current implications concerned the attitudes of men to their wives accepting employment. This study was a replication of one completed in the United States. The most relevant comparison drawn indicates that more Hungarian males than American approved of their wives working. In addition, three-quarters of the Hungarians as opposed to two-thirds of the Americans thought it appropriate that women employed at the same job as men should obtain equal wages. Attitudes are one thing, and realities are another, and the issue of disparity in wages and opportunities for women has by no means been solved in Hungary: One of the issues brought forth to the summer session of the 1972 Parliament had to do with the apparent divergence in wages between men and women performing the same jobs.

Another interesting study dealt with the emigration desires of the remnant of the Jewish population. The unsurprising result of this survey is that one-half of the then discernible and resident Jewish population in Budapest were interested in leaving, with the countries of first choice being the United States and what was then Palestine. These sentiments are readily understandable, given the recent history of European Jews. What is not clear is the reasoning of the remaining 50 percent of this Jewish sample who had no firm intention or plans for leaving Hungary.* One possible explanation available, aside from the obvious one of questioning the reliability of the survey, is that the end of fascism gave hope that a truly new era for Jews had begun. There were strong indications in several areas[28] that the resurrection of Jewish spiritual life and communal institutions was progressing rapidly. The government took a very strong stand

---

*Other evidence indicates that in 1946 some 108,500 Jews were interested in emigrating, while only 31,500 planned to stay.[27]

against anti-Semitism, but, given the nature of the indoctrination that had been carried on for many years, the everyday actions of the population could not be monitored. Thus for some Jews a new life was seen as possible in Hungary; for others, emigration was the only way to achieve a new beginning.[29]

The institute was founded at a time when there was great optimism in Europe. The old order had been destroyed, and the means were felt to be at hand to create a social structure that would not follow the old patterns. However, as time went on, the initial enthusiasm that sought to generate a more responsive social and political order was dampened. These high hopes were expressed by the then president of the institute, Dr. Gyula Ortutay, who placed considerable emphasis on the reciprocal nature of the impact of public opinion on the nation's leadership.[30]

> This public opinion Institute assumes the responsibility for two tasks. On the one hand the political leaders obtain a knowledgeable glimpse of the workers' opinions. On the other hand, we give the public the opportunity to express its views on problems.

There were no direct controls over the direction of research. The researchers in the institute had a free hand in determining what issues and problems existed and the nature of the questions asked. This free interplay of information and ideas would, it was hoped, have a positive effect on the nature of decision making and the general development of the nation. This liberal reverie was short-lived, since freedom of investigation was considered a refutation of historical materialism, as defined by orthodox Marxism-Leninism and interpreted under the influence of Stalinism by Stalin's East European disciples.[31] For the next several years, until what now appears as the inevitable explosion of 1956, the situation in all of Eastern Europe was characterized by an increasingly doctrinaire and coercive perspective. Channels of information, even as limited as that provided by the institute, were seen as unnecessary, if not outright offensive and subversive to the goals of the leadership.

1956

The revolution of October 1956 signaled the beginnings of a new direction in statecraft in Hungary. Faithfulness and commitment to Party dogma has been slowly replaced by a more compromised and less insistent measure of political redemption. In a manner analogous to the shift of religious groups, from a sectarian posture in opposition to the world, to a "churchly" understanding of the need to maintain continuity through time,[32] Hungary's political leadership had veered away from an attempt to indoctrinate and control motivation consistent with a preordained formula to a perspective in which individual motives are defined as simply another adjunct of an administered milieu. This change in perspective from enforced direction to manipulated management has not in reality reduced the importance of the Party or of politics. It has, however, deflected the centrality of the prescription for the development of socialist man from moral suasion to the more neutral gospel of technique. This pattern is by no means unique to Hungary. In varying degrees, this subtle approach to domination is increasingly the preferred strategy throughout Eastern Europe. This alteration is exemplified in the Soviet Union in the move away from the terror and coercion of the Stalinist period to the more collective and bland orientation of Brezhnev and Kosygin.

Of the socialist bloc countries, the fact that Hungary has perhaps progressed further along this path is in large measure attributable to Janos Kadar, the first secretary of the Hungarian Socialist Workers' Party. Since assuming the mantle of leadership, with the help of the Soviet Union, Kadar has managed to effect a downgrading of ideological concerns in combination with a firm intention to resolve manageable issues. He has steered a course away from potentially divisive questions for which no solution is available, to ones in which the promise of some clarification exists. His famous pronouncement "Those who are not against us are with us" had had the result of coopting and uniting various potentially dissident elements behind him.

This organizing thrust has further resulted in the development of a newer, less explosive vocabulary to engage problems and issues. It may not be too far off the mark to say that the sense of reality Kadar has promulgated parallels the manner in which Alcoholics Anonymous saves alcoholics from their potentially self-destructive impulses. One basic element in this perspective relies on recognition of the constituents of the environment that cannot be modified, and within which action must take place. Once recognized, these limits will allow for a considerable range of options, while becoming increasingly invisible and taken for granted. For example, the facts of the situation indicate that there is little possibility of the Soviet Union's leaving Eastern Europe, either as the result of military action, as Hungary's experience exemplifies, or through the path of negotiation, as evidenced by the events in Czechoslovakia in 1968. This kind of evidence, which cannot be argued away and which it would be fruitless to debate, serves to make the Soviet presence at least acceptable and removes it as a pretext for debate. There exist a large number of other potentially divisive issues, which, if solutions were really attempted, would cost more to solve than the tactic of treating them matter-of-factly, as part of the set in which the drama takes place. The scenario dictates that all the players recognize that there are few if any alternatives to the structure created since 1956.

Kadar's "reality orientation" has been to downplay politics as the arena in which collective goals can be achieved[33] and to place the potential achievement of goals in the nonideological hands of planners and technical experts. Experts, by definition above traditional divisions and animosities, are the source from which national unity and progress will be drawn. The ascent to "true socialism" will thus be on the basis of incontrovertible technical criteria with none of the awkwardness of the dialectic. With no possibility of release from the tensions imposed by this emphasis, Kadar's early phrase, which heralded a relaxation of ideological concerns, has more recently been replaced by *Ez van ezt kell szeretni*, which, loosely translated, means, "This is what there is. Love it!"

An offshoot of this general emphasis on planning has been to upgrade the political planner from the role of preacher-to-sinners to a technical expert who offers facts, hypotheses, and testable propositions rather than revealed truths. This has resulted in considerable stress being placed on media specialists and social scientists in general who are now responsible for securing the data on which decisions in the areas of social policy are based. One measure of the impact of these new techniques and the ability to gather information quickly, and at some considerable savings in cost, has been to downgrade the older means of ensuring political reliability, which rested on trusted Party workers writing mood reports (*hangulat jelentes*). These inefficient traditional reports, which are still being produced, are supposed to offer information on individual commitments and attitudes at schools, plants, factories, and in neighborhoods. They are processed up the chain of command with the acknowledged result that they are more often than not quite useless. Their uselessness, in addition to their high relative cost, has been one significant factor in enhancing the attractiveness of the new techniques. The general ineffectiveness of these older procedures has been obvious for quite some time, and it is likely that they will be reduced in importance if not phased out completely. Having said this, it requires no major insight to note that changes in procedure are not easily achieved. A large literature exists that indicates that the easy adaptation of more effective techniques in organizations is not an automatic process, given the variety of commitments made to established ways.[34]

The strain to achieve greater efficiency, lower costs, and more information is, however, pervasive. In a paper published in a Party journal, Karoly Grosz,[35] the director of the Agit-Prop Department of the Central Committee presents the case for the establishment of these new sources of data collection. He argues that in order for agitation work to be effective, more must be known about public opinion and the psychological dimensions of political attitudes, perspectives, and behavior. This work, he continues, is crucial to the determination of effective propaganda work. The director of the Mass Communications Research Center, Tamas Szecsko, supports the fundamentals of Dr. Grosz's argument by underscoring the notion that the development of "Socialist Democracy" relies to an important extent on better and more effective knowledge on the part of the leadership about the wishes, needs, and desires of the public. Szecsko argues that the achievement of an efficient social system relies on continual inputs of information that have been gathered by reliable and valid procedures, which will stand the test of scientific scrutiny.[36]

More recently at a conference on Public Opinion Research and Mass Communication held in Budapest in March 1971, at which representatives of all the socialist countries of Eastern Europe took part, Dr. Szecsko emphasized the need for a mass communications network in which new qualities must be established that will aid the development of "socially progressive elements."[37] The specific constituents composing these new elements are not defined. However, the intent of the remarks makes it clear that what is foreseen are more rationally oriented individuals who are hard-working, educated, informed, and politically acquiescent and who will have no interests that conflict with the goals of the collectivity. The manner in which these long-range goals will be achieved are left moot, but "the tools are felt to be available for providing the key to uncovering the basic human processes of man's place, role, and opportunities in society."[38]

The solution to the ideological dilemmas and frustrations that have characterized previous patterns of decision making is through accenting the malleability and predictability of the human psyche. The social sciences play an instrumental role in serving the "decision makers by exploring and becoming acquainted with the processes of society" and then supplying a body of systematized "knowledge on the basis of which political decisions may become more rational and optimal."[39] This recent support for the social sciences has resulted in several social research institutes being initiated, refurbished, or expanded.

Of these, the Social Science Institute of the Party (Tarsadalom Tudomanyi Intezet) is the most direct channel to decision making in applied areas. However, the areas of policy research are too ramified and broad to be encapsulated in a single center. Other institutes are also seen as providing crucial skills in a variety of areas. The foremost of these, the Sociological Research Institute, reorganized from the Sociology Research Group, has doubled its staff since 1968. The lack of training facilities has been overcome to some extent by the establishment of a Department of Sociology at Eotvos Lorand University, which secures its instructional staff from several research institutes, as does the small Department of Industrial Sociology, which has existed for several years at Karl Marx University.

These developments in social research have not been a random activity. They have been the result of a deliberate policy on the part of an ascending element within the Party hierarchy who have discovered the potential of technical research as a means of escaping the morass of traditional ideological debate. Whether or not this "end of ideology" thesis will be followed by the antithesis of criticism of the "nonideological" values of technique as in the debates inflaming major sectors of the social sciences in North America is of some concern.[40] At the moment, the argument is posited that if the social sciences do not fulfill their technical role as objective sciences, they will devolve into criticism based on subjective notions of the social order.[41] The social sciences will then revert to social philosophy and not be useful as a planning tool. Consequently, the onus is on the social sciences to generate more valid and reliable techniques and to be continually on guard against subjective bias. The response to problems generated by technique is, then, to ignore them, as they are not scientific and emanate only from subjective views of conditions, and to continue the quest for the perfect method, which will aid in the ultimate aim of achieving the organization of socialism.

THE NEW PUBLIC OPINION CENTER

One of the recently established social science research institutes is the Mass Communications Research Center of the Hungarian Radio, which houses both Mass Communications and Public Opinion Research groups. The placing of both research groups under one roof is seen as facilitating communication between them. The resulting cross-fertilization, it is hoped, will enhance the testing of the impact of mass media as an agent supplying both information and interpretive perspectives. This linkage between mass media and public opinion research is one that has a long tradition in North America[42] and is currently very common in Eastern Europe generally.*

The steps leading to the development of this institute go back to 1959, when Poland took the lead in reorganizing public opinion research in the Eastern bloc.[43] In the early 1960s, three articles in Hungarian journals heralded the beginnings of official acceptance of public opinion in Hungary. The first was a general article on social science methodology,[44] the second was an article on the reaction of young people to jazz,[45] and the third was a survey study on the uses of leisure and moral and political concerns.[46] At about this time an article was also written by Sandor Szalai in *Elet es Irodalom*,[47] (Life and Literature), in which he argued that sociology as developed in the West had eclipsed anything so far produced in Hungary. Szalai's article generated considerable protest, and while a debate concerning his views was in progress, modifications in the dominant ideological perspective were taking place to justify the existence and the importance of social research.[48]

Direct institutional support for social research was evidenced by the formation of a small, minimally supported Public Opinion Research Group established in 1959. Much of the work of this group was tied directly to the media, with results published at odd intervals in *Radio es TV Szemle* (Radio and Television Journal). Large-scale opinion research was little in evidence in this journal

---

*The perspectives currently directing research activity in the area of public opinion show a superficial similarity to the views expressed by Dr. Ortutay in 1947. The crucial difference rests on the fact that now opinion research is encapsulated within the organizational structure of the state and is not free from direct political controls.

as the reports published were concerned mainly with the development of radio drama, television reporting, and production problems. In 1963, the title of this review was changed to *Magyar Radio Modszertani Ertesito* (Hungarian Radio Information Methods Bulletin). The material in this publication consisted almost exclusively of foreign articles translated into Hungarian. Some issues were devoted exclusively to bibliographies of new material on radio and television production and the results of audience research studies. Even given the relaxation of concern about social science as manifested by the appearance of these journals, caution still surrounded the justification of social research.

The first outward sign of the shift in the definition of social research work, from a concerned but skeptical toleration to supportive acceptance was coincident with the organization of the Sociology Research Group in 1963. While support for large-scale studies was not as yet forthcoming, a new journal, *Kozvelemeny Kutatas* (Public Opinion), was organized, and the atmosphere generated by its presence indicates that opinion research now had a secure niche in the ideological fabric. This journal, more of a house organ for the Public Opinion Research Group than a professional publication, was brought out irregularly. The studies presented in it dealt with audience research focusing on such diverse topics as musical tastes and porgram preferences of overseas Hungarians. The first study was a rather innocuous one that dealt with the effectiveness of the Radio Information Service. In this report, it was discovered that those who completed more schooling and lived in larger urban areas placed a higher value on the informative character of radio broadcasts as compared to those with less schooling who lived in rural areas. Among those defined in the survey as intellectuals,* the authority of the radio is somewhat lower than among other occupational categories. The explanation for this finding centers on this group's greater awareness of other sources of information, such as books and magazines, in contrast to those lower in the socioeconomic scale who are less knowledgeable about sources of news and informative material.

Relatively little change in the structure and organization of public opinion research took place until 1969. Concomitant with the reorganization and re-constitution of research in this no-longer sensitive area, as a whole panoply of bureaucratic legitimacy has developed. Currently in the Mass Communication Research Center, there are 19 professional workers, in addition to 30 interviewer supervisors and approximately 500 part-time interviewers throughout the country. Much of the research of the center is directed specifically to audience research, with considerable attention directed to investigating the impact and patterns of television viewing. This interest in audience research parallels his-

---

*This is a difficult category to translate into English as it encompasses white-collar workers, along with teachers, professionals, and intellectuals.

torical developments in research in North America and is seen as performing the function of sharpening methodological and analytic skills in the more delicate areas of policy research.

In addition to staff increases, there has also been a marked increase in the number of publications including articles and books that report different aspects of the center's work. There is now enough available material to obtain some clues as to the general direction of the work undertaken. Two aspects of the work are available for comment: published material organized and directed autonomously by the center, some of which is in English, and studies completed under contract to the Agit-Prop Department of the Central Committee. These latter surveys normally have a circulation limited to the members of the Agit-Prop Department, but some of the work has recently been published in a volume presenting the results of several studies sponsored by the center.[49] While the completed and published work of the center is not extensive, an overview of the major available studies allows for an appreciation of some of the problems and issues focused on in opinion research in Hungary.

PUBLISHED SURVEY STUDIES

There is currently a standing panel of 2,000 listeners and viewers who fill in a monthly report on their listening habits.[50] Consistent with this audience survey work are the by-now traditional studies devoted to musical taste, the uses of free time, and the prestige of Hungarian information media. In addition, there is also considerable attention devoted to methodological problems, such as interviewer effects, question formulation and sequence, and the psychological aspects of the refusal and inability to answer questions.[51]

One study that dealt with the impact of television on social relations in villages[52] showed that television owners go less frequently to the films than nonowners. Aside from this finding, no fundamental changes have as yet appeared in the lives of the rural agricultural workers surveyed. However, a tentative conclusion drawn from the study points to the greater passivity of nonviewers in community affairs than viewers.

In the studies dealing with the ranking of Hungarian information media, respondents of all strata evaluate the radio more favorably than either television or the press, a pattern not fundamentally different from that found elsewhere.[53] However, listeners and viewers in the villages evaluate radio and television more highly than in Budapest. The explanation for this difference in ranking is suggested as due to the fact that in villages television is in far less competition with other media than in urban areas.

The studies that provide the greatest amount of information on the current views, attitudes, and opinions of the Hungarian population are the surveys of the level and structure of economic and political knowledge. These studies are viewed by Party officials[54] as basic sources of information, and a variety of such surveys have been completed since 1966.[55] The general concern of these studies is directed to examining the differences between strata in information levels. The results obtained point to education as the single most important factor, explaining 43 percent of the variance in information levels, with occupation a close second explaining 39 percent, and newspaper reading, television newsreels, and radio broadcasts explaining 20 percent, 17 percent, and 8 percent, respectively.[56] These results show that while the media play a role in providing information, their import is filtered through the stratification system and differentially affects segments of the population.[57]

In a paper summarizing three studies, on housing, internal politics, and awareness of the issues debated by the 10th Party Congress, Edit S. Molnar[58] draws the conclusion that, in general, upper-strata individuals are more aware of issues than those lower on the socioeconomic scale. The paradoxical point is made that, while radio and television are listened to and watched more frequently by agricultural workers with less than eight grades of education than by the better-educated sectors of the urban population, they appear less well-informed than their urban compatriots. In addition, the less well-educated also report greater satisfaction with the availability of information. The argument advanced to explain this incongruity centers on the life-styles of the different strata and the concomitant differences in the use to which the media is put. The more educated who are concerned with a broader range of issues use the media more selectively, while the less well-educated rely on the media more for entertainment than information.

In another article in this same vein, Miklos Tomka[59] raises the question as to how individuals react and define the political and/or nonpolitical content of issues and events. The general conclusion drawn is that more distant issues appear more political than those concerns that affect day-to-day life.[60] The more obvious variables such as income, sex, and rural and urban residence do not appear significantly related to the conception of the political content of events. What is crucial is again the level of education, with those with more education better able to define and distinguish more clearly between what constitutes political as opposed to nonpolitical issues. Other factors related to greater political awareness are Party membership and occupation. Party members see far more political content to trade union elections and the work of factory planning committees and the National Trade Union Councils than do non-Party members. In a parallel manner, white-collar workers differentiated issues as more political than did laborers.[61] Among workers who are less than 30 and over 50, there is a far lower readiness to define issues as political than among those between the ages of 35 and 50.[62]

The importance of personal contact as contrasted to the impersonal quality of mass media as a source of information is given support in a study completed in the city of Jaszbereny in 1970.[63] This study was concerned with discovering the sources of information used by citizens in a smaller city and the perception of their role in local affairs. Of the residents surveyed, 52 percent believed they played little or no role in local affairs, while 75 percent of the local council members believed that they played a significant role. In attempting to uncover the background to this differential attitude, the authors were directed to seeking out the sources of information about local affairs on which the mass of the population relied. The discovery made was that 64 percent relied primarily on informal word-of-mouth contacts, as opposed to either formal channels of communication or the media.[64] This relatively low use of media is even further exaggerated if poster advertisements in public areas are not accepted as falling within the defining limits of mass media. Further, while 45 percent avail themselves of formal institutional sources of information, fully 30 percent claim it is unnecessary to both obtaining information by other than word of mouth.[65] One additional result of this survey indicated that, although council meetings are legally required to be publicized, only about one-third of those questioned knew when the last council meeting had been held. One significant finding brought out in this study is that few local means of information directly related to the ongoing concerns of the population are available. In focusing on this, the authors of the study report that 65 percent of the residents want a local daily paper.[66] Of the segment of the population supporting this proposal, a large proportion came from among the best informed and most active in local affairs.

In a study that focused on the beliefs that various strata have about the nature of the standard of living of others,[67] it was shown that those who live in small villages know more about the life of city dwellers than the reverse.[68] The city, then, is much closer to the village than is the village to the city. The evidence marshaled for this generalization is suggested by the fact that 8 percent of the sampled Budapest population was unable to estimate the average income of factory workers, while 11 percent of the village population could not do so. The reverse situation holds when these sectors were asked to estimate the incomes of workers on cooperative farms, with 29 percent of the Budapest population and only 9 percent of the village population unable to make a judgment. Although the argument centers on negative responses, the judgment made is that villagers are less hesitant to make income estimates on the urban population than are the latter on the income of villagers. In the pursuit of this argument about the greater knowledge of villagers, stress is laid on the demographic consequences of the shift in rural manpower[69] to the major industrial concerns during the 25 years since 1950. This migration pattern has created a major crisis in urban housing in that housing was a relatively neglected area of investment in contrast to the investments made in heavy industry.[70] Largely because of this situation, large numbers of factory workers are "commuters" from villages where, through their network of ties, they are better able to inform their friends and relatives of the realities of urban life. By way of contrast, city dwellers show considerably more knowledge about the standard of living abroad than they do about the rural-urban links in Hungary.[71] This general lack of knowledge about the society in which they live is manifested by the fact that although subsidization and control of food costs have been a factor in Hungarian life for more than two decades, only 9 percent of the urban population surveyed knew that the cost of food production is more than the price.[72] Even among white-collar workers and managers, only 33 percent were aware of this situation.[73]

The more general point of this study is that the nature and extent of personal relationships has a far greater impact on the awareness of life-styles of other strata than what is claimed as the objective characteristics of the situation. The old dictum of W. I. Thomas, that if men define situations as real, then they are real in their consequences,[74] is an old insight, but in terms of the technical rationality dominating the centralized system in Hungary and in much of Eastern Europe, it is quite new.

The recent discovery of the deficiencies of a rational model in predicting behavior is seen in the current research on efficiency in industrial plants. One of the new series of studies directed to this general area has been concerned with the effective functioning of work groups in factories.[75] The result of these studies has been to point out the necessity of recognizing that various strata do exist in factories and that by no means are workers to be taken as a homogeneous group solely interested in maximizing their incomes. The various strata of workers are separated by interests and values that have developed from a myriad of sources involving their particular social situations and prospects for the future. Informal groups as a manifestation of these interests develop and play a considerable role in productivity. The important consequence of these studies and of those conducted by the Public Opinion Center of the Hungarian Radio, is to point out the assumptions of the planners' rational model. Any attempt to impose a model of productivity or information dissemination that does not take into account the conflicting interest of subgroups within industrial enterprises and the nature and extent of personal relationships is likely to result on the one hand in lower productivity and on the other hand in important information not reaching its intended target.

Changes in opinions and attitudes on the New Economic Mechanism (NEM) are a source of several studies. Shortly after the introduction of this revision in economic management in 1968, few, when asked to specify the nature of these alterations in the organization of economic affairs, could do more than hint at it in a rather oblique manner.[76] Despite the generally superficial level of information, the atmosphere surrounding the consequences of the reform were quite favorable. High hopes existed among a significant proportion of the population (65 percent) that the reform would entail a rise in the standard of living. Of this group, 59 percent counted on the changes being manifested within two to five years, 18 percent felt that the changes would be evident within five years, while 12 percent felt two years to be a sufficient time period for changes to occur.[77]

One of the most intriguing areas studied in this survey was the reaction to changes in the determination of wage levels. A consequence of the NEM was to give greater leeway to individual firms and plants to set their own wage levels in order to obtain the manpower necessary to their functioning. This created the possibility of a far greater range in income than was the case previously. To test reactions to this prospect, the question was asked:[78]

In your opinion should differences in incomes be greater, identical or smaller than now in jobs involving various degrees of responsibility?

The responses were as follows:

	Distribution of Answers of Active Wage-Earners
Differences should be greater	22%
Differences should be the same	22
Differences should be smaller	48
Don't know/no answer	8

Another question that focused on wage differentials on the basis of educational qualifications gives a somewhat different picture of the perspectives of the population:[79]

In your opinion, what should be aimed at in the future: to make differences in the incomes of more or less educated people greater, identical, or smaller than at present?

	Answers of Active Wage-Earners
Differences should be greater	37%
Differences should be as they are	28
Differences should be smaller	27
Don't know/no answer	8

The authors of this study did not combine these tables to show the percentages that felt that both education and job responsibility were legitimate bases for salary discrimination. From these data, it appears that wage differentiation on the basis of educational attainment is more acceptable than job responsibility.

Several years have passed since the above study was completed, and in a more recent study[80] concerned with the opinions on the standard of living, we can judge the consequences of a more mature impact of the NEM. One of the questions asked and responses are:[81]

In your opinion are the differences in the standard of living in Hungary large, middling, or small?

43%	Large
48	Middling
3	Small
6	Don't know/no answer

In further breaking down these opinions, it was found that those with more schooling and higher incomes were more predisposed to assuming that standard-of-living differences in the population are large. Pursuing the same line of questions, the authors of the study went on to ask:[82]

In Hungary, do you think the differences in standard of living should be greater, less or the same?

Differences should be smaller	70%
Differences should be the same	13
Differences should be greater	6
Don't know/no answer	11

The age group between 18 and 25 felt most strongly about the reduction of differences, with 87 percent responding in this manner. The general sentiment toward minimizing differences was elaborated when 41 percent of those who thought differences were small thought they should be smaller still, while 88 percent of those who answered that large differences exist thought the differences should be smaller.[83]

These two studies, although asking somewhat different questions, show striking differences in the acceptability of differences in the standard of living. It is a debatable point whether one can conclude from these data that the initial support for the NEM has been completely superseded by a heightened concern for the inequalities created. To examine further this aspect of the NEM, respondents in this latter study were requested to specify what was entailed in the term "standard of living." The authors reflect that in the response to this question, the majority of the population hold to a very narrow definition of the term, while fully 24 percent could not respond in any meaningful way when asked to define it.[84]

In a further examination of the data, 32 percent compare their life situations to their own past, while 31 percent compare themselves to their parents, and 47 percent focus on their fellow workers, friends, and acquaintances or their own age cohort.[85] Those who focused on the past as a focal point for comparison were in general less educated, older, from smaller towns, and considerably less knowledgeable about world affairs than those who directed their attention to those with comparable life chances. In searching for the nature and acceptance of life situations, a question was asked that found 62 percent expressing satisfaction, 28 percent partly satisfied, and 10 percent dissatisfied with their circumstances.[86] Those who are most satisfied consisted largely of those who compared their own situations to the past, were older, had less schooling, and lived in smaller urban areas or villages. The younger, with more schooling and higher-level occupations, felt most dissatisfied. The consensual picture of the earlier study is partially upset by these results, which indicate some disaffection on the part of those who have, on objective grounds, benefited most, while those who expect less are apparently more appreciative.[87]

The current acceptance of the changes introduced by the NEM then appears to be somewhat less than enthusiastic, compared to the initial attractiveness of the shift away from a highly centralized and directed system. The authors of the earlier study did forsee the possibilities of stress in the continual accommodation to mutations in the ordering of the system and suggested a specific role for the media:[88]

> It has become possible that the mass media should do useful work in the future in the strengthening of consensus connected with current events as the overwhelming majority of the society has favorably reacted to the first phases of the process. At the same time, efforts to change the opinion of the minority to dissipate reservations should be increased, and mass communications media must take a greater part in this activity. The task of public opinion polling is again to build up a way for "feedback" on a national scale, to explore social reflection continually and with an ever greater frequency.

The guidelines for the media are clear—to explain, and more broadly to take a hand in "selling" policy in accord with the precepts advanced by the spokesman for the Party, the Agit-Prop Department.[89] This grand design entails an acceptance of stratification differences as a natural if not unfortunate fact, while at the same time seeing one of the major results of media exposure as organizing and directing responses to agree with what is defined as the general good by technical experts.[90]

It is becoming increasingly clear that the impact of the media is not direct but is mediated through more personal and immediate sources. This inability of the media to generate greater effects by itself is not unknown to the Party leadership. One of the important conditions now seen as necessary to develop is means of information that will reach those who are relatively untouched by the sources of available information. In accord with this, the director of the Agit-Prop Department has called for a greater effort on the part of those who are better informed—Party members and interested and active non-Party members to help those less well-informed to draw appropriate conclusions.[91]

The relationship between the state and citizen has led one well-known Hungarian economist to define and interpret the role of public opinion and the guiding hand of the government in the following manner:[92]

When making decisions the government pays increased attention to the interest of groups affected by them. The general intention is to coordinate the social optimum with the various group interests to avoid contradictions arising from the implementation of the decision. . . . The anticipated reaction of public opinion to decisions to be made is given increased consideration. . . . It follows that influencing public opinion (by the press, television, radio, publications, scientific discussions, etc.) has acquired added importance.

This stated role of public opinion suggests that the techniques of shaping, manipulating, and coordinating reactions to policy may not be markedly different from the perspectives seen as characteristic of capitalist societies. One capable researcher has argued, on the one hand, that[93]

The decisions of modern capitalist societies are anti-democratic not because they do not take public opinion into consideration but just because they do. This only seems to be a paradox: one of the essential features of political manipulation is just to create public opinion in order to get a consensus for the preplanned decisions.

On the other hand, a comparable role is predicted for the agit-prop work in its preparation of the populace prior to the implementation of important decisions.[94] The significance of reliable and authoritative information on the basis of which informed judgments on decisions can be made is not lost sight of in the Hungarian milieu, and more instruction is seen as necessary in order to control information flow on proximate levels.[95]

Public opinion research in Hungary is an agent of guidance and control over reaction to changes in the structure and organization of the state. This transaction between opinions and control is perhaps more a consequence of the stress placed on planning as opposed to traditional ideological conceptions. In a highly complex system, whatever its ideological base, surprises can be costly. Given the centrality of planning in industrial systems in general,[96] assumptions on the consequences of policy decisions and the problems associated with their implementation are variables that cannot be neglected. In the West, particularly in North America, a value consensus involving political stability is assumed in the planning and control of markets for goods and services. In Hungary, and in all of Eastern Europe, such a consensus is not as yet taken for granted. The apparent aim of public opinion research is to be a formative factor in its creation. In order to generate this unity, increased stress is given to the gathering of information on what is perceived and altering it, so that disjunctions and contradictions are leached out. It is at this juncture that the handmaidens of policy, the social scientists, enter the scene to discover and organize data for policy makers so that all consequences, both intended and unintended, will be comprehended.

METHODOLOGICAL PROBLEMS IN AGIT-PROP RESEARCH

In 1970, a study was completed on the attitudes toward the changes in rent payment policy.[97] This study was oriented, aside from the collection of data, to the development of methodological procedures that would allow for quick and relatively uncomplicated public opinion studies of internal political questions. A plan was constructed for further studies and eventuated in what is called the "Omnibus" series. The plan consisted initially of politically oriented studies that would be conducted quarterly using national samples. As it developed in 1971, the first year of the plan, national samples were used only in the first and last quarter of the year, while strata-specific studies on teachers and factory workers were completed during the middle of the year. At the moment the results of these studies are not available as they are circulated only to members of the Agit-Prop Department. However, the titles of 14 studies completed during the year have been published, as has a discussion of the methodological problems involved. This summary of material does provide a view of some of the difficulties of doing research of this order in Hungary.[98]

The major results of these surveys point out that the correlation between social demographic characteristics and opinion configurations are of a most general and relatively trivial nature. The most responsive social category is the urban, white-collar, educated male who is also the most extensive user of mass media, and consequently the best-informed and most able to respond to questions. This paucity of informed respondents suggests a major difficulty in the use of simple random samples. The results of these surveys indicate that, by the time an adequate number of codable responses are obtained, one-quarter to one-half of the original sample is eliminated either because they have no opinion or because they will not answer the questions.[99] It is concluded from this that most of the populace, particularly those in the lower strata, women, and the majority of non-Party members, who together make up the vast majority of the population, are still very defensive about openly stating their opinions. There are assumed to be two sources of this response inhibition: (1) many feel that they will be sanctioned if they offer their opinions openly, and (2) many feel that their opinions have relatively little importance and that only the opinions of the Party and government leadership carry any weight. Immediate and local concerns are areas in which opinions are easier to elicit than issues of a national or international character. These latter issues are too far removed from the lives of those involved to be in any way capable of involving or generating opinions.

Several suggestions have been postulated for coping with these difficulties, suggestions that involve primarily a more detailed list of those who may be more sensitive and responsive to the problems under discussion than the traditional categories. In addition, sample bases of more than the 500 usually interviewed are seen as necessary, in order to obtain at least a minimal base from which reliable generalizations can be obtained.[100]

Some interviewer-effect problems are also noted.[101] It is suggested that interviewers ought to strive to understand the schedules better and that their training ought to encompass this. Finally, it is suggested that untried questions, without being subjected to a pretest are not likely to be informative, given the varied problems in eliciting responses. One suggested way out of the dilemma of trying to obtain opinions from a poorly informed population is to develop strata-specific schedules. But this solution is seen as likely to create as many problems as it solves, as it reduces the comparability of responses.

These procedural difficulties are evidence of some considerable strain between what is seen as necessary in policy terms and what is in fact possible, with a suspicious, skeptical, and uninformed population.

SUMMARY

The study of public opinion in Hungary is not without problems. While the attempt is made to modernize the country and to make the institutional structure more responsive to the needs and demands of the population, the older cultural style, in which the regimes of Eastern Europe looked upon their populations with mistrust, is not likely to be eradicated in a few short years. The more recently developed approach of "managerial Marxism,"[102] although not unique to Hungary, accepts the importance of structure, planning, and organizational skills as necessary to the raising of the standard of living and shows little concern for or interest in alienation or anomie, except insofar as these traditional sociological conceptions may present intrusions into the smooth functioning of whatever is planned. Problems are defined as manageable by the cultivation of efficiency in the industrial sector, and the elevation of a technically cognizant and informed consciousness on the part of an acquiescent citizenry. One informed student of the social sciences in Hungary has commented:[103]

> There is . . . a major interest in the responses of the population, both positive and negative, to new structural arrangements. Thus by remaining sensitive to the opposing elements in all human activity (the dialectic), sociologists in Eastern European countries hope also to identify responses which detract from improvement of the human condition.

Few would argue that one of the fondest hopes of all mankind is to improve the human condition, and it is fair to impute this motive to the social scientists and the officialdom of Eastern Europe. However, while the consideration of the general good is a pervasive quality, the specific detailed definition of its operation devolves upon an administrative elite. There are no illusions about the capacities of the working classes to affect major changes. They remain the sources from which data are to be obtained. However, the definition of what attitudes and opinions ought to be and the decision as to how best to generate these responses are in the hands of a select few.[104] The dilemma of working in this environment and the alternatives available to the social scientist are discussed by Andras Hegedus, ex-director of the Sociology Research Institute of the Hungarian Academy of Sciences:[105]

> In the European Socialist countries, including Hungary, the kind of social science which treats the present faces the dilemma of whether to become an apologetic science influencing behavior, or to provide the analysis and at the same time the criticism of the conditions that have developed. Some demand that it be the former, some the latter; the scholar who undertakes the former may often gain considerable material advantages, whereas the reader who prefers to interpret the responsibilities of sociology may often invite censure, not excluding material disadvantages.

Rewards are thus available to those who will play their limited technical role; those who choose the path of an autonomous critical discipline will at best not be compensated or recognized for their efforts. One result of this controlled research is that many topics cannot be touched upon, much less researched without the very real possibility of serious consequences. For example, there is no open discussion of the power of the Party bureaucracy and the legitimacy of the Party or the government and their potential fallibility. To raise questions of this order would be tantamount to questioning the authority of historical materialism as compared to the potential virtues of bourgeois democracy. These and other issues lie below the surface, although at odd moments there is some attention devoted to the more general nature of the form of society that affects the construction and formation of opinion. In an atypical case, one researcher has argued that the genesis of public opinion depends on "a fully developed commodity production and market, free citizens in the bourgeois interpretation, a split of society and state, power and rule."[106]

Sensitive questions are not often raised, as answers may appear that threaten the stability of the structure. However, while this orientation to research has resulted in some disappointment in the material unearthed in the surveys completed for both researchers and those developing policy, the crucial aspect at the moment is not the results but that attempts to study public opinion exist at all. The investment in research is complicated by the felt necessity to control and direct, but on another level very little is actually known about the values and goals of the population. One of the residual effects of this work may very well be a better picture of what Hungarians are really concerned with as opposed to what the directors of the system believe they ought to be interested in.

One proposition that appears to offer a reasonable perspective on the conditions of life in Hungary is suggested by the studies completed to date, which show a lack of interest in politics and considerably more interest in and knowledge of economic issues.* This suggests that a process of depoliticalization may be taking place paralleling that which many have argued characterizes the West. In the West, the withdrawal from collective goals has been traced to the disillusionment with technical rationality. Technical virtuosity, it is argued, has resulted in a disenchantment with public symbols, which no longer provide a sense of solidarity and commitment to the established order.[108] Given this, greater attention has been directed to the "self" and to the private sphere as the arena in which "ultimate meaning" is sought. In the East, the public sector is beyond justification, since the elitist managerial structure with its lack of accountability places the issue of the public good beyond reach. It can be further argued that as a consequence of this increasing distance and invisibility of the elite structure, in both the East and the West, new vistas are opened for the masses of the population, provided their attention is directed to individual rather than collective interests. In the West, the acceptability of encounter therapy and the proliferation of exotic religious groups and ideologies in addition to the continued deification of consumerism constitute some evidence of this pattern. In Hungary, more staid alternatives are available in foreign travel, weekend cottages, and public entertainments of various sorts, which are at the moment more available than elsewhere in Eastern Europe.

The legacy of bitterness inflicted by political and ideological diatribes has, at least in Hungary, been replaced for the moment by envy and rivalry in the accumulation of goods. This is a step that presents some dangers, particularly to the remnants of the Jewish community, who were for many years the public objects of considerable speculation on the sources of inequality. Although overt anti-Semitism is under control, the memories remain vivid among Jews of the price paid in lives for the high visibility of past success. For the moment, however, the potential resurgence of inflammatory and disruptive conceptions are held in check by techniques that coopt the various strata with the promise of more privileges, goods, and services.

The relative tractibility of the population in Hungary, due to these attempts to control potential schism by managing and raising the standard of living, has not as yet altered the conventional wisdom on the nature of the regimes in Hungary and in Eastern Europe. The limited analytic vocabulary of

---

*Some evidence exists that points to a marked difference in levels of political and economic information between strata. Intellectuals and those in managerial positions are considerably more knowledgeable on political and economic affairs than those in other strata, particularly homemakers. However, the level of economic knowledge in general appears higher than political knowledge. The argument advanced to explain this discrepancy is that economic affairs are closer to the particular sphere of everyday interests than is politics.[107]

motives confuses lack of political concern with potential disloyalty. This confusion is exemplified by one study, which concludes:[109]

> This study has shown that the younger generation is at least as Western-oriented as their parents' generation. Large-scale audience surveys reveal that young people tune into Radio Free Europe in as large numbers as do older people. Both of these findings point in the same direction: time is not working for the Communist system. The legitimacy of Communism, Socialism, People's Democracy continues to be rejected in favor of Western political values. This is of predictive relevance in assessing further relations between the rulers and the ruled and the entire long-range course of events in Eastern Europe.

The error in this conclusion lies in the assertion that the lack of legitimacy of political values in Eastern Europe means that the population longs for a Western democratic government. An alternative explanation, which appears to fit the situation better, is that acceptance rather than legitimacy is accorded, as the regimes provide a necessary stability in which self-interest can be maximized. This does not mean that a more representative political structure is not desired, but simply that what currently exists is more acceptable than the initimidating moralizing that took place in the years prior to 1956 and in the fascist autocracy that preceded it. Modernization is not the same as political democracy, and, as the realistic prospect for political democracy remains limited, the free flow of goods is preferred to dogmatism, and this is the only basis at the moment for progress.

The lot of the citizenry in a social order that apotheosizes technique is political impotence and disinterest, and this is reflected in the surveys conducted by the Hungarian Radio's Public Opinion Center. But this impotence and invisibility of the population allows planners to simplify their assumptions in addition to making politics inconsequential to the masses. The result is a "mass society," in which elites and masses are unavailable and inaccessible to one another.[110] The role of public opinion surveys in this situation is something of an exercise in futility, as policy formulated by the elites is unrelated to the interests of the masses. However, to allow greater influence to the masses in policy determination is fraught with the danger of the possibility of creating "publics" that will demand access to the decision-making process. The current stand-off in Hungary between the elites and potential publics is tenuous, but it appears as if everyone fears the hazards of questioning the situation too closely. Consequently the public policy of creating a rationally ordered society continues with public opinion research showing, if nothing else, that at the moment no political interests are developing to disrupt what has been achieved to date.

NOTES

1. No all-inclusive and definitive work on Hungarian sociology has yet been written. Some material that specifies in more detail the contemporary as well as the historical outlines of development are Kalman Kulcsar, "The Past and Present of Hungarian Sociology," in Hungarian Sociological Studies, *Sociological Review*, Monograph no. 17, ed. Paul Halmos and Martin Albrow, February 1972, pp. 5-37; Kalman Kulcsar, "Sociology in Hungary," *New Hungarian Quarterly* 12, no. 41 (Spring 1971): 58-66; Herman R. Lantz, "Sociology in Hungary: Impressions and Appraisal," *New Hungarian Quarterly* 13, no. 46 (Spring 1972): 134-46; Gabor Kiss, "History of the Development of Sociology in Hungary from 1945," *American Sociologist* 2, no. 3 (August 1967): 141-44; Karl Mannheim's role in the early period of sociological development in Hungary is sketched in Lewis A. Coser, *Masters of Sociological Thought* (New York: Harcourt, Brace, Jovanovich, 1971), pp. 441-47; for a concise statement on Hungarian social structure during the interwar period see John Kosa, "Hungarian Society in the Time of the Regency, 1920-1944," *Journal of Central European Affairs* 16 (October 1946): 253-65.

2. For more detail on this period see, Istvan Dekany, "Rapport sommaire sur l'evolution de la sociologie depuis 1920 en Hongrie," *Revue Internationale de Sociologie* 46, nos. 1-2 (1938): 53-61.

3. See John S. Shippee, "Empirical Sociology in the Eastern European Communist Party-States," in *Communist Party-States: Comparative and International Studies*, ed. Jan F. Triska (Indianapolis: Bobbs-Merrill, 1967), pp. 282-336; Kulcsar, "Past and Present of Hungarian Sociology," op. cit., p. 14; Zoltan von Bezeredy, "Die Lage der Soziologie in Ungarn," *Kolner Zeitschrift fur Soziologie und Social-psychologie* 13, no. 4 (1961): 770-76.

4. Kulcsar, "Past and Present of Hungarian Sociology," op. cit., p. 10.

5. Gyula Rezler, "Magyar Varos-es Uzemszociografia a Ket Vilaghaboru kozott: merleg es Visszatekintes" (Hungarian Urban and Industrial Sociography Between the Two World Wars: An Evaluation and Review), *Szociologia* 1, no. 4 (1972): 556-72.

6. Gyula Rezler, *A Magyar Nagyipari Munkassag Kialakulasa, 1848-1914* (Budapest, 1938).

7. Rezler, "Magyar Varos-es Uzemszociografia," op. cit., p. 565.

8. An excellent summary of pre-World War I intellectual ferment in Hungary can be found in David Kettler, "Culture and Revolution: Lukacs in the Hungarian Revolutions of 1918-1919," *Telos*, no. 10 (Winter 1971), pp. 35-92.

9. Kulcsar, "Sociology in Hungary," op. cit., p. 59.

10. Kulcsar, "Past and Present of Hungarian Sociology," op. cit., p. 7.

11. Klara Szabo, "A Radio Kozvelemeny Kutatas Magyarorszagon," *Tanulmanyok* (Radio Public Opinion Surveys in Hungary) 2, no. 5 (1970), Magyar Radio es Televizio Tomegkommunikacios Kutatokozpont; and Paul H. Schiller, "A Hungarian Survey on Sympathetic Attitudes," *International Journal of Opinion and Attitude Research* 1, no. 3 (September 1947): 85. A recent survey of the impact of radio during the interwar period can be found in *Tanulmanyok a magyar radio tortenetebol 1925-1945* (Studies in the History of the Hungarian Radio, 1925-1945) (Budapest: A Tomegkommunikacios Kutatokozpont Kiadasa, 1975).

12. Ferenc Bekes, "Adalekok a Hazai Intezmenyes Kozvelemenykutatas Tortenetehez" (Contribution to the History of Institutional Public Opinion Research), *Statisztikai Szemle*, July 1971, pp. 745-57.

13. Schiller, op. cit., p. 86.

14. M. Lacko, *Arrow-Cross: National Socialists, 1935-1944* (Budapest, 1969); Hannah Arendt, *Eichmann in Jerusalem* (New York: Harcourt Brace Jovanovich, 1965), pp. 194-202; Raul Hilberg, *The Destruction of the European Jews* (Chicago: Quadrangle, 1961), pp. 509-54; Jeno Levai, *Zsidosors Magyarorszagon* (Budapest, 1948).

15. Hilberg, op. cit., p. 509. For an analysis of the current situation of Jews in Hungary see, Paul Lendvai, *Anti-Semitism Without Jews* (Garden City, N.Y.: Doubleday, 1971), pp. 301-25.

16. Hungarian Press Service, "A Magyar Kozvelemenykutatas Eredmenyei, 1947," (Results of Hungarian Public Opinion Research 1947), mimeograph, Budapest, 1947.

17. Ibid., p. 2.

18. "Hungarian Institute of Public Opinion Research," *International Journal of Opinion and Attitude Research* 1, no. 2 (June 1947): 100.

19. Bekes, op. cit., p. 747.

20. "A Magyar Kozvelemenykutatas Eredmenyei, 1947," op. cit., p. 10.

21. "Hungarian Institute of Public Opinion Research," op. cit., p. 100.

22. *Mai Magyarorszag 1965* (Hungary Today, 1965), (Budapest: Central Statistical Office, 1966), pp. 15-16.

23. The original studies were reviewed in the Parliamentary Library in Budapest. Two excellent summaries dealing directly with the work of this institute are Szabo, op. cit., and Bekes, op. cit.

24. Lacko, op. cit., p. 70.

25. Ibid., p. 71.

26. Ibid., p. 72.

27. Nehemiah Robinson, ed., *European Jewry Ten Years After the War* (New York: Institute of Jewish Affairs, 1956), pp. 67, 74.

28. Ibid., p. 63.

29. Hungary today exhibits on balance a high degree of immunity from politically inspired anti-Semitism. Lendvai, op. cit., pp. 301-25.

30. Bekes, op. cit., p. 753.

31. Shippe, op. cit.

32. H. Richard Niebuhr, *The Social Sources of Denominationalism* (New York: Henry Holt, 1929); Max Weber, "The Social Psychology of the World Religions," in *From Max Weber*, ed. H. H. Gerth and C. Wright Mills (New York: Oxford University Press, 1958), pp. 267-301.

33. Laszlo Jotischky, "Hungary, 15 Years After," *New Society*, May 20, 1971, pp. 862-64.

34. Alvin Gouldner, "Organizational Analysis" in *Sociology Today*, ed. Robert Merton, Leonard Broom, and Leonard S. Cottrell, Jr. (New York: Basic Books, 1959), pp. 400-429.

35. Karoly Grosz, "Gondolatcseret Minden Emberrel!" (An Exchange of Views with Everyone),*Tarsadalmi Szemle* no. 5. 8-9 (1970): 81-92.

36. Tamas Szecsko, "A Propaganda Rendszere: Gondolatok a Tomegbefolyasolasrol" (Propaganda Systems: Thoughts on Mass Influence), *Tarsadalmi Szemle* no. 10, (1969): 93-103.

37. Tamas Szecsko, ed. *Public Opinion and Mass Communication, Working Conference—Budapest* (Budapest, 1971), p. 10.

38. Kulcsar, "Sociology in Hungary," op. cit., p. 63.

39. W. F. Robinson, "Hegedus, His Views and His Critics," *Studies in Comparative Communism*, April 1969, pp. 124-25.

40. Alvin Gouldner, *The Coming Crisis of Western Sociology* (New York: Basic Books, 1970).

41. Kulcsar, "Sociology in Hungary," op. cit., p. 62.

42. Bernard Berelson and Morris Janowitz, eds., *Reader in Public Opinion and Communication* (New York: Free Press, 1966), passim.

43. Andrzej Sicinski, "Public Opinion Surveys in Poland," *International Social Science Journal* 15, no. 1 (1963): 91-110; Andrzej Sicinski, "Development in Eastern European Public Opinion Research," *Polls* 3, no. 1 (1967): 1-10; Eve Merriam, "Socialist Gall-

ups: Opinion Surveys Behind the Iron Curtain," *Monthly Review* (October 1969): 205-11.

44. K. Kulcsar, "Egy Szociologia Vizsgalat Modszertani Tapasztalatai" (Methodological Experiences Gained in a Sociological Study), *Valosag*, no. 5 (May 1960).

45. Agnes Losonczi, "Zene es Kozonseg: Egy Uzemi Vizsgalat Tapasztalatai" (Music and Its Audience: Experiences Gained in a Factory Study), *Valosag*, no. 1 (January 1963).

46. Miklos Szanto, "Egy Kiserleti Felmeres Modszertani Tapasztalatai" (Methodological Experiences Gained in an Experimental Study), *Magyor Filozofiai Szemele* 5, no. 3, pp. 355-78.

47. Emilia Wilder, "Opinion Polls," *Survey*, no. 48 (1963), p. 128; von Bezeredy, op. cit., p. 770.

48. K. Kulcsar, "A Kozvelemeny mint Szociologiai Jelenseg" (Public Opinion as a Sociological Phenomenon),*Magyar Filozofiai Szemle*, no. 3 (1962), pp. 243-70.

49. *Az Informaciotol a Kozeletig* (From Information of Public Life), ed. Tamas Szecsko (Budapest, 1973). A full list of titles published by the Center is available in Tamas Szecsko, ed., *Public Opinion and Mass Communication—Working Conference, Budapest* (Budapest, 1971), pp. 207-13.

50. Szecsko, "Introduction," *Public Opinion and Mass Communication*, op. cit., pp. 9-11.

51. Edit S. Molnar and Ferenc Bekes, "The Public Opinion Research Department of the Hungarian Radio and Television," *Social Science Information* 7, no. 5 (October 1968): 15-29.

52. Ibid., p. 22.

53. Ibid., p. 23.

54. Grosz, op. cit., pp. 81-92.

55. Molnar and Bekes, op. cit.

56. Ferenc Bekes and Balint Suranyi, "Some Methodological Considerations Following from a Survey Measuring the Level of Political Knowledge," in *Radio and TV Review*, Special Issue for the Varna Conference, 1970, pp. 62-66.

57. Ferenc Bekes and Balint Suranyi, "Politikai Ismeretszint es Tarsadalmi Retegzodes"—Kulonlenyomat a Korszeru Statisztikai Torekvesek Magyarorszagon (Political Knowledge and Social Stratification—a special publication of current statistical activity in Hungary), pp. 487-92.

58. Edit S. Molnar, "Velemenyalkotas es Informacioszerzes" (The Creation of Opinion and the Acquisition of Information), in *Az Informaciotol a Kozeletig* (Budapest, 1973), pp. 25-50.

59. Miklos Tomka, "Milyen messze van a Politika" (How Distant Is Politics?), *Az Informaciotol a Kozeletig* (Budapest, 1973), pp. 161-75.

60. Ibid., p. 167.

61. Ibid., p. 171.

62. Ibid., p. 172.

63. Robert Angelusz and Laszlo Varadi, "Kisvarosi Kozelet 1970" (The Public Life of a Small City 1970), *Az Informaciotol a Kozeletig* (Budapest, 1973), pp. 179-227.

64. Ibid., p. 182.

65. Ibid., p. 183.

66. Ibid., pp. 191-92.

67. Zoltan Jakab, "Jovedelmek es Hiedelmek" (Incomes and Beliefs), in *Az Informaciotol a Kozeleltig* (Budapest, 1973), pp. 126-60.

68. Ibid., p. 152.

69. Ibid., p. 153.

70. Gyorgy Konrad and Ivan Szelenyi, "A Lakaselosztas Szociologia Kerdesei," in *A Szocialista Varosok es a Szociologia*, ed. Ivan Szelenyi (Budapest, 1971), pp. 344-68.

71. Jakab, op. cit., p. 156.

72. Ibid.

73. Ibid.

74. W. I. Thomas and Florian Znanecki, *The Polish Peasant in Europe and America* (New York: Dover, 1958), pp. 1-86.

75. L. Hethy and Cs. Mako, "Differential Incentives and the Structure of Interests and Powers," *Hungarian Academy of Sciences*, Research Group for Sociology, 1970; L. Hethy and Cs. Mako, "Obstacles to the Introduction of Efficient Money Incentives in a Hungarian Factory," *Industrial and Labour Relations Review* 24, no. 4 (July 1971): 541-53.

76. Ferenc Bekes and Zoltan Jakab, "Hungarian Public Opinion and the New System of Economic Management as Reflected by a Poll," *Radio and TV Review*, Special Issue for the Varna Conference, 1970, pp. 77-85.

77. Ibid., p. 79.

78. Ibid., p. 83.

79. Ibid., p. 84.

80. Peter Makara and Istvan Monigl, "Eletszinvonal es Kozgondolkodas, in *Az Informaciotol a Kozeletig*, ed. T. Szecsko (Budapest, 1973), pp. 107-25.

81. Ibid., p. 123.

82. Ibid., p. 124.

83. Ibid.

84. Ibid., p. 112.

85. Ibid., pp. 114-15. The percentages total to more than 100 percent as respondents could compare themselves to more than one group.

86. Ibid., p. 117.

87. Ibid., p. 122.

88. Bekes and Jakab, op. cit., p. 85.

89. Molnar, op. cit., p. 31.

90. Tamas Szecsko, "Everyday Communication Situations and Public Opinion," *Radio and TV Review*, Special Issue for the Varna Conference, 1970, pp. 7-21.

91. Grosz, op. cit., p. 85.

92. Jozsef Bognar, "Initiative and Equilibrium: Major Political and Economic Issues in Hungary," *New Hungarian Quarterly* 11, no. 37, p. 27.

93. Szecsko, "Everyday Communication Situations and Public Opinion," op. cit., p. 17.

94. Molnar, op. cit., p. 31.

95. Ibid., p. 31.

96. J. K. Galbraith, *The New Industrial State* (Boston: Houghton-Mifflin, 1967).

97. Ferenc Bekes and Edit. S. Molnar, "Az 1971 Evi Omnibusz Felmeresek Modszertani Tapasztalatai" (Methodological Experiences Gained with the 1971 Omnibus Surveys), *Modszertan*, MRT Tomegkommunikacios Kutatokozpont 3, no. 7 (March 9, 1972): 4.

98. The first Omnibus surveys were completed in March 1971: and their titles are: (1) A Kozel-Keleti Valsag (The Middle-East Crisis); (2) A Diplomata Rablasok (The Kidnapping of Diplomats); (3) A Lengyel Esemenyek Visszhangja (The Reaction to the Events in Poland); (4) A Kepviselo-es Tanacstagi Valasztasok (The Election of Representatives and Council Members); and (5) A Foberlok Velemenye a Lakasfelmeresek Tapastalatairol, a Felmerest Vegzok Magatartasarol (The Opinions of Renters on Their Experiences with Housing Surveys, a Survey of Concluding Attitudes). In November 1971, the second Omnibus series was completed and the titles of the nine studies in this series are (1) A Kozel-Keleti Valsag (The Middle-East Crisis); (2) A Politikai Erdeklodes Jellege (The Characteristics of Political Interest); (3) A Politikai Tajekozodashoz valo Viszony (Correlates of Political Information); (4) A Velemeny-Nyilvanitas Ertelmenek Megitelese (Judgment of the Understanding of Expressed Opinions); (5) Az Orszag Gazdasagi Helyzetenek, az Elets-

zinvonalnak es a Nemzetkozi Helyzet Alakulasanak Elorebecslese (The National Economic Situation and the Formation of Prejudgments on the Standard of Living and the International Situation); (6) A Hazai Hirkozlo Eszkozokkel Valo Elegedettseg (The Adequacy of the National News Media); (7) Hosszu Haj es Tiki-Taki (Long Hair and Tiki-Taki—that is, a game in which two plastic balls on a string are bounced off one another); (8) Orszaggyules, Ifjusagi Torveny, a Felnottevalas Kriteriumai (Parliament, Youth Laws and the Criteria of Adults); and (9) A Fock Jeno Beszederol Valo Tajekozottsag (Information on the Speech of Jeno Fock, the Prime Minister).

99. Bekes and Molnar, "Az 1971 Evi Omnibusz Felmeresek Modszertani Tapasztalatai," op. cit., p. 6.

100. Ibid.

101. Ibid., p. 7.

102. Lewis Feuer, *The Conflict of Generations* (New York: Basic Books, 1969), p. 513.

103. Herman R. Lantz, in *The State of Sociology in Eastern Europe Today*, ed. Jerzy J. Wiatr (Carbondale, Ill.: Southern Illinois University Press, 1971), Foreword, p. xi.

104. Milovan Djilas stressed just this point in *The New Class* (New York: Praeger, 1959).

105. Andras Hegedus, "Hungary," in *State of Sociology in Eastern Europe Today*, op. cit., p. 84. The recent exile in 1975 of Ivan Szelenyi and the silencing of the Lukacs group consisting of Agnes Heller, Georg and Marisa Markus, and Mihaly Vajda is indicative of a shift in emphasis in Party circles away from a benign toleration of criticism to a more apologetic stance.

106. Robert Angelusz, "To a Definition of the Concept and Structure of Public Opinion," in Szecsko, ed., *Public Opinion and Mass Communication*, op. cit., p. 51.

107. Szecsko, "Introduction," *Az Informaciotol a Kozeletig*, op. cit., p. 11; Ferenc Bekes, "A Lakossag Politikai es Gazdasagi Ismereteirol," *Az Informaciotol a Kozeletig*, op. cit., pp. 51-83. Additional support for this conclusion can be found in Peter Toma and Ivan Volgyes, *Politics in Hungary* (San Francisco: W. H. Freeman, 1977), pp. 143, 153-59, 173. A review of some American studies on this theme appears in Robert E. Lane and David O. Sears, *Public Opinion* (Englewood Cliffs, N.J.: Prentice-Hall, 1964), pp. 57-71.

108. Robert Nisbet, "Radicalism as Therapy," *Encounter* 38, no. 3 (March 1972): 53-64; Thomas Luckmann, *The Invisible Religion* (New York: Macmillan, 1967), pp. 69-117.

109. "Attitudes Toward Key Political Concepts in East Europe," Audience Research Department of Radio Free Europe, Washington, D.C., December 1969, p. 104.

110. William Kornhauser, *The Politics of Mass Society* (Glencoe, Ill.: Free Press, 1959).

6

OPINION, REALITY,
AND THE COMMUNIST
POLITICAL PROCESS
Walter D. Connor

The subjective experience of possessing esoteric knowledge, unshared by others, often conduces to intolerance, or a contemptuous tolerance, of the opinions and attitudes of the uninitiated. In the political sphere, when the knowledge in question is that of the dynamics of social and political development—when a group experiences the heady feeling of mastery over the sole scientific understanding of the laws of social progress and conflict—it is unlikely that the group will readily attend to dissenting opinions or objections from those whose understanding is pre-, or un-, scientific. When, in addition, such a group feels a moral imperative to aid the historical process, to push toward the known (and generally utopian) endpoint with whatever resources it may possess, its tolerance of opposition, or of the ignorance of the mass, will be small indeed.

Such has, in part, been the experience of the Marxist-Leninist ruling elites in the nations with which previous chapters have dealt. The Leninist contempt for (mass) spontaneity as opposed to (elite-initate) consciousness, for mere trade union consciousness satisfied by incremental benefits versus revolutionary commitment to the overthrow of a social order, was amply reflected in the Soviet experiment carried out under Stalin. Whatever policy it pursued, the regime could justify it in the framework of ideology, citing historical necessity and long-term benefit whenever short-term stringency resulted, and the leaders ascribed opposition to faulty consciousness, the backwardness of the mass, or sabotage by classes resisting the proletariat's attempt to dump them on history's rubbish heap.

The partial recapitulation of the Soviet experience in the East European states after World War II contained many of the same elements. But here, with the exception of Yugoslavia and Albania, much of the motive force for social transformation came from the dominant USSR, whose historical experience (raised to the level of an ideology valid for all) the new Communist regimes were forced to reproduce, whatever the differing national traditions, developmental levels, and consciousness of their subjects. Public opinion was not consulted, except as a base for action designed to preempt its logical thrust when it seemed to indicate lessening fortunes for Communist rule.*

Ideology, of course, was not the only pretext for ignoring or failing to consult mass opinion in earlier years of the Soviet and East European regimes. Convinced ideologues there were, no doubt, among the Communist groups that fought for and attained power; but there were also many to whom ideology was but a mode of expression, of communication, and a cloak for the quest and retention of power, which were their real driving forces. And the problems of power were real ones. Whether or not the new leaders regarded the citizenry as generally benighted, ideologically illiterate, it was clear that in most cases Communist parties could only claim minority support among the populace. Thus, public opinion was ignored—not only because of its lack of ideological/ scientific maturity, but also, and mainly, because it did not support the complex of Communist objectives.

With varying mixes of carrot and stick, accommodation and coercion, the Communist regimes muddled through their early years, cloaking whatever real chasm existed between public opinion and state policy under the mantle of propaganda, poster art, assertions that state and people—except for bourgeois elements surviving from the old order—were united in conviction and commitment, marching resolutely toward a new, achievable utopia.

It is tempting to speculate on the state of mind of various elements of the Communist leaderships in these years of system-building. The propagation of the notion of monolithic, supportive public opinion behind regime actions was of a piece, of course, with the tendency to inflate the magnitude and speed of attainment of all achievements in the construction of a new order. At the same time, the presence of dissident, conspiratorial groups and minorities was recognized, both in the sense of real perceptions that remnants of the old bourgeoisie were unlikely to be enthusiastic supporters of the new regime, and also in an inventive sense—the fabrication of conspiracies against the state and the drawing into the toils of investigation, arrest, hard labor, and death to people who had done nothing.[1] While the invention of political deviation was more characteristic of the USSR in the 1930s than of the East European states later, all engaged in it to some degree, providing the negative examples by which public opinion was to be aroused to a distrust for internal enemies and those of the West.

_____

*Thus, Gitelman noted earlier that the opinion poll results in 1947, which indicated lessening support for the Czech Communist Party, were a factor possibly hastening the onset of the 1948 coup.

These are external facts. What did they indicate about true leadership perceptions? Probably many things—though, lacking autobiographies as we do, we are unlikely ever to reach a very high order of specificity. In some measure, certainly, the leadership—especially the men at the very pinnacle—became convinced of the reality of public support for all their governments did, cultivating the view of the outside world they found most comforting. Happy cooperative peasants, a stern, purposeful, and loyal working class, and a new socialist intelligentsia being created out of them were the major components of this picture. Much of it was illusionary, but some was real—opportunities for education, occupational mobility, and other benefits did, indeed, create support for the new regimes, in the Russia of the 1920s and 1930s and later in Eastern Europe. Strangely enough, the leadership probably was less aware of the sources of support, the "normative resources" it was creating, than it might have been.*

The forced-draft industrialization in the USSR, undertaken for defensive purposes just as Peter the Great had earlier sought the modernity of the Europe of his time for the same reason, and the parallel drives later in Eastern Europe undertaken in the necessary emulation of the one, allegedly proven path to socialism, seemingly might have little to do with public support, since they imposed stringencies on the population that led to downturns in the general living standard. Yet, implying as they did the movement of peasants into regularly paid blue-collar work and the urban environment, and the ascent of some workers and peasants to positions of prestige and moderate power, they did create support. Of this support, the leaders of the time were unsure. Those who had not accepted the picture of supportive populations were, in their darker movements, probably too concerned with the manifestations of discontent, discovered or created by their security agencies and networks of informers, to view clearly, or even investigate, the impacts of the larger processes of modernization.

Through the web of positive and negative misimpressions of the public mood, evidence of a more realistic, if no less ambitious and transformational, outlook was manifest in the extraordinary efforts of the agit-prop establishment and mass media to influence public opinion, control it, and thus bring it into that state of correspondence with official ideology already proclaimed as real. Clearly, some in the leadership understood the necessity for purposeful political socialization on a mass scale; others attended to it intermittently, and large

---

*One doubts, for example, that Stalin and his subordinates could have been aware, in the 1930s, that free education and medical care and government ownership of major industry were sources of considerable support for the regime. It remained for a different sponsor, through the refugee interviews of the Harvard Project on the Soviet Social System,[2] to demonstrate this.

numbers of paid and volunteer agitation and propaganda workers* were detailed to complete the task. The means were crude enough and depended little on prior empirical research into public opinion. But they were parts of a real enterprise and provided an indication that public attitudes were, even to regimes still relying heavily on coercion, of some interest.

Leadership attention was, however, badly divided, as it could not but be, and only a moderate amount, in all, went to monitoring the state of mind of the masses. Factional struggles, external concerns (especially critical linkages with the USSR for the East European states), and the physical aspects of industrialization claimed most of it. The reckoning was yet to come, but come it would, at different times in different countries, but for much the same reasons.

THE RECKONING: PEOPLES AND REGIMES

The death of Stalin—who had shaped the USSR into the distinct type of entity it was and whose stamp lay on the East European satellites as well—could leave nothing quite as it had been. His Soviet successors faced the adjustment to a necessarily new way of ruling without him—for many a not unpleasant prospect—and the satellite leaders faced the prospect of arriving at some kind of reconciliation, however halting and conditional, with their own populations. The riots in East Berlin, Plzen, and Poznan indicated that the task would not be easy.

The USSR, where this peculiar form of modern despotism had first emerged, moved slowly into the so-called thaw. Survivors of the camps returned, terror abated, and gradually the regime came to acquaint itself with some of the textures of popular feelings: no polls, simply the gradual development of informal links and networks wherein intelligentsia could now speak somewhat frankly to leaders, workers give voice to grievances on the factory floor without fear of arrest for ideological sabotage, peasants vent the frustrations of a generation of life at the margins of survival. The East European states moved at different paces. In Poland, never really "Stalinized" and spared the blood purge other satellite states experienced in the early 1950s, discussion and debate reemerged in the media and cafes. Literary journals assumed a new pointedness (as with

---

*The growth of the agit-prop bureaucracy and its implications have been generally rather ignored. Bureaucracies develop their own interests, and one is tempted to wonder whether, in today's mature socialist systems, calls for "increasing the consciousness of the masses" are not in large part a manifestation of this bureaucracy's attempt to guarantee its own continued relevance, command of jobs and resources, and other benefits, long after the populations in question have been (according to one's view) either won over or sufficiently depoliticized to prove fairly trustworthy.

Adam Wazyk's painfully retrospective "Poem for Adults" in 1955), and the protagonists of empirical social science reemerged to assert claims to legitimacy or, at least, toleration. Hungary by 1955 had come, perhaps, a shorter way, but stirrings there as well hinted that the deformations of Stalinism lay heavy on the people and that the costs of Rakosi's rule had been high. Only Czechoslovakia, among the countries covered here, seemed frozen. Paradoxically, the only state in the area with a tradition of liberal democracy now languished under Novotny's anachronistic but firmly entrenched Stalinism.

With the year of revolt, 1956, the situation changed, such that there could never be the possibility of going back quite all the way. Khrushchev's denunciation of Stalin justified the beliefs of many, disoriented those who had been true believers, and set the stage for an upsurge of national communism and pure, anti-Russian nationalism, which resulted in the Hungarian revolt and the Polish October. Though the first failed and the second succeeded from the perspective of the late 1950s, both were, in fact, profoundly important. We have seen the emergence of a consultative style on many issues in the Poland of 1956-63, via the development, inter alia, of a substantial polling enterprise, while Kadar's 1961 declaration that "he who is not against us is with us" was clearly a sign that Hungary was now "stabilized" after the post-1956 years of oppression. At the same time, it was an admission that the regime per se had no roots in public sympathy but would have to seek a mode of accommodation on a potentially wide range of nonpolitical issues in order to get the country moving. This, in turn, implied something of a learning process, wherein the Kadar regime, in its characteristically unobtrusive way, would go about finding out what its subjects might want and go some way toward delivering, as long as those wants were limited to items of a noncontroversial sort.

Kadar's profferal of a truce came shortly after the beginnings of public opinion polling in the USSR (1960). There, as we have seen, the start was slow, and the legitimization of such inquiry was probably aided greatly by the resurgence of social research already underway in Poland—a country firmly in the Soviet bloc, whatever the divergence in internal policies that separated the "feel" of everyday life in Warsaw and Krakow from that in Moscow and Leningrad.

Well into the 1960s, Czechoslovakia remained dormant. Foot-dragging, then grudging half-compliance with Khrushchev's demands for de-Stalinization left Novotny still in charge of an unreconstructed polity when Khrushchev fell in 1964. Brezhnev and Kosygin—men of the "party of stability" if nothing else—did little to push him further. Novotny apparently presided over a stable monolith. But simmering Slovak resentments, economic disaster in 1963 and its later consequences, and perhaps, general fatigue, all created cracks in its facade. Economic reformers, permitted to talk of economics, expanded their concerns, a slow engagement of other intelligentsia followed, and by 1967, before the accession of Dubcek, the establishment of a public opinion research institute legitimized a new linkage between state and people that was to develop far and fast in the first months of 1968.

Thus, in different cadence and at different junctures, the Soviet and East European regimes emerged from the frozen solidity of Stalinism and stepped unsurely onto new ground, where the masses, hitherto silent save for the public opinion put in their mouths by those who spoke for them, would be permitted, to varying degrees, to use their own tongues.

What had happened, one can argue, is that various elements of the elites, political and otherwise, with either the power to act or the impetus to press for action, had recognized a use, or uses, for public opinion. This recognition had administrative, political, and what may be called moral-ethical aspects.

A more rationalized, regular administration of state operations of all sorts required more information about public perceptions and desires. As Huszczo notes, it was the press in Poland that first attempted to gather feedback from its presumptive audience, for there was no point in transmitting messages no one was listening to—and "circulation" figures in a Communist state scarcely provided an adequate answer to the question "Are we succeeding?" Later, Moscow's *Izvestiia* and *Liternaturnaia gazeta* would similarly seek reader opinion on what was most, and what least, interesting in those newspapers.[3] In communications, and in other consumer areas, little resistance arose to the notion that the public could be reasonably consulted on matters over which they exercised a clear, if diffuse, influence.

More important, and more controversial, were the political aspects. The rhetoric of political leaders in Communist states had always had a populist ring—with the crisis of 1956 and those that shook Czechoslovakia later, new political leaders of a reformist tinge had a stake in appealing to the support of public opinion, and citing the approval manifested, in support of their policies and in legitimation of their own performance as leaders. The specialist cadres— the functional elites whose concerns focused on policy choices political leaders would have to make—similarly had an interest in manifestations of public opinion supportive of their views, which might move the choices in a desirable direction. Thus, a combination of strategic-tactical political concerns and policy concerns of a more substantive nature exerted some pressure toward seeking the validation (or at least the appearance thereof) of state actions, proposed or in process, through a tapping of public views. Particularly in periods of instability or leadership transition, as Gitelman observed earlier, public opinion could play a significantly supportive role for a program or a leader, and, despite the general restrictions on the expression and influence on public opinion under socialism, at such times some will seek to make use of it.

Finally, a moral-ethical dimension exists here, which should be neither under- nor overestimated. Some elements of the leaderships and some elements of the intelligentsia felt it a moral imperative that the public should be consulted, that the democratic aspect of socialism had been, but should not remain, a sham. The bloodshed and trauma of forcing unpopular policies on the populace pricked some consciences in retrospect, while others, in a new atmosphere of decompression, gave voice to convictions they had suppressed but not abandoned. Actually, two dimensions were involved: for some political leaders, a new relationship with the masses was a clear desideratum, one that—if it did not mean that public opinion would determine government actions (for such, in any case, it did not even do in the Western liberal democracies)—would allow public opinion to indicate, ahead of time and thus allowing official reconsiderations, what governmental actions it might deem abhorrent and therefore resist: no small matter. Some intelligentsia, on another plane, saw also the possibility of transformation of the political system through the new channels of polling—a constant upward flow of information from the mass to the elite—in which their own roles, as conductors and articulators, would be major ones. Thus the Polish researcher Anna Pawelczynska saw public opinion research as a "mouthpiece for democratic standards in public life,"[4] and in the much more turbulent Czechoslovakia of 1968, Adamec asserted that it would "aid in the process of democratization,"[5] while Jaroslava Zapletalova addressed directly the interests of reformist political leaders in arguing that the "organs of the social system gain from this research one of the safest supports of their decisions."[6] The larger changes hinted at by a growing interest in, and tolerance for, public opinion were ones that many of the intelligentsia supported, and in their attempts to institutionalize public opinion research, they saw a realistic possibility of bringing those changes closer.

The political and moral-ethical dimensions peaked, certainly, in the Prague Spring of 1968. However delayed reform was in Czechoslovakia, when it finally came, it drew on a national resource unique among the socialist states— a political tradition of liberal democracy. The most egalitarian wage and salary system in Eastern Europe had helped to keep the Czech masses quiescent, each making his own peace with the system in a Schweik-like manner. But, in the end, it was not enough to compensate for democracy lost, and intelligentsia and workers coalesced around a program that, if enacted, would have transformed the nation.

(Yugoslavia, though it falls beyond the boundaries of this book, provides another interesting example of elite-mass linkages and rather free expression of public opinion through institutionalized channels. A political history very different from that of Czechoslovakia left Yugoslavia with few of the underpinnings of stable democracy, and, as the interwar years showed, it could scarcely support a democratic system. Yet, socially, underdeveloped Yugoslavia, like modern Czechoslovakia, had a democratic strain in its lack of a traditional, native agrarian upper class. Its Serbo-Montenegrin core tradition, that of a peasant "nation in arms," was quite different from the traditions of elitist Poland or Hungary and was amplified in the Partisan movement from which the new Communist Yugoslavia was born. This national mobilization, not beholden to Soviet military intervention, gave a different tone to the Yugoslav revolution, which, in part, both provoked the 1948 break with the USSR and provided critical domestic support for the regime's solitary course thereafter. The Yugoslav model, actually a model-in-process throughout most of the period since 1948, has developed limited but real democratic potential via the self-governing bodies, though their structure weights popular control heavily in favor of the modern sector, leaving the peasantry permanently outvoted.[7] Though not a society with the civil-libertarian potential Czechoslovakia manifested in 1968, Yugoslavia does represent a peculiar pattern of gradual adaptation of one-party regime to real public opinion input, and thus has distinguished itself from the societies with which we deal here.)

These, then, were aspects of the moves toward admitting the force and potential of public opinion in the context of Communist regimes. Opinions were forthcoming, and with them some interesting, and disquieting, reflections of the long impact of those regimes on their subjects.

OPINION EMERGENT

While it is undoubtedly the case that opinions—products of a certain amount of reflection and assessment—can only emerge when life provides some respite from a constant struggle to ensure material/physical survival, such opinions need not affirm, by their emergence, that the supply of material goods in the broad sense is sufficient. And material complaints were plentiful in responses to opinion surveys.

In broad terms, dissatisfaction was linked with occupational status. For all the rhetoric exalting the working class and, to a lesser extent, the peasantry as strata upon which Communist rule based itself, it was from these sectors that complaints about living standards and the conditions and quality of work life welled up most impressively. Peasants pointed to the hardships of the rural-farm environment, which left them in their traditional place at the bottom of the hierarchy of status and reward. Ominously, Polish, Soviet, and other researchers found that younger and better-educated peasants were least adjusted to the prospect of a life in agriculture and most likely to migrate from the countryside—depleting disproportionately the very component of the rural population upon which the governments needed to rely for effective mechanization of agriculture, broader use of sophisticated farming techniques, and so on.

Workers, in a broad range of inquiries, showed elements of the "blue-collar blues," as Huszczo noted earlier. While dissatisfaction with low wages was most marked among unskilled and semiskilled laborers, and moderated in the case of some skilled workers whose wages were relatively high, all could find cause for dissatisfaction: the monotony of the productive process, sometimes harsh work conditions, and the hierarchical organization of the factory, which left workers no more autonomous under socialism than under capitalism. The constant problems of absenteeism, drunkenness, and the like were well known to officials and economic planners, and these expressions of workers' malaise provided some explanation of their persistence.

Guaranteeing adequate living standards has been a matter of great concern to Communist regimes, however much their economic policies in the early years were geared toward the heavy reinvestment that necessarily lowered average living standards or delayed their rise. As Blumstock's chapter on Hungary indicated, the termination of the short life (1945-48) of the Institute of Public Opinion sponsored by the Hungarian Press Agency was probably closely connected with the falling-off of public perceptions of improvement in living standards in the 1947-48 period. The new regime had benefited from the positive perceptions of 1946-47 changes, when its economic tasks were mainly "restorative," but such could not hold as the regime went about beginning the business of a thorough Sovietization of the economy.

It should be emphasized, however, that the years of hardship, of the beginnings of socialist construction, were years also of necessarily great social mobility. If the average—statistically aggregated—Warsaw worker or Budapest professional in fact earned less in real terms in, say, 1951 than in 1939, one should remember that he was not the same person he had been. The early years of socialism saw the working class swell in size through the recruitment of peasants and their sons from the labor-rich countryside and saw the administrative strata expand through induction of former workers (and to a lesser degree peasants) to fill posts newly created, as governments assumed a multiplicity of functions. For these *novi homines* who came to dominate the strata, their mobility generally meant clear upward movement. If the perquisites of intelligentsia and workers were not what they were before socialism, they were better than what workers and peasants faced if they remained in the strata of their origins. Their frames of reference were not those of the old intelligentsia or proletariat. Hence, the indicators of average decline in real wages and living standards were not so vitally relevant to them; the impact of declining standards had been moderated by mobility.

Both promise and threat are implied here, for, as Blumstock further indicates for Hungary (whose situation is probably rather typical in this respect), standards of comparison and frames of reference are again changing.[8] The introduction of the consumer-oriented New Economic Mechanism (NEM) in 1968 prompted increased inquiry into levels of satisfaction and expectancy, and the results have given Hungarian officials food for thought. Those who compare their current situations in material terms with the past are, of course likely to find that Hungary of the 1970s is a more comfortable place than its counterpart of the 1940s and 1950s. But those who do tend to be older, less-educated, and dwellers in the smaller towns and countryside. Their relative satisfaction, while no threat to the government's stability, reflects rather limited expectations.

The young, the urban, the better-educated represent the future with which leaders, in Hungary and elsewhere, must contend—and these are more demanding, less able or willing to use the past as a frame of reference, and altogether less satisfied with the material life socialism has provided.

There is, then, dissatisfaction aplenty in the socialist populations over bread-and-butter issues. Though virtually all the states have seen progress toward standards that seem affluent in comparison to the 1950s, the subjective reflections of economic progress are not so clear. Polls and other forms of social research indicate malaise, but so do the more traditional channels. Letters to the press, complaints, and even the satirical journals the governments themselves produce attest to the many varieties of dissatisfaction. Polish events in 1970 and 1976 gave evidence of the risk of destabilizing consequences attendant upon governmental failure to read the public mood correctly, and as, however gradually, the relevant basis of comparison becomes both more contemporary and more Western in focus, throughout the socialist states,* all the regimes may find opinions disquieting as they explore them.

The "spiritual" side of socialist life, as reflected in opinion and other social research, has also provided regime officials, propagandists, and ideologists with indications of divergence from the ideal. Religion, though its power varies from country to country, is far from dead. And, where it shows clear evidence of weakening, the cause seems to lie more in the complex of changes attendant on urbanization and increased levels of formal education, rather than in the success of governmental programs promoting scientific atheism. If the trend is away from firm religious commitment, it is toward agnosticism—much as in the West— rather than toward a new, characteristically Marxist world view. Adaline Huszczo's chapter paints a picture familiar to anyone acquainted with Poland, wherein historical realities, anti-Russian attitudes, and a still rather traditional social structure make a country more Catholic than Communist. It seems unlikely that Party and government leaders could have been surprised by figures from the later 1950s indicating that over three-fourths of respondents classified themselves as Catholic and that more than two-thirds of university students did the same. The early accommodations of the post-October period had, after all, seen state recognition of the fact that public opinion was more influenced by

------

*Here, as Bogdan Denitch observes,[9] Yugoslavia's peculiar post-1948 history has made it an early case of frustration born of comparison with the West. Against a Balkan, or more generally East European-Soviet, backdrop, material standards on the average are good indeed, but few Yugoslavs see any relevance in such comparisons. They are drawn to those with the West, by which they still suffer. The USSR's still considerable degree of isolation, and its relative success in both managing material expectations and keeping these focused on a domestic-historical dimension have been in substantial measure elements of stabilization in the sphere of Soviet mass opinion.

Catholicism than any other system of beliefs. Grudgingly, the government had to accommodate itself to the discrimination that open nonpracticers might meet in informal social life.

Though such facts could have been anticipated in Poland, studies in other countries may have come as more of a surprise. Czechoslovakia's religious tradition is neither so strong (reflecting a trend of Czech free-thinking and an essentially secular state in the interwar years) nor as unitary (with Czechs divided between Protestantism and Catholicism and Slovaks overwhelmingly Catholic) as Poland's, yet evidence there in the 1960s pointed to only a moderate decline in belief and commitment. The 1968 study of Slovak religiosity cited by Gitelman[10] showed believers amounting to almost three-fourths of the adults polled. While the smallish gap between peasants (approximately 91 percent) and workers (about 73 percent) on this score was disquieting to a regime that had pitched so much of its rhetoric and economic policies at the workers, comfort could be taken from the fact, given Slovakia's historical backwardness, most workers were not far, temporally or psychologically, from the peasantry. More interesting, in a way, was the roughly 54 percent of white-collar functionaries who also declared themselves believers, since this stratum is generally most subject to pressures to conform to official images of good (nonreligious) citizenship. Czechoslovak history of the post-1948 period, except for the brief reform interlude of 1968, showed no parallel to the Polish compromise with Catholicism. In this context, such figures are not unimpressive. As in Poland, the Czechoslovak researchers also were drawn to conclude that religious identification in a general sense, persisted though an individual might not adhere to all church doctrines, and that religious nonidentification signaled no automatic enrollment in the ranks of officially approved atheism. Religious dropouts ended most frequently in an indeterminate, agnostic status, with no real evidence to indicate that this was a way station on the route to atheistic commitment.

If official Marxism-Leninism has had hard going in vanquishing religious survivals, evidence also shows that those who cite no religious commitment (and thus, presumably, carry no baggage preventing the adoption of a secular outlook) are likely to develop idiosyncratic views neither religious nor orthodox Marxist. Polish research in the late 1950s showed Warsaw University students favoring "some form of socialism" by more than two-thirds (these necessarily including some religious believers) while virtually the same share of the total denied being Marxists. Socialism in this sense seems mainly an economic reality, not a point of strong ideological engagement. Students favored government control of heavy industry, policies that guaranteed against unemployment, and so on, but not all aspects of what socialist governments had done (an interesting point, as we shall see, given the tendency of regime apologists to place all aspects of government under the mantle of socialist "achievements"). Their endorsements seem, on balance, rather pragmatic; the researchers themselves concluded that students' value systems reflected the "relative unimportance of social and political principles."[11]

Elsewhere, though our evidence is thinner, things are likely to be similar. Certainly, Kadar's dictum that "he who is not against us is with us" is, inter alia, confession and acceptance of the fact that Hungarians in the mass, while likely to accept certain fundamental features of a socialist economy, are hardly to be mobilized or educated into a principled Marxist-Leninist outlook. And, though the USSR makes no such candid admissions, impressionistic evidence as well as research on Soviet emigres suggests that while some economic features of socialism are quite highly valued, others are not. The terror of the Stalin years led to a surface and to some degree internal secularization of outlook and hence abandonment of institutional religion (the risks of adherence including, at some points, death). But the emergent amalgam was a humanistic, private value system far from that commitment and readiness to follow governmental objectives out of deep unshakable conviction that the Soviet state had, for a time, sought to inculcate. All in all, value systems of individuals, groups, and strata in the socialist states manifest varying degrees of accommodation and resistance to the official blueprints of what values should be—a diversity perhaps no less broad than that of many Western societies, but highlighted here by the fact that the socialist regimes, unlike those of the West, have such blueprints and continue, if with less intensity than before, to attempt to build from them.

From the sphere of values and ideology, a logical step brings us to popular evaluation of the nature and functioning of socialist political structures themselves. Of the countries surveyed here, only Poland, in a halting way and for a short time, and Czechoslovakia, for an even shorter time but in a quite revolutionary way, have given their citizens the opportunity of speaking directly to political issues, from the general place they would assign the socialist period, in moral-historical terms, in their countries' long chronicles, to more specific questions of the success of one-party, highly centralized systems in meeting various concrete and not-so-concrete needs of the citizenry.

Taken at face value, the manifestations of historical judgment in public opinion polls have been devastating. In a 1968 poll noted earlier by Gitelman,[12] only 3 percent of Czech respondents saw glory or progress best realized in the 1948-67 period, while many more voted for the Prague Spring itself (21 percent) and the interwar republic of Masaryk and Benes. Slovaks had less reason to favor the latter period, rating it equally at 17 percent with the post-1948 socialist regime. But 36 percent of the Slovaks nominated the Prague Spring as the best period of their history. It would be hard to find more expressive rejections of historical experience.

A path of greater indirection was followed by Polish researchers who in 1967 investigated the interests of respondents in various periods of Polish and European history. The presocialist interwar period, again, was rated highest in interest, along with the Polish activities in World War II, while the creation and growth of socialist Poland rated low.[13] If historical interest in this sense be a reflection of positive nostalgia, then the Poland of Pilsudski, of the colonels, still has an attraction, even for those who never experienced it and who would probably find much to object to if they had.

The reverse side of the political coin, however, shows widespread support for some of the fundamental changes that Communist regimes have introduced and consolidated. State ownership and control of heavy industry, of natural resources and their use, are not seriously challenged, whether because the public evaluation of these characteristics is positive in essence, or because the majority of the people have known no other set of arrangements and affirm the reality they do know. Thus, even at the peak of Czech reformist sentiment in July 1968, the poll reported earlier by Gitelman revealed that only 5 percent responded positively to the question "Do you wish us to return to capitalism?," while 89 percent answered no. (In fact, a fairly widespread nationalization of heavy industry had, with an apparently good deal of mass support, preceded the 1948 coup: an earlier indication that economic socialism was not something to which the Czech masses were generally opposed. Dubcek's 1968 program, appropriately enough, was socialism with a human face; the dehumanized aspect of the 1948-67 period was the political, rather than the economic, in the eyes of most citizens.) Similarly, as we already noted, uniersity students polled in Warsaw expressed, in the clear majority, the preference for some form of socialism. In truth, little evidence can be marshaled to suggest that either in Poland or Hungary in 1956, or Czechoslovakia in 1968, was socialism as economic principle and general mode of organization a target. The basically prosocialist convictions expressed cast in a curious light the rhetoric of antireform leaders who have denounced proposed changes in political operation and structure as "assaults on socialism." It was not socialism but his own style of leadership and party monopoly that a Novotny, for example, defended in asserting that reformists would not be permitted to destroy socialism, to lay their hands on "what the working class had achieved." No large constituency opposes socialism; some do oppose the structure and operations of Communist regimes; but regime leaders find it convenient to label the latter as opponents of socialism (and hence, of guaranteed employment, socialized medicine, welfare provisions, and so on), to give credibility to their own antichange positions and to drive a wedge between the working-class/peasant mass and the generally elite or middle-class advocates of new directions in socialist governance.

Much, then, of what public opinion research has revealed might cause disquietude among Communist leaders, and more in some countries than in others. But, when the manifestations of public sentiment contained in such research are taken as a whole, something else, equally important, emerged from which the same leaders might take courage. This was the general evidence of mass apoliticism, of the predominantly private, everyday orientations people had preserved through economic privations, the restructuring of societies, and decades of political communication exhorting them to become consciously and firmly political.*

If this meant that the rhetoric of permanently mobilized, loyal masses was only rhetoric, it also provided some reassurance that mass demands were not likely to be formulated in directly political terms. Polish students, as we saw, showed a decline in political interest as the Gomulka regime moved away from the heady days of 1956—partly, no doubt, because little they could welcome was happening in politics. Yet, if interest had remained high, would Gomulka's restabilization have proceeded so well? Czech students in a 1966 poll showed little concern or resonance with the Communist Party—only 7 percent thinking that it ever influenced the majority of students. The apoliticism might have seemed galling to Novotny, but the stability of 1966, in retrospect, had to be infinitely preferable to a period of peak political interest in 1968—the period in which he fell. As in Poland, the reversal of reform must account in part for a lessening of Czech interest in politics shown in a poll taken almost a year after the Soviet invasion:[14] But would normalization have proceeded more smoothly if students and others, once engagés, had not slipped back into quiet privatism? (The damage of politization, coming from the only source it seemingly could—a lively reform movement—was further evident in that 18.2 percent of the student respondents in this 1969 poll did favor the capitalist system—a higher percentage than might have been gotten in 1967 or 1968, and evidence of real revulsion at the post invasion regime, if not of any recrudescence of capitalist ideology.)

No Communist leader, Soviet or East European, has made such an eloquent invitation to apoliticality as did Kadar with his declaration that neutrals were also "with us." But one is inclined to think that they all, in fact, appreciate the evidence that, for the most part, their subjects are still just that: subjects, and not yet real participants, nor striving to be so, in systems where authentic participation of the sort evoked in Czechoslovakia in 1968 threatens the destruction of those systems.

Opinion polling, as virtually all the previous chapters show, has not grown into a mass enterprise in the socialist states. Much of the polling that does occur produces results for internal use only—data to be guarded from the public eye. The prime reason seems to be that Communist regimes, however great their need for conformation, and however sophisticated their appraisal of the high costs of

---

*This is of course, a broad judgment. Published Soviet polls, certainly, did not aim deeply into the political convictions of the mass: Whether more probing questions would have yielded answers less conventionalized for the most part than those I cited in an earlier chapter is hard to tell. Even better-constructed questions, however, such as those in some of the Polish inquiries, seemed on the whole to elicit little evidence of a politicized mass.

reliance on coercion in its absence, are not ready, nor perhaps in a position, to accommodate themselves to what opinion might demand, if the critical questions were posed squarely, and if the resultant answers were broadly publicized. To say this is not to hedge on the earlier characterization of the mass as apolitical, but only to emphasize that broad, free inquiry into the public mood would be an important element in a process that could politicize the populations of socialist states.

REALITY ENDURING

The data from opinion polls reported in this volume have told us something about the moods, thoughts, and strivings of the socialist public (whether it is really a "public," a collection thereof, or a mass—a question raised at various prior points—is one we need not dispose of here). The fate of the public opinion polling enterprise, as an open activity, is equally revealing. Opinion emerged, for a time, in each of the countries we consider here—not only to the attention of their respective regimes, but also into the consciousness of the broader, better-educated strata who would follow the publication of poll results. Now, for the most part, opinion research is not an open enterprise: an indication that the basic realities of Communist regimes, whatever public opinion may or may not communicate, endure. While the regimes are more interested now in public opinion than in the past, they are no more ready now than before to submit to it, to be guided by it, in those areas where basic political decisions are made. Alex Inkeles, more than 25 years ago, noted the necessary interest the Soviet regime took in public opinion, and the regime's parallel concern that it use, manipulate, control public opinion—not the reverse.[15] His observation remains true today, even allowing for all the changes that have occurred in the intervening time.

Opinion research continues, but it has been further politicized—not in the sense of regime demands that researchers cook their results to produce favorable and reassuring pictures, but in the tightening of control over the institutions and personnel involved in the research, and in the reservation of the results of that research to governmental and party bodies that make use of them. Opinion research is today less a matter of academic·entrepreneurship, much less a matter of public discussion and publication, than in the years immediately following its emergence. This is the essence of its politicization.

Both the value and the limits of opinion research as an auxiliary tool of governance are probably clearer to Communist political leaders today than ever before. Well done, it can reveal aspects of the public mood and temperament, of mass beliefs and convictions, more reliably and cheaply than alternative modes of data collection. It can, therefore, provide some of the social and economic intelligence that increasingly bureaucratized regimes must rely upon to conduct their business. Problems of public reaction to legal change, to shifts of emphasis in educational, consumer, and housing policies, and to other matters of governmental initiative can be anticipated on the basis of good opinion data, and this is no small thing.

Opinion research, however, cannot provide the key to unlock peoples' souls. However many problems in the public consciousness it pinpoints, it cannot show how to change that consciousness, how to resocialize an apathetic or recalcitrant mass into monolithic support for a regime. Of course, such seems no longer to be the objective of the governments in any case; whether, and to what degree, the returns of polling convinced them of this and made them ready to settle for a mass apoliticism as the bedrock of stability is an interesting question, but one impossible to answer here.

The human context of polling—the posing of meaningful questions to members of the population on an individual basis—may, as argued at various points in this book, boost morale, make an individual feel that his opinion is a matter of interest and will be taken into account. But this, too, carries its dangers, in that it may make for greater attention to certain policies, their ups and downs, on the part of a public otherwise unlikely to follow them so closely. An intererested and attentive public may be a more difficult management proposition than an apathetic one, and of this potential price for gathering information socialist leaders are probably aware.

Most important of all, however, the results of opinion research alone cannot tell decision-makers exactly what to do. The critical, and therefore most important decisions, are made in a sphere beyond that of administrative rationality. Data alone cannot indicate the way, especially when the data of public opinion, which indicate what the public seems to prefer, run counter to equally real and convincing data on other real-world problems and constraints in the context of decision.*

The Communist regimes in the USSR and Eastern Europe have opted for stability as the main *desideratum* of internal politics. Concessions of many

---

*The problems of the Gierek regime in Poland are interesting in this respect. As one well-connected Pole reported the situation in 1976 to me, government-sponsored and controlled opinion research indicated that mass response to the rises in food prices intended for midyear would likely be quite negative. Given the precedent of 1970—the December riots that spelled the end of Gomulka's rule—this was clearly "social intelligence" indicating large risks involved in raising prices. On the other hand, economics had to be taken into account. The distortions of the Polish price system, the only-too-evident deformations in the subsidized sale prices of foodstuffs, were damaging in a real, and sharply felt, way—especially to economists and leaders who had to take the total picture into account. In June 1976, the regime was swayed more by the arguments on the economic than on the opinion side. The announcement of price increases was, of course, followed by riots and disorder, leading to a rescinding of the increase. The economy's problems persist.

sorts—to consumerism within the material capacities of the economies, to lack of political commitment and interest as long as these do not show risks of transformation into antiregime activism—have been made, by leaders emulating, to one degree or another, Kadar's example of 1961. As long as the masses accept the inevitability of the regimes and their current architecture, the regimes can afford the concessions—or, until recently, they could. The commitment to "no change" is not one to increased coercion, but to a preservation of the status quo, wherein the regimes promise no heroic accomplishments on their part and demand no heroic labors from the population on theirs. To the degree that this very secularized style of regime-population relations endures, it will do so on the basis of mass apoliticism, a corresponding mass conviction that they are impotent with respect to bringing about changes, or having an effect on the political system, and a level of expectancy of material reward and gradual improvement in living conditions moderate enough so that the regimes can satisfy the mass.

These conditions, as I have argued elsewhere,[16] seem to be present in the USSR, and likely to persist there for some time. But the picture is less clear in the East European states. Will those populations remain apolitical, convinced of their impotence, and materially satisfied? The Communist regimes have changed, but moderately; their populations have changed more, raising interesting possibilities. While I do not intend to close on a note of social change (education, industrialization, urbanization, and so on) forcing political change as mass opinions focus and accelerate demands (we have seen too many examples of the stability of regimes to subscribe to a logic of necessity), some of the possibilities of rupture in the secular exchange relationship that links regimes and peoples in Eastern Europe do require discussion.

First, Communist regimes have, on balance, benefited from the fact that, in the systems they replaced, opinions counted for little, and few articulated them. The pre-Communist political cultures were generally of a parochial-subject sort; the new regimes made some effort to mobilize the populations into a subject-participant mode, wherein participation would be guided, organized, and supportive. Success has been partial at best, but the results have been, from the regime viewpoint, endurable. Stability may be threatened today, however, by diverse processes of change. The extremes are represented by Bulgaria and Romania, on one end, and Czechoslovakia (and, perhaps, the unique case of Yugoslavia) on the other. The Bulgarian and Romanian political cultures are still, evidently, of a subject sort, using the term loosely to indicate little departure from apoliticism and generalized conformity. Both are stable states, likely to remain so, even though Romania must face protracted stringencies as a consequence of the 1977 earthquake's damage to the economy. Neither Romanian nor Bulgarian regimes have seen fit to encourage much by way of opinion research, and the weight of history is heavy enough to permit a suggestion that "opinions" may still be luxuries to a large percentage of the populations there.

In Czechoslovakia, the events of 1968 proved that the bases of a participant political culture had not been eradicated in the years since 1948 but needed
only a favorable climate to reemerge and even find some rapid organizational
expression. The Soviet intervention crushed the mechanisms of change, but the
Czechoslovak leadership is on notice that the national political culture is not
supportive of the current political system. The threat of force and the consumerism supported by Soviet funds to turn Czechs and Slovaks to more material,
everyday concerns keep the state together in an uncertain stability.

Hungarians, perhaps, have fewer illusions than other East Europeans:
Generally well-served materially by the New Economic Mechanism, their politics
is subdued, a measure of internal liberalism in return for the abandonment of
romantic, anti-Soviet aspirations. Hungarian political culture is hard to characterize, still anti-Russian certainly, but given over for the time more to adjustment
to economic opportunities than to continuing attention to politics. Here, perhaps, stability is most rooted in economic performance, and thus far it has
sufficed to keep the population quiescent. But a sharp worsening of the economic situation might well raise the specter of disorders.

In Poland, that specter is real, palpable: Twice in the last decade large disorders have been provoked by failures in the economic sphere, and stability is
perhaps a misplaced word here. Polish political culture—not only the continuing
claim of the intelligentsia, Communist and non-Communist, to some participant
role, but also increased working-class consciousness and militancy on bread and
butter issues—can no longer be regarded as supportively apolitical.

The emergence of working-class militancy in Poland brings us to the
second force for instability in Eastern Europe: the long-term consequences of
the social mobility that economic development induced. Earlier, we noted the
stabilizing effects of this process—the drawing-off of peasantry into the working
class, the ascent of workers and peasants into the nonmanual strata, which by
confronting large numbers of mobiles with improvements in their personal situations, balanced the effect of decline in average living standards of strata and gave
many a stake in the new system. The longer-term effects, different in their
impacts, are two. First, viewed *en gros*, socialist economic development has expanded the relative size of population groups more likely to challenge, or make
demands upon, the regimes—notably the intelligentsia and the working class,
especially the stratum of skilled workers. At the same time, it has decreased the
share of the most traditional, least readily mobilizable category, the peasantry.
However disgruntled peasants were with early socialist policies in Eastern Europe, their localism, lack of organizational expertise, communications, and so on
made them unlikely launchers of a *jacquerie*: They provided, then, as majorities
or near majorities of the population, a fairly stable base. Paradoxically, peasants
in states like Hungary and Czechoslovakia today are doing better, relative to
other strata and absolutely, in the material sphere than ever before, but the
benefits to the regimes have lessened as the peasantry comes to represent a de-

creasing minority of the population. Intelligentsia and workers, better paid on the whole, have shown signs of restiveness ranging from the subtle and halting to the increasingly sharp confrontations in Poland. These groupings, in the modern sector of the economy, and especially the industrial workers, are critical to economic performance and thus to political stability. Their moods no longer guarantee either of these.

Why this is the case is a complex question, but the other mobility-related factor may provide a partial answer. While the intelligentsia and working classes of the earlier socialist period were composed predominantly of persons upwardly mobile, such is less the case today. Those beginning careers as intelligentsia or workers are now more likely to have grown up in these strata and lack the frame of reference of lower starting points, which would make their current situations seem great improvements. Peasant and rural criteria are no longer applied to their material situation by young workers; young intelligentsia see little relevance in judging theirs by working-class standards. When such favorable evaluative contexts disappear, both intelligentsia and workers can find much to hold negative opinions about, much cause for dissatisfaction: in the slow growth of housing supply, consumer goods and services, and other material benefits. Fewer and fewer recall Stalinism as a political context, which tends among the intelligentsia especially to amplify desires for more freedom, to travel to the West, and so on. The substantial easing of terror and liberalization of the last 20 years means little compared to the distance yet to be covered, the restrictions that remain. Thus the very success of economic development has produced groups more likely to articulate dissatisfaction with the regimes under which they live.

Still, not too much emphasis should yet be placed on the political versus material issues—Polish workers, for example, have different central concerns than the intelligentsia, and they are of a more bread-and-butter variety, as are mass concerns throughout Eastern Europe. The third potentially destabilizing factor, then, which in its effect on public opinion may be ominous for the regimes, is the uncertainty that they can go on bettering the material lot of populations that have grown to expect modest but cumulative improvements in their material conditions. Recent history has given evidence of many threats to economic performance. Externally, Western recession and inflation drove up the price of Western imports and decreased demand for socialist exports, while the price of Soviet-supplied petroleum for the essentially resourceless East European economies has escalated dramatically, forcing them to export more to the USSR. Western loans and credits are less available to East European states already heavily in debt to hard-currency lenders. Internally, economic reform has been halting in most countries, and the distortions of artificial price systems continue to create major problems. The reality today is one of prospective "hard times": Poles from 1971 to 1975 enjoyed a pace of material improvement that exceeded plan targets, but the prospective figures for the plan to 1980 neither promise so much, nor is it even clear that these can be delivered.

To the extent that the legitimacy of Communist regimes is based mainly on a secular principle of meeting mass expectations in the material sphere in exchange for their quiescence on political matters, that legitimacy may face a real threat. Expectations are not so limited as they once were—for some East Europeans, the affluence of Western Europe is an increasingly relevant frame of reference. Evidence mounts that the regimes will find it difficult in the future to meet even the modest expectations of rates of improvement that still prevail. As this evidence comes to be reflected in a public opinion less confident of material gain as the quid pro quo for working and living quietly, the material issues become, however gradually, politicized. And with this process, new possibilities arise that cannot but trouble leaders reluctant to return to coercion, but for whom the future may provide no alternative except a restructuring of the mechanisms of their rule in a more democratic direction—an alternative neither they, nor the Soviet leaders, are ready to accept.

To record all these difficulties is not, finally, to conclude that the socialist regimes have failed. Basic elements of socialism in the economic sphere have, as noted earlier, found a broad acceptance among the populations of the nations discussed in this book. That public opinion on many more ideological issues has not been effectively transformed is not so much a measure of the inadequacy of media, education, agit-prop, and other socialization agencies as a testimony to the magnitude and perhaps, impossibility, of such a task. If the picture I have drawn, of regimes increasingly willing to tolerate, and settle for, mass apoliticism rather than commitment is an accurate one, this is of course an accommodation Western democratic nations have also lived with and survived by.

The political realities in the Communist states endure, as they have for more than a generation. The regimes face difficulties today, as they did in the past. Thus far, their record has been one of impressive stability, judged in the context of the post-World War II world, and that record cannot be ignored. The destabilizing trends we have examined represent contingencies that the regimes must perforce face, but in a manner we cannot confidently predict. Mixes of coercion and accommodation may, as in the past, prove adequate to surmount the difficulties. Certainly, it would be going far to say that the regimes are already in crisis. Whatever objections those whose orientation in political values is Western may raise to the socialist regimes, it may be that history will record them as successes, on the main criterion it uses—endurance. It cannot yet record them as failures.

NOTES

1. See Walter D. Connor, "The Manufacture of Deviance: The Case of the Soviet Purge, 1936-1938," *American Sociological Review* 37, 4 (August 1972): 403-13.

2. See Alex Inkeles and Raymond A. Bauer, *The Soviet Citizen: Daily Life in a Totalitarian Society* (Cambridge: Harvard University Press, 1961).

3. On these newspaper polls, see Ellen Mickiewicz, "Policy Applications of Public Opinion Research in the Soviet Union," *Public Opinion Quarterly* 36 (Winter 1972-73): 566-78.

4. Anna Pawelczynska, "Zalozenie i problemy badan opinii publicznej w Polsce," *Kultura i spoleczenstwo* 10, no. 1 (1966), as cited by Huszczo, in chap. 2.

5. Cenek Adamec, "Verejne mineni v objektach vyzkumu," *Reporter* 3, no. 14 (April 3-10, 1968): 8, as cited by Gitelman, chap. 3.

6. "Rozhovor o verejnem mineni," *Nova mysl* 12 (December 1968): 1511, as cited by Gitelman, chap. 3.

7. See Bogdan Denitch, *The Legitimation of a Revolution: The Yugoslav Case* (New Haven and London: Yale University Press, 1976).

8. See Peter Makara and Istvan Monigl, "Eletszinvonal es Kozgondolkodas," in T. Szeczko, ed., *As Informaciotol a Kozeletig* (Budapest, 1973), pp. 114-15, 117, as cited by Blumstock, chap. 5.

9. See Denitch, op. cit., p. 143.

10. P. Prusak, "Some Results of a Survey on Religiousness in Slovakia," *Sociologia*, no. 1 (1970), Radio Free Europe (RFE) Czechoslovak Press Survey, no. 2308, p. 5, as cited by Gitelman, chap. 3.

11. Zofia Jozefowicz et al., "Students: Their Views of Society and Aspirations," *Polish Perspectives*, nos. 7-8 and 11-12 (1958), p. 42, as cited by Huszczo, chap. 2.

12. "Ustav pro vyzkum verejneho mineni CSAV," *Vztah Cechu a Slovaku k dejinam* (Prague, 1968), pp. 15-17, as cited by Gitelman, chap. 3.

13. W. Wernic, in *Tygodnik Demokraticzny*, September 10, 1967, RFE, Polish Press Survey, no. 2041, as cited by Huszczo, chap. 2.

14. F. Motycka, "Notes on a Public Opinion Poll," *Tribuna*, August 6, 1969, RFE, Czechoslovak Press Survey, no. 2249, p. 5, as cited by Gitelman, chap. 3.

15. Alex Inkeles, *Public Opinion in Soviet Russia* (Cambridge: Harvard University Press, 1950), p. 24.

16. Walter D. Connor, "Generations and Politics in the USSR," *Problems of Communism* 24, no. 5 (September-October 1975): 22-27.

INDEX

Academy of Sciences, Czechoslovakia, 86–87, 90

Academy of Sciences, Hungary, 159

Academy of Sciences, Poland, 41, 43, 66, 68

Academy of Sciences, USSR, 125, 126

"Action Program," 90, 98

Adamec, Cenek, 9, 18, 19, 84, 86, 87, 89; democratization function of polls, 173

Agit-Prop Department (Hungary): calls for poll research, 145; commissions research, 149; control of media, 155; molds public, 155-56

Agit-Prop Department (USSR), 8; directs research, 117; molds public opinion, 169-70

"agricultural circles," 55, 77

Albania, 6, 9, 167

All-Union Institute for the Study of the Causes and Elaboration of Preventive Measures of Crime (USSR), 115

apoliticism, 120, 179; benefits regime, 182; in Bulgaria, 183; and "consumerism," 182-84; in Czechoslovakia, 180; in Poland, 180; in Romania, 183; tolerated, 180, 182, 183, 186; in USSR, 180 (see also, political participation)

Apter, David, 104-05, 106

attitudes toward public opinion (see, Communist public opinion policy)

Benes, Eduard, 94, 178

Bienkowski, Wladyslaw, 69, 71

Blumstock, Robert, 174, 175

Bolsheviks, 105. 121

Bratislava, 27, 86

Brezhnev, Leonid, 144, 171; spurs research, 125

Brno, 86, 99

Budapest, 146; residents polled, 136, 137-38, 141, 149, 151; war destruction, 139

Bulgaria: political culture, 183-84; political participation, 22; scholars criticize West, 12; social science, 8, 10

Catholics (see, Roman Catholicism, Poland; poll research, Czechoslovakia)

Chalasinski, Josef, 41, 68-69

Chikin, V., 113, 122-23

cohort analysis, 92-93, 120

Communist policy toward poll research (see, policy toward poll research in Communist countries)

Communist public opinion policy, 5-6; Amalrik's observation, 2; Bolshevik, 1; compared with West, 6-7; in Czechoslovakia, 83-84, 89-90, 97, 168-69, 178; dictated by ideology, 168; dictated by objectives, 168; early Soviet bloc, 85, 167–170; in Hungary, 15, 171; Lenin, 2; in Poland, 73, 74, 178; roots of differences, 7-8; Stalin, 2; in USSR, 28, 30, 126-27, 168-69; Western view, 1, 31-32; in Yugoslavia, 173-74 (see also, concept of public opinion, poll research's function in Communist countries, public opinion's function in Communist countries)

concept of public opinion, Communist: Bolshevik, 1; Bulgarian, 12-13, 14-15; as guiding norm, 110; Hungarian, 15; "identification premise," 1, 3, 15; Lenin, 2; Marx, 2; Marxist-Leninist, 17, 18; monist-traditionalist, 13-17; pluralist-modernist, 13-17; Romanian, 12, 16; some scholars, 14; Soviet, 1, 3, 12, 14-15, 17, 117; Stalin, 2; as terror's equivalent, 21; as view of majority, 14-15; Yugoslav, 14-15

consumerism, 182-83, 184, 186

Councils Republic, 132-33

CPSU (Communist Party of the Soviet Union), 30, 106; participation in public work, 121; on public opinion, 2, 6, 117; quality of political education, 118-19; relation to masses, 105–07; on religious attitudes, 46-47; Twentieth Party Congress, 46-47 (see also, poll research's function in Communist countries: in USSR)

ABOUT THE AUTHORS AND CONTRIBUTORS

WALTER D. CONNOR directs Soviet and East European studies at the Foreign Service Institute, U.S. Department of State, and also serves as a Senior Fellow at the University of Pennsylvania. He received the Ph.D. from Princeton in 1969, and from 1968 to 1976 taught in the Department of Sociology and the Center for Russian and East European Studies at the University of Michigan.

His first book, *Deviance in Soviet Society*, was published in 1972; his *Socialism, Politics and Equality* will be forthcoming in 1978. He has been the recipient of grants from the American Council of Learned Societies, the International Research and Exchange Board, and other bodies. His articles have appeared in *Problems of Communism*, the *American Sociological Review*, *Comparative Studies in Society and History*, and other journals here and abroad.

His writings in this book reflect his own thoughts, and do not constitute expressions of U.S. government views or policies.

ZVI Y. GITELMAN is Associate Professor of Political Science at the University of Michigan, and a member of the Center for Russian and East European Studies there. He received his Ph.D. in 1968 from Columbia University.

A specialist in Soviet and East European politics, he is the author of *Jewish Nationality and Soviet Politics* (1972), a contributor to *Change in Communist Systems* (1970) and other collective volumes, and to *Problems of Communism*, the *Journal of Politics*, and other journals. A recipient of grants from the Rockefeller Foundation, the American Council of Learned Societies and other organizations, he has also served several terms as visiting professor in the Department of Political Science at Tel Aviv University.

ROBERT BLUMSTOCK is Associate Professor of Sociology at McMaster University, Hamilton, Ontario. After an undergraduate education at the City College of New York, he received the Ph.D. from the University of Oregon in 1964.

A frequent traveler in Hungary, Professor Blumstock has received research grants from the Canada Council and the Social Science Research Council of Canada. His articles have appeared in the Hungarian journal *Szociologia*, the *Canadian Review of Sociology and Anthropology*, and other journals.

ADALINE HUSZCZO received the BA degree from the University of Michigan in 1968, and in 1970 an MA in Journalism and the Certificate in Russian and East European Studies from the same university. A working journalist, she joined the *Ann Arbor News* in 1972, and has served as Features Editor since 1974.

POLITICAL DEVELOPMENT IN EASTERN EUROPE
Jan F. Triska and
Paul M. Cocks

EDUCATION AND THE MASS MEDIA IN THE SOVIET
UNION AND EASTERN EUROPE
edited by Bohdan Harasymiw

SOCIAL SCIENTISTS AND POLICY MAKING IN THE
SOVIET UNION
edited by Richard B. Remnek

CURRENT RESEARCH IN COMPARATIVE COMMUNISM:
An Analysis and Bibliographic Guide to the Soviet System
Lawrence L. Whetten

PERIODICALS ON THE SOCIALIST COUNTRIES AND ON
MARXISM: A New Annotated Index of English-Language
Publications
Harry G. Shaffer

THE INFLUENCE OF EAST EUROPE AND THE SOVIET
WEST ON THE USSR
edited by Roman Szporluk